CONTENTS

KU-195-935

	Introduction	
1	Introduction to computer accounting	2
2	Looking after the computer and the data	22
3	Setting up the company in Sage	38
4	Setting up records for Customers and Suppliers	50
5	Setting up the Nominal Ledger	70
6	Selling to customers on credit	84
7	Buying from suppliers on credit	98
8	Customer and supplier payments	106
9	Cash receipts and payments	124
10	Bank accounts and recurring entries	136
11	Reports and routines	152
12	Corrections and adjustments	172
13	Sales invoicing – further aspects	188
14	Double-entry book-keeping and manual systems	204
	Extended Exercise – Interlingo Translation Services	219
	Sage printout checklist	242
	Index	273

ACKNOWLEDGEMENTS

The author wishes to thank the following for their help with the reading, production and design of the text: Mike Gilbert, Maz Loton, Jon Moore and Charli Wilson. Particular thanks must go to Debbie Board for her patience and expertise in the technical editing, updating of the text and test running the Sage tasks. The author also wishes to thank Hania Lee for further test running of the Sage tasks.

Thanks are also due to Microsoft UK and to Sage (UK) Limited for their kind permission to use screen images within the text. It should be noted that Osborne Books Limited is a company which operates completely independently of Sage (UK) Limited.

THE AUTHOR

Michael Fardon has had extensive teaching experience on a wide range of banking, business and accountancy courses at Worcester College of Technology where he also set up and ran computer accounting courses, using Sage software. He now specialises in writing business and financial texts and is currently General Editor at Osborne Books.

THE CONSULTANT

Debbie Board spent twenty-six years in the commercial sector before becoming a teacher and assessor of accounting in further education. While working in the commercial sector she was responsible as director and office manager for the introduction of computerised accounting in a multi-million pound business. She currently works in South Devon as a part-time AAT tutor and as the accounts manager of a small independent tool hire company.

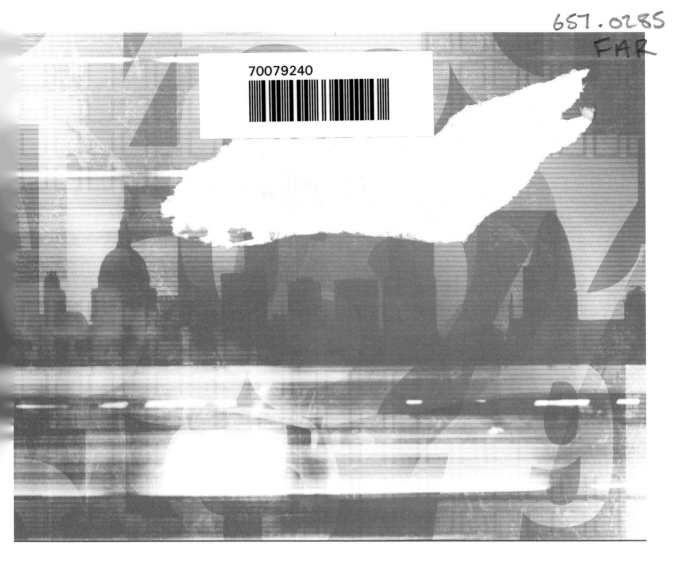

Computer Accounting

Third edition

for courses based on Sage Accounting software

Michael Fardon

Debbie Board (consultant)

RECEIVED

osborne
BOOKS

Published by Osborne Books Limited
Unit 1B Everoak Estate
Bromyard Road
Worcester WR2 5HP
Tel 01905 748071
Email books@osbornebooks.co.uk
Website www.osbornebooks.co.uk

Graphic design by Richard Holt and Jon Moore

Printed by CPI Antony Rowe Limited, Chippenham

British Library Cataloguing in Publication Data
A catalogue record for this book is available from the British Library

ISBN 978 1905777 563

INTRODUCTION

Computer Accounting has been written to provide a Sage-based practical study resource for students taking first-level courses offered by Awarding Bodies such as OCR, City & Guilds (Pitman) and IAB.

The major feature of this **third edition** is the use of **Sage 50 Version 15**, which at the time of writing is widely used by businesses and by training providers.

The **text** of *Computer Accounting* contains clear and practical explanations of how to set up and run a Sage system. A Case Study – Pronto Supplies Limited – runs through the chapters.

Many of the teachers consulted in the writing process mentioned the need for an understanding by students of the theoretical background to computer accounting – in particular the use of financial documents and double-entry book-keeping. The documents are explained as they are encountered in the text and a chapter on double-entry book-keeping is included at the back of the book to help students who may not be studying it as part of their course.

The **processing activities** at the end of the chapters in this book have all been tried and tested a number of times. Trial balances and audit trails have been included periodically and also at the back of the book so that account balances and transactions can be checked. The end-of-chapter activities progressively build up the various processes needed to set up and run a Sage system.

The **Interlingo Extended Activity** at the end of the book is designed for extended study purposes and is standalone.

Invoicing has been treated flexibly in the text so that batch entry can be used if the teaching centre does not want to (or cannot) set up a full invoicing function.

Throughout this book the **standard VAT rate of 17.5%** has been used. This rate applied at the time of writing and inputting the Sage transactions, but users of this book should note that it does vary from time-to time.

Michael Fardon

Spring 2010

1 INTRODUCTION TO COMPUTER ACCOUNTING

chapter introduction

■ Computer systems involve
  • *hardware – the equipment*
  • *software – the programs that run the computers*

■ *There are a number of different types of computer programs used by businesses and other organisations:*
  • *word processing*
  • *databases*
  • *spreadsheets*
  • *email management*
  • *accounting packages*

■ *Computers require input of data – which can either be carried out manually from sources such as financial documents or can be imported from other computer systems.*

■ *Computers also output data in the form of 'hard copy' printouts and electronic data which can be emailed or exported to other computer programs.*

COMPUTER HARDWARE

Computer **hardware** is the equipment on which the programs will be run.

There are two main ways of setting up the hardware – a standalone system and a network.

standalone system

A typical standalone system uses a single computer with a screen, mouse, a hard disk for data storage and a printer. This computer is likely be linked to the internet by phone line. This type of system is useful for a small business when only one person needs to operate the computer at any one time.

network and intranet

A **network** comprises a number of computer workstations linked to a server (which holds all the data) and other equipment such as printers and scanners. This type of system is likely to be used by a larger business or organisation (such as a college IT centre) where a number of operators need to access the system and its data at the same time. A network will often give employees direct access to the internet through an **internet** service provider.

When a network is set up, it is also possible to establish an **intranet**. This is an internal website which operates through the network and enables employees to share data, documents and internal web pages. An intranet cannot be accessed by unauthorised outsiders (except for 'hackers' who are successful in breaking in).

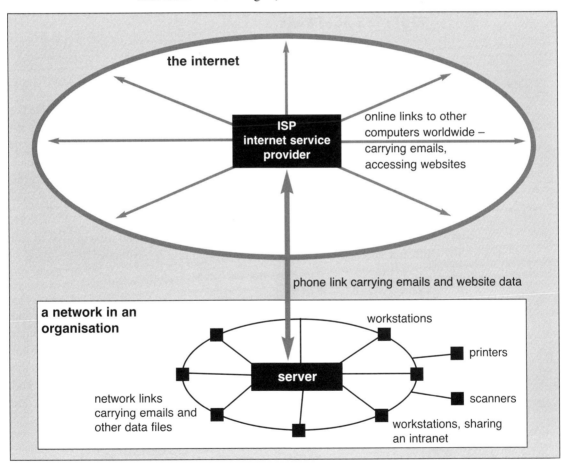

printers

All computer systems need a printer to produce 'hard copy' such as letters, financial documents and management reports. The old-fashioned form of printer is the dot matrix printer which prints text as a series of dots using a printer head with pins. This is useful if you need multiple copies of documents such as invoices. Nowadays better quality printing can be achieved by using an inkjet or laser printer. These printers can produce high quality multiple copies if required.

data storage and back-up

It is very important that the data held by the computer is backed up regularly and stored away from the premises or transmitted to another location. Data can be backed up onto a variety of storage media, eg tape, portable hard disk, USB memory stick, CD and DVD. All systems should therefore have some form of data storage facility or be able to transmit data to another location.

COMPUTER SOFTWARE

Windows operating systems

The program – the **software** – that makes a computer work is known as the operating system. Most business computers are PCs (personal computers) and laptops which run the Windows operating system which is a Microsoft product. Another Microsoft product is the Office suite of programs which includes the Word word processing program, the Excel spreadsheet and the Access database.

Standard 'off-the-shelf' accounting programs such as Sage 50 are also designed for use on Windows, and it is this system which we will refer to and illustrate when explaining computer accounting in this book.

types of software

We will now outline the different types of software used in businesses and other organisations and then explain how they 'fit in' with computer accounting packages such as Sage. It may be that you are already familiar with these types of program. Even so it is a good idea to read through the next few pages to remind yourself of the exact function of the packages and see how they can be integrated with computer accounting software. The common types of program are:

- word processing
- databases
- spreadsheets
- email managers
- accounting packages
- web browsers

WORD PROCESSING

Word processing programs – including Microsoft Word – enable you to

- enter text
- format text, eg set it out in columns, add bullet points
- change and edit text
- set up tables

Word processed text can be saved and printed out in the form of letters, memos, reports, and notices. Word processed text can also be sent electronically either on disk or as an attachment file on an email. Some of the text in Osborne Books publications is first input in Word and sent to Osborne Books on disk or by email. It is then imported into a page set-up program.

Word processing programs can be linked up with other programs. For example the names and addresses from a computer accounting package can be imported to 'mailmerge' into a set of letters sent out to customers.

Similarly, names and addresses of customers entered in a word processing or spreadsheet program can be transferred into a computer accounting package to set up account details. The text format used is known as comma separated text (see page 10 for a practical illustration of this).

The screen below shows how the original version of some of the text on this page was set up in Word and then imported into a page set-up program.

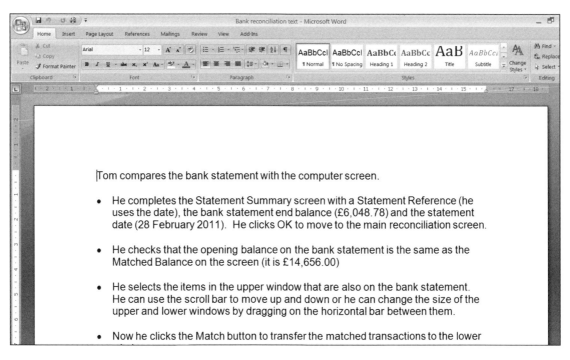

DATABASES

A computer database enables you to input and store information in an organised way so that it can be readily accessed, sorted and exported. A database is essentially an electronic filing system which takes all the hard work out of sorting and retrieving information.

Imagine, for example, your business does not have a computer database. It keeps the names and addresses of 250 customers on cards sorted alphabetically by surname and kept in a plastic box in the office. Suppose

- you drop the box on the floor and all the cards get out of order, or
- you are asked to identify all the customers who are based in Nottingham

These two situations will take a long time to sort out if the records are kept on cards. If this information were stored on a computer database . . .

- the records could automatically be sorted alphabetically by surname
- you could ask the computer could to search the field which contains the town or city name which is 'Nottingham'

Note that two terms are used here:

- a **record** is a set of information which corresponds to each card in a card index – here it is a customer record which is likely to contain the name of the customer, address, telephone number, and email
- a **field** is a part of the record (normally a box to fill in on the computer screen) which contains a specific piece of information, for example, customer surname, town, telephone number, email

A customer record is shown in the screen below. Note how the information is stored in different fields. In particular, note how the address is a series of fields. The 'City' field is one of these.

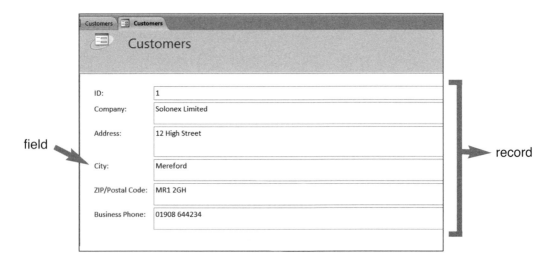

using data

Databases are very useful if you wish to record and make use of significant data relating to your business or organisation. For example, assume that the 'Customers' record shown on the previous page is part of a list of the people and organisations to whom a business sells its products. It could be expanded with further fields to record information such as:

■ date last contacted

■ status – eg target customers (those who have not ordered)

■ details of products sold

The 'Customers' file could then be accessed and searched to produce lists, for example, of customers not contacted within the last six months, target customers and customers who have bought a particular product.

The possibilities offered by a database apply in many areas. The index of this book, for example, was created by a database which sorts word fields alphabetically.

SPREADSHEETS

calculations

A spreadsheet is a grid of boxes – 'cells' – set up on the computer, organised in rows and columns into which you can enter text and numbers. It enables you to make calculations with the figures. The computer program will work out the calculations automatically once you have entered an appropriate formula in the cell where the result of the calculations is required.

The major advantage of a spreadsheet is that if you change any of the figures the computer will automatically recalculate the total, saving you much time and effort.

Spreadsheets are used for a variety of functions in organisations:

■ producing invoices – working out costs of products sold, calculating and adding on VAT and producing a sales total

■ working out budgets for future expenditure

■ working out sales figures for different products or areas

A commonly used spreadsheet program is Microsoft Excel. The example on the next page shows regional sales figures input into Excel. Note that the rows are numbered and the columns have letter references. The total sales figure appears in the cell (box) which therefore has the reference of B10.

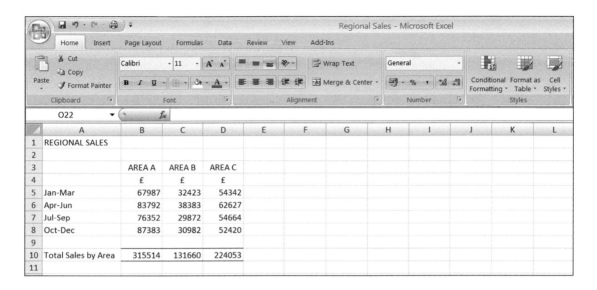

producing graphs and charts

Another function of the spreadsheet is its ability to produce graphs and charts from the figures in the spreadsheet grid. All that you need to do is to select the appropriate figures and the computer does the rest through its charting function. Look at the screens below and on the next page which use the Sales figures illustrated in the screen above.

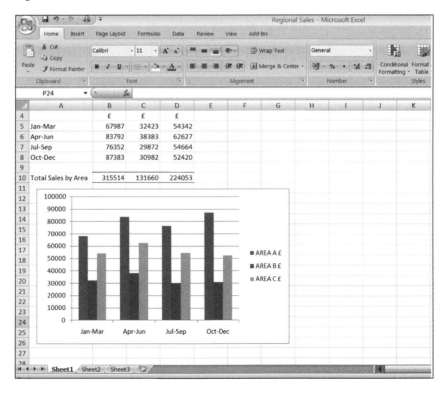

using the chart

The chart can then be copied and pasted into a Word processing document, in this case a Sales Report memorandum.

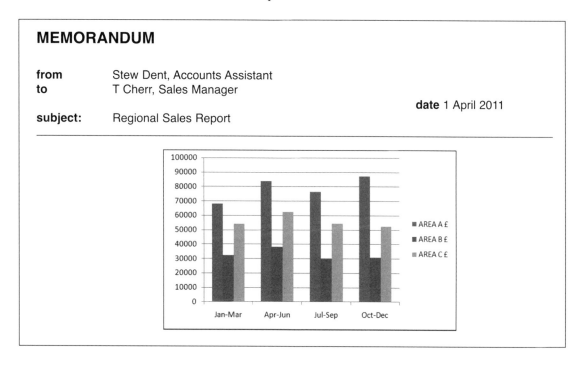

MEMORANDUM

from   Stew Dent, Accounts Assistant
to   T Cherr, Sales Manager

                                                    date 1 April 2011

subject: Regional Sales Report

EMAIL MANAGEMENT

Most businesses and other organisations are now online and can send and receive external emails. Some businesses and other organisations are also networked through an intranet and can send emails internally. Another important computer program is therefore the email management system. A commonly-used example is Microsoft Outlook Express. The screen below shows the outbox. In this case a message has been sent to Osborne Books, the publishers of this book.

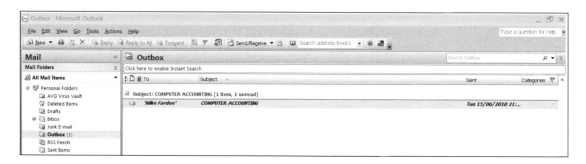

uses of email and attachments

Email is a very useful and inexpensive means of sending messages electronically, not only within a business, but also externally to customers and suppliers.

Email also acts as a link between many different types of computer program. Not only can a message be relayed in text form, email can also be used to transfer word processing, database and spreadsheet files from one computer to another in the form of an attachment file. Documents – orders and invoices for example – can be generated on the computer and sent by email attachment to suppliers and customers.

Data can also be transferred from one program to another after it has been converted into **CSV** format ('Comma Separated Values') which transforms text into a continuous line of data like this:

'which,transforms,text,into,a,continuous,line,of,data,like,this'

electronic documents and EDI

Data and documents – eg financial documents such as orders and invoices – can also be sent electronically through **Electronic Data Interchange** (EDI) programs. This form of transfer employs specialised software. The process is reliable, fast and efficient and often used by supermarket chains in ordering and paying for goods and also increasingly by bookshops ordering books (like this one) from publishers.

INTRODUCTION TO COMPUTER ACCOUNTING PACKAGES

a growth area

Although some organisations, particularly small businesses, still use paper-based accounting systems, most are now operating computerised accounting systems.

Small and medium-sized businesses can buy 'off-the shelf' accounting programs from suppliers such as Sage while larger businesses may opt to have custom-designed programs. Computer accounting programs are easy to use and can automate operations such as invoicing which take so much time and effort in a manual system.

links with traditional book-keeping

If you are studying on a book-keeping or accounting course, your study is likely to concentrate initially on paper-based systems. The reason for this is that when you use a paper-based system you have to do all the work manually and so you can understand the theory that underlies the system: you prepare the documents, make entries in the accounts, balance the cash book, and so on. You know where all the figures are entered, and why they are entered. If you know how a paper-based system works, you will be in a much better position to be able to understand the operation of a computer-based system.

comparison with other computer programs

Computer accounting packages – such as the Sage 50 series of products – make use of many of the functions of the other types of computer program already described in this chapter.

Most computer accounting packages contain:

■ word processing functions – eg the facility to write memos and notes

■ a series of databases – eg details of customers, stock items held

■ calculation facilities – eg invoices where the operator inputs figures and the program automatically generates VAT amounts and totals

■ charting and graphing facilities – eg charting of activity on a customer account

FEATURES OF COMPUTER ACCOUNTING

facilities

A typical computer accounting program will offer a number of facilities:

■ on-screen input and printout of sales invoices and credit notes

■ automatic updating of customer accounts with sales transactions

■ recording of suppliers' invoices

■ automatic updating of supplier accounts with details of purchases

■ recording of money paid into bank or cash accounts

■ recording of payments to suppliers and for expenses

Payroll can also be computerised – using a separate program.

management reports

A computer accounting program can provide instant reports for management, for example:

- an aged debtors' summary – showing who owes you what and for what periods of time
- activity reports on customer and supplier accounts
- activity reports on expenses accounts
- VAT Return

advantages of a computer accounting program

Computer accounting programs, like the other computer programs outlined in this chapter, are popular because they offer a number of distinct advantages over paper-based systems:

- they save time
- they save money
- they tend to be more accurate because they rely on single-entry input (one amount per transaction) rather than double-entry book-keeping
- they can provide the managers of the organisation with a clear and up-to-date picture of what is happening

computer accounting and ledgers

The 'ledgers' of a business are basically the books of the business. 'The ledgers' is a term used to describe the way the accounts of the business are grouped into different sections.

There are four main ledgers in a traditional accounting system:

- **sales ledger** contains the accounts of debtors (customers)
- **purchases ledger** contains the accounts of creditors (suppliers)
- **cash book** contains the main cash book and the petty cash book
- **nominal ledger** (also called general or main ledger) contains the remaining accounts, eg expenses (including purchases), income (including sales), assets, loans, stock, VAT

A diagram illustrating these ledgers is shown on the next page. The structure of a computer accounting system is based on these ledgers. It may also include stock control and be linked to a payroll processing program.

A ledger-based computer system is designed to be user-friendly in Windows software. In Sage 50 regular tasks can be performed by clicking on the Task options on the vertical panel on the left of the screen. These options change

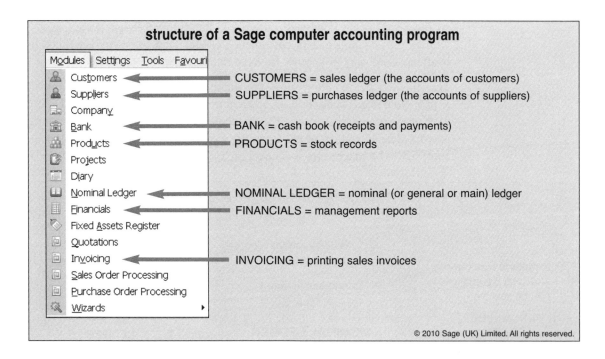

according to the module button selected at the bottom of the panel. The full range of modules within Sage (shown below) is accessed through the Modules drop-down menu on the menu bar. The notes to the side explain what the various modules are. Note that computer accounting packages vary in levels of sophistication; you may be working with one that does not include product records or invoice printing.

Please note that the screens shown in these chapters may not necessarily be exactly the same as those on your computer because programs are regularly updated. This should not be a problem, however, because the basic principles of using the software are likely to remain exactly the same.

computerised ledgers – an integrated system

Before we look at the various functions on the toolbar, it is important to appreciate that a computerised ledger system is **fully integrated.** This means that when a business transaction is input on the computer it is normally recorded in two accounts at the same time, although only one amount is entered. Take the three transactions shown in the diagram below:

■ a business buys from a supplier on credit (ie the business gets the goods but will pay later)

■ a business sells to a customer on credit (ie the business sells the goods but will receive payment later)

■ a business pays an advertising bill

At the centre of an integrated program is the nominal ledger which deals with all the accounts except customers' accounts and suppliers' accounts. It is affected one way or another by most transactions.

The diagram below shows how the three 'ledgers' link with the nominal ledger. Note in each case how an account in the nominal ledger is affected by each of the three transactions. This is the double-entry book-keeping system at work. The advantage of the computer system is that in each case only one entry has to be made. Life is made a great deal simpler this way!

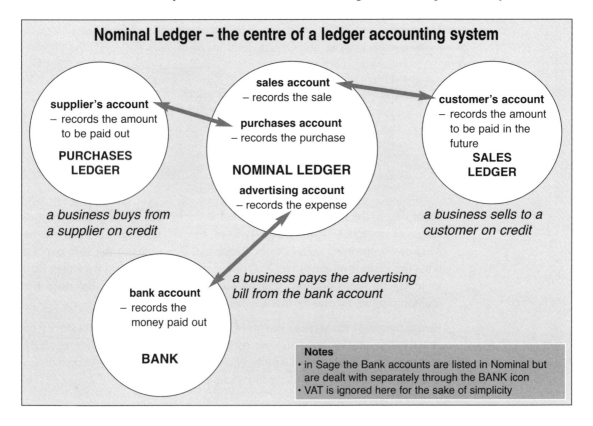

INPUT INTO A COMPUTER ACCOUNTING PACKAGE

manual input

Input into a computer accounting package is normally made direct on screen from source documents or other data. If you are not familiar with financial documents, please read pages 85 to 89 before proceeding any further.

Typical transactions which form the 'bread and butter' of computer accounting input include:

- processing **sales invoices**, often in runs of several transactions known as 'batches' – the invoices are either produced before input or they can be input and printed out by the computer

- inputting **credit notes** from authorised documentation which says why the credit note has to be issued and a refund made – again the credit notes may be produced separately and used as a basis for input, or they may be printed out by the computer

- inputting **bank receipts** (money paid into the bank) – for example cheques or BACS payments received from customers in settlement of accounts due; the source document in this case is the remittance advice which comes with the cheque or advises the BACS payment

- inputting details of **new customer accounts** – this is the input of text onto what is effectively a database screen in the computer accounting package; this might happen if the sales team has been very successful and obtained a number of new sales

There are, of course, many other types of transactions which you will input on the computer, but these are common examples. We will cover the input procedures in much greater detail in the individual chapters of this book.

importing data

Text files such as Customer and Supplier details can be imported into a computer accounting package from other programs such as Microsoft Office or other accounting programs.

authorisation and checking

Each organisation will have its own procedures to make sure that the data input is accurate and authorised. Source documents – invoices received, for example – may have a stamp placed on them with boxes for the initials of

- the person checking the document

- the person authorising the input – often as part of a 'batch' of invoices

- the computer operator

- the person who checks the input against the source document

This ensures that accuracy is maintained. Each individual takes responsibility for a particular stage in the process and any errors can be traced to that individual.

OUTPUT FROM A COMPUTER ACCOUNTING PACKAGE

Output of data from a computer accounting package can take a number of different formats and can be used in a number of different ways.

printouts

The familiar form of data output from a computer is the paper printout. This is often referred to as 'hard copy'. There are a number of different forms of printout:

- day-to-day lists of items processed, eg a list of invoices produced on a particular day, a list of cheques issued to pay suppliers

- financial documents such as invoices and credit notes

- reports for management, eg activity reports on accounts, aged debtors analysis (a list of who owes what – highlighting overdue accounts)

A printout of sales invoices produced is shown below.

Pronto Supplies Limited

Day Books: Customer Invoices (Detailed)

Transaction From:	1						N/C From:		
Transaction To:	99,999,999						N/C To:	99999999	

Dept From:	0
Dept To:	999

Tran No.	Type	Date	A/C Ref	N/C	Inv Ref	Dept.	Details	Net Amount	Tax Amount	T/C	Gross Amount	V	B
48	SI	05/02/2011	JB001	4000	10023	1	1 x 17" monitor	400.00	70.00	T1	470.00	N	-
49	SI	06/02/2011	CH001	4000	10024	1	1 x printer lead	16.00	2.80	T1	18.80	N	-
50	SI	06/02/2011	CR001	4001	10025	1	1 x Macroworx	100.00	17.50	T1	117.50	N	-
51	SI	08/02/2011	KD001	4002	10026	1	2 hrs consultancy	120.00	21.00	T1	141.00	N	-
							Totals:	636.00	111.30		747.30		

End of Report

---

faxed data

Data or documents which have been printed out may in some circumstances be faxed. This often happens when it is a copy of the original data that is needed. When, for example, a business is chasing up its customers for overdue payments it may be given the classic lame excuse by the business that is late in paying:

'Oh – we didn't receive your invoice in the first place – can you fax us a copy please?'

emailed data

Most current computer accounting packages have the facility for data to be exported to an email management program so that it can be emailed direct to the person who needs the information. Sage, for example, allows you to send invoices and statements direct to customers. Printouts and reports previewed on screen can be emailed directly to external email addresses.

exporting data direct to other programs

Most current computer accounting packages also allow you to export data to spreadsheet and word processing programs. Sage allows you to:

■ export data to a Microsoft Excel spreadsheet, eg a list of the nominal accounts and their balances – this data will be placed direct into a spreadsheet grid from the Sage screen and can then be manipulated as required

■ email reports in various formats from reports previewed on-screen

■ export data in the form of a mailmerge to a Microsoft Word word processing file – for example, if a business wants to send a letter advertising a new product to all its customers, it can export the names and addresses from the customer details in the computer accounting program to a letter file in Word which will then print out personalised letters to all the customers

■ export data files to your accountant

The example below shows Customer files being exported for mail merge.

■ Organisations using computer systems can either use a single standalone machine or a network of computers linked on an intranet. Many computer systems are now linked externally to the internet.

■ Most computer programs – word processors, databases, spreadsheets, email managers and computer accounting packages – are designed so that you can interchange data from one to another.

■ Computer accounting programs combine the functions of a number of different programs – they act as database and spreadsheet and can generate text and data for use in other programs.

■ A computer accounting program can record financial transactions, generate financial documents, provide management with financial reports and generally make running and managing the finances of any organisation a more efficient process.

■ Computer accounting programs are based on the ledger system of book-keeping and link together accounts for customers (sales ledger), suppliers (purchases ledger), bank (cash book) and other payments, receipts and items owned or owed by the organisation (nominal ledger).

■ Input into a computer accounting program is normally carried out manually on the keyboard. Many programs will now accept data imported from other programs.

■ Output from a computer accounting program can be on paper (hard copy), can be faxed or sent by email or direct to other programs, a spreadsheet for example.

hardware	the computer equipment on which the computer programs run
software	the computer programs which enable the computer to work and carry out its functions
intranet	a linked network of computers within an organisation
internet	computers linked up externally by phone line with other computers on the worldwide web (www)
word processor	a computer program which allows text to be entered and manipulated on screen
database	a computer program which acts as an electronic filing system, storing data so that it can be sorted, searched and organised efficiently

record	a set of information stored in a computer database, eg a name and address
field	a part of a database record which contains a specific category of information, eg a postcode
spreadsheet	a computer program which stores text and numbers on a grid system of columns and rows and enables calculations to be performed on the numbers
CSV	Comma Separated Values is a special format of text used to transfer data from one computer program to another – the fields/pieces of data are separated by commas
email management	a program which enables the computer to send and receive emails and to organise messages sent and received
EDI	Electronic Data Interchange (EDI) is a system which enables data and financial documents to be sent electronically from computer to computer - eg from supermarket to supplier
ledgers	the books of the accounting system which contain individual accounts – the sales ledger, for example, contains the individual accounts of customers who buy on credit (ie they pay later)
integrated system	a computerised accounting system which links together all the ledgers and accounts so that a transaction on one account will always be mirrored in another account
double-entry book-keeping	the method of manual book-keeping from which the integrated system has been developed – it involves the making of two entries in the accounts for every financial transaction
hard copy	a paper document containing data – often a printout from a computer
data export	the transfer of data from one computer program to another

STUDENT
ACTIVITIES

note

Many of the practical functions of computer programs described in this chapter will form the basis of tasks in activities in later chapters. The activities which follow here will develop your general understanding of the way computer programs work together.

1.1 What is the difference between computer hardware and computer software?

1.2 What is the difference between an intranet and the internet?

What are the advantages to an organisation of using an intranet?

Can you think of any disadvantages to an organisation of using an intranet?

1.3 Describe the main functions of the following programs (ie what they 'do'):

(a)   a word processing program

(b)   a database program

(c)   a spreadsheet program

(d)   an email management program

1.4 Give one example of the use of the four programs in 1.3 in all of the three businesses listed below. Try and think of different examples for each.

(a)   a local car garage

(b)   a travel agency

(c)   an independent financial advisor

1.5 What is the difference between a field and a record in a database program?

1.6 Why is a spreadsheet program so useful if you want to

(a)   make a financial plan which involves inputting figures which might vary?

(b)   illustrate trends in figures that you have input?

1.7 How can you send an invoice electronically?

1.8 What are the main features of a typical computer accounting program?

1.9 Name the ledgers in an accounting system. Describe the type of accounts that they hold.

1.10 What is the main difference between a computer accounting system and the traditional double-entry book-keeping system? Why should this difference also be an advantage of a computer accounting system?

1.11 List four types of transaction that are commonly input into a computer accounting system.

1.12 What different forms of output are available to a computer accounting system?

What forms of output are likely to be used by a business from its computer accounting system in the following circumstances:

(a) the business needs reports to be stored for at least six years so that they can be viewed by auditors, or HM Revenue & Customs investigators who may visit the business

(b) a customer (who is not online) phones up to request an up-to-date statement of account which is needed that day

(c) a sales rep who is online via her laptop emails to ask for an up-to-date list of customer contacts

(d) the sales department wants to send out a standard letter announcing a new range of products to the customers who have accounts on the computer accounting system

chapter introduction

■ Before looking in detail at the setting up of a computer accounting system it is important to establish the principles of good housekeeping for computers. In other words, knowing how to look after the computer hardware and software and avoid losing either the equipment or the data held on it.

■ The issues we will look at in this chapter include:

- the importance of making visual checks when starting up the computer

- the use of passwords and access rights to the computer accounting system

- logging onto the computer and dealing with dates

- saving and backing up data

- restoring data in Sage

- getting help when things go wrong

- closing down

- password protection

- dealing with security risks

- legal regulations relating to computer operation

COMPUTER CARE

An organisation that uses computers will have invested thousands of pounds in buying equipment and in training staff to operate it. A business that fails to look after the equipment and the data that it holds is potentially throwing this money down the drain.

What are the dangers? They relate both to the equipment and to the data. In the first part of this chapter we will explain the importance of treating the equipment with care when turning it on, running it and closing it down. The second part of the chapter deals with the importance of protecting the data itself from viruses, hackers and unauthorised access from employees.

STARTING UP A COMPUTER SYSTEM

There are a number of visual safety checks that you must perform when starting up a computer system.

hardware components

Are all the hardware components there? Check to see if the main processing unit and peripherals such as screens, printers, back-up drives and scanners are in place and have not been moved by a cleaner or removed for maintenance, or worse still, by a thief!

If there is a problem, you should refer it to someone in a position of responsibility who will be able to deal with it. Clearly if equipment is missing, it will need to be dealt with urgently.

have you checked the power supply?

power plugs

Is everything plugged in correctly? Check the following:

- are the mains plugs in place and is the electrical supply up and running?

- check any power supply surge protectors are correctly in place (these protect against surges in current which might damage sensitive electronic devices such as computers)

- are the mains plugs plugged in properly?

If there is any problem here you should either fix it yourself if you are able, or refer it to someone in a position of responsibility who will be able to deal with it.

peripheral plugs and cables

In a standalone system (one computer on its own) the main processing unit should be connected to a variety of devices such as mouse, keyboard, monitor and peripheral units such as printer, scanner and back-up device such as a zip drive.

A quick visual check will tell you whether these devices are all securely plugged in.

You should also check that the internet connection is plugged in.

are you connected?

If you are working on a network system you will need to check your work station connections. Peripheral devices such as printers may be situated elsewhere in the office and will not be connected directly to your machine. In this case you will be able to check on screen once the computer is up and running.

Lastly, and very importantly, check that cables are not positioned dangerously, where people could trip over them and possibly injure themselves. This is part of your general responsibility under the Health and Safety regulations which apply in the workplace. You may be able to deal with dangerous cabling yourself, or, if you are not able to put it right, you should refer the problem to someone in a position of responsibility who will be able to deal with it.

powering up

When all these checks have been carried out, you should switch on the computer(s) in the usual way and hopefully experience a trouble-free session operating the computer system.

USING PASSWORDS

Before getting going on the computer you are likely to have to use **passwords** to enable you to gain access to:

- the computer itself, for example if you are using a workstation on a network – this is a **system password**
- particular computer programs, some of which may enable you to access sensitive or confidential information – eg the accounting software – this is a **software password**

We will deal with the security aspect of passwords later in this chapter. We will concentrate here on the practical aspects of passwords as part of the starting up procedure.

system passwords – logging on

logging onto the system

If you are working on a network you have to 'log on' as a user before you can use a computer workstation. You may have to give a user name and also a unique password. The user name will normally show on the screen as you input it, but the password will show as a series of dots or asterisks. The example on the left shows someone logging onto a computer in the production department. Logging on is a simple process, and you may well be familiar with it because it is normally used when you log onto the internet.

software passwords – accessing a program

Passwords are also needed to protect sensitive and confidential data held on the computer system. This is particularly important in the areas of staff records and also in the case of financial data processed by computer accounting programs.

One solution to the problem of unauthorised employees gaining access to sensitive financial data is the use of **passwords** to gain access to the computer program. Many larger businesses will employ a number of people who need to operate the computer accounting system; they will be issued with an appropriate password. Businesses can also set up **access rights** which restrict certain employees to certain activities and prevent them from accessing more sensitive areas such as the making of payments from the bank account.

When an employee comes to operate, for example, a Sage computer accounting package, he or she will be asked to 'log on'. In the example from Sage 50 shown below a person called Tom enters his log on name and a password (COBBLY).

The screen from Sage 50 (see below) shows that Ben has partial access to the Sage accounts. He is allowed to deal with Customers, Suppliers, the Nominal (Main) Ledger, Products and Invoicing. He cannot, however, access the Bank records.

LOGGING ON AND DEALING WITH DATES

the different dates

One potential problem area for the operator of a computer accounting system is the use of dates when inputting. There are a number of dates that need to borne in mind:

- the actual date – most people can manage this concept
- the **system date** – this is the date that the computer thinks is the actual date – the computer is normally right
- the **program date** – the date which you can instruct the accounting software to use as the actual date
- the **financial year** start date – the month in which the financial year of the business starts

logging on and using dates

When you log on and start using the computer accounting software, you should check that the date shown at the bottom of the screen is the date you want to use for your input.

The date shown here will be allocated to any transactions that you input into the computer. Normally this is the **system date** (the date the computer thinks it is).

You should then ask yourself if you want your transactions to be allocated any other date. This might be the case if . . .

- you are inputting a batch of transactions which went through last week – for example a number of cheques received from customers – and you want the transactions to show on the records as going through last week
- you are in a training situation and you have been given a specific date for input

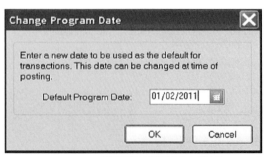

If you are using Sage software in these cases you should change the **program date** through the SETTINGS menu. The program date lets you set any date to be 'today's date'.

This new date will appear against every transaction you make that day and will remain in force until you exit from the program, after which it reverts to the system (actual) date.

financial year

A business will use a financial year for accounting purposes. The financial year, like the calendar year, may run from January through to December. But the financial year can start anytime during the year; some businesses end their financial year on 31 March or 30 June, for example. When setting up the data in a computer accounting program you have to state when the financial year starts. In Sage this is done from the SETTINGS menu:

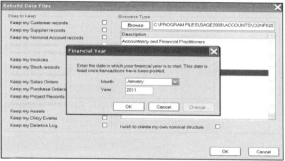

The financial year is important for the management of the business. The end-of-year routines run on the computer provide the data from which the end-of-year financial statements and management reports can be produced.

SAVING AND BACK-UP

The computer accounting program you are using will tell you when to Save your work. This is normally done after inputting a group of transactions and before passing on to the next task.

backing-up files

You will also need to **back-up** the data generated by the computer. There is no set rule about when you should do this, but it should be at least at the end of every day and preferably when you have completed a long run of inputting.

back-up media

If you are working on a network, you can normally save to your files, to your work station's hard disk and also to the server. If you have a standalone computer system, the back-up files should be saved to some form of storage device. This may take the form of a disk drive in the workstation itself or it may be an external drive.

Data can be backed up onto a variety of media:

- writable or rewriteable CDs (cheap and disposable)
- tape drive
- portable hard disk drive
- writable or rewriteable DVDs
- USB memory stick

Another back-up option is to send files by email and keep them secure at a remote location, although this option would be limited by file size.

back-up in Sage

Back-up in Sage is carried out from the FILE menu, or on the prompt when you close down. The screen gives you a choice of file name (by default the date) and asks to which drive you want the data saved. In the Sage screen shown below it is an external USB drive.

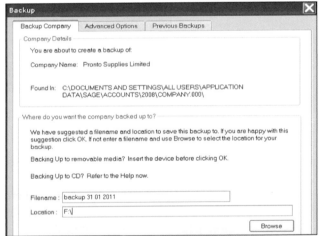

If you are using Sage you are recommended to run the ERROR CHECKING routine from MAINTENANCE (from the FILE menu) before backing up. This will check the data files and ensure that you do not back-up any corrupted data. The screen after a check looks like this:

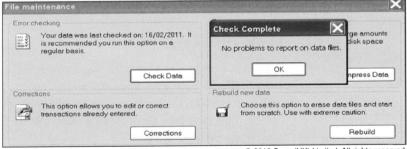

back-up policy

It is important that an organisation works out a systematic policy for back-up of its data. This should involve:

- more than one back-up held at any one time
- back-up media held off the premises
- periodic back-up (eg back-ups at the end of each month) stored securely

One solution is for the business to keep a set of back-up media (eg tapes) for each working day, labelled with the name of the day.

At the end of each working day the data is backed up on the appropriate back-up media, which are kept securely on site, preferably under lock and key.

As a further security measure, a second set of back-ups could be kept as an off-site security back-up. These would be backed up at the end of each day and taken off-site by an employee.

With this system in place the business has double security for its valuable data.

It should also be mentioned that the back-up media should be replaced periodically (every three months, for example) as they wear out in time and the data can become corrupted.

restoring data from a back-up

In the unfortunate event that the accounting data on your computer has been corrupted, you can **restore** the data from an earlier date from the appropriate back-up media. This is carried out in Sage from RESTORE in the File menu. Note that all the data is restored in this process; it is not possible to restore selected files. You should then run ERROR CHECKING routine from FILE MAINTENANCE to make sure the restored data is not corrupted.

GETTING HELP

A computer system that goes wrong can be very frustrating, not only for the organisation, but also for the customers that deal with it. Try booking a holiday at a travel agent when the 'system is down'.

If there is a problem, it should be fixed as soon as possible. If you cannot deal with it yourself, you should know where you can get help.

The type of problems that you are likely to encounter include:

*   hardware faults – eg a printer that jams, toner that runs out
*   software faults – program files that become corrupted
*   corrupt data or deleted or overwritten data files which stop your normal work flow

hardware failure

There will be times when you have equipment failures. If this happens, the problem should be referred to the person in the organisation who deals with the equipment. Many businesses will have back-up computers which can run the software and which can be loaded with your last back-up data. There may also be 'on-site' support provided under contract by the supplier of the hardware.

software failure

Software problems can be more complex. If it is a case of not knowing how to carry out a particular operation, refer the matter to someone who does. Help is always at hand through HELP menus, on-line support or telephone technical support to which the business is likely to have subscribed. If a program crashes, it may be necessary to restart the computer. If the program refuses to work after repeated attempts, it may have become corrupted, in which case it may need to be re-installed by a technician.

corrupted, deleted or overwritten data files

Problems can also be caused if a data file you are using

*   becomes **corrupt**, ie it becomes unusable and will not open or print, or both
*   gets **deleted** by accident when you are tidying up your computer desktop and sending what you think are redundant files into the recycle bin
*   is accidentally **overwritten** by an older version of a file, and in the process wipes out the work you may have done on the file

In these cases you have to rely on your back-up files.

CLOSE DOWN

Closing down the computer system correctly is important because a variety of problems can arise if the correct procedures are not followed.

When you wish to shut down you should:

■ exit each program by using the 'quit' command – this will warn you if you have any unsaved files still open and will enable you to save your work; it will also make sure that the program starts up properly next time the computer is used

■ use the correct command from the operating system to close the computer down

If you are using a work station on a network and need to keep the computer turned on – perhaps for someone else to use – you should log off, making sure that all your files are closed, saved and backed up.

DATA SECURITY

dangers to the data

The data held on the computer is irreplaceable once lost and so must be kept securely both on the computer system and also in the form of back-ups.

Back-up systems have already been discussed in this chapter. An essential element of data security is the maintenance of a foolproof back-up system and the secure location of back-up media, both on-site and off-site.

The data must be kept securely and protected from unauthorised users outside and inside the business:

■ people such as competitors or criminals outside the business may try to gain access to the data either directly (through 'hacking' if the computer is linked to the internet) or through an employee who can be persuaded to obtain the information

■ employees of the business may try to access the data in order to work a fraud – through the payroll, for example, or by making bogus payments to external bank accounts which they control

In this section we look at the various precautions that can be taken to minimise these risks.

PASSWORD PROTECTION

We have seen earlier in this chapter that passwords are needed to access:

■ the computer system itself (system passwords)

■ the software run on the computer system (software passwords)

The organisation can also increase security by ensuring that passwords are changed regularly and also that they are 'unbreakable'.

basic rules of choosing an individual password

1   Do not use the word 'password' (it does happen!)

2   Combine letters and numbers if possible.

3   Do not use your own name or date of birth.

4   Make it so that you can remember the password easily and avoid forgettable combinations such as z9ad2w8y7d — try the name and birthday of your first girlfriend/boyfriend, Lisa0511, for example, but avoid using similar details relating to your present partner (because people will guess them).

5   Never write the password down where people can see it, and never put it on a post-it note stuck on the computer monitor (it does happen!)

When you have chosen a password, make sure that nobody stands watching you when you are logging on; the password appears as dots on the screen, but people can work out what you are typing on the keyboard.

An organisation should ensure that if there is any suspicion that a password has been 'leaked', there should be a wholesale change of passwords.

IDENTIFYING SECURITY RISKS

Data on computer file needs to be protected against:

■ **corruption** – ie when the file goes 'wrong' and does not work properly – either because of a virus or because of poor storage facilities

■ **loss** – when the file is deleted, accidentally or intentionally – by an employee or by a virus introduced from outside

■ **illegal copying** – by an employee copying a program or by someone 'hacking in' from outside through the internet connection

Clearly the threats to data therefore come both internally, from employees, and externally, from hackers or viruses.

protecting data from internal risks

Much of the data held on computer file is sensitive and confidential in nature, for example:

■ payroll details of employees

■ financial details relating to customers

It is an unfortunate possibility that employees may be persuaded or paid by outsiders to obtain this information. As a result all employees should take reasonable precautions to prevent data that they are working from being used in this way. For example:

■ if you leave your computer, do not leave sensitive data on screen, or the program running

■ use a screensaver

■ use passwords wherever possible

■ if you print out a document with confidential information on it, do not leave it on the printer (or the photocopier!)

Another internal risk is **illegal copying** of computer data – often program files – by employees who 'borrow' disks to take home or 'lend' to friends. The answer here is to keep these types of files under strict control. A business using software will in any event have been granted a **licence** to use it, and any unauthorised copying will be a breach of that licence.

Careful and safe **storage** of computer data on various forms of media is also important. Heat and radiation can damage files held on disk, and the surface of CDs and DVDs can easily be scratched, causing corruption and data loss.

protecting data from external risks

External risks to data include:

■ thieves who steal data by stealing the computers on which it is held – computer laptops are particularly vulnerable

■ external hackers who access files within an organisation by 'hacking in' from the internet and accessing files held – often on a network

■ viruses sent into the computer system, either on a disk or through the internet

Protection against thieves can be achieved by rigorous security at the premises. CCTV is now commonly used to guard against crime. Laptops away from the premises should be kept under lock and key wherever possible, and preferably not left in cars. Hackers can be kept at bay by a 'firewall' on the internet portal of a computer network. A 'firewall' is software which keeps out all external interference and unwanted emails.

Computer viruses are dealt with in the next section.

VIRUS PROTECTION

Computers are vulnerable to viruses. A **virus** is a destructive program which can be introduced into the computer either from a disk, USB memory stick, an internet download, email attachment or from another computer.

Some viruses are relatively harmless and may merely display messages on the screen, others can be very damaging and destroy operating systems and data, putting the computer system completely out of action. Most computers are now sold already installed with virus protection software which will:

- establish a **firewall** to repel viruses
- check for existing viruses
- destroy known viruses
- check for damage to files on the hard disk
- repair damage to files on the hard disk where possible

This software should be run and updated regularly so that it can deal with the latest viruses.

The screen below shows a virus protection program scanning the hard disk of a computer. As you can see, it has not yet found any infected files.

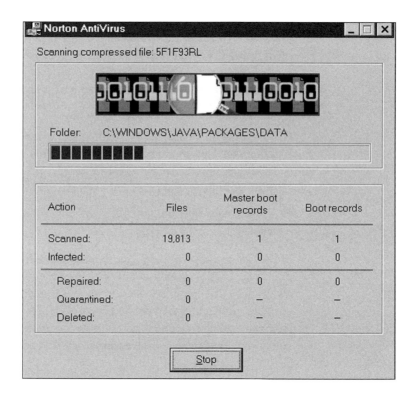

precautions against viruses

There are a number of precautions which you can take against viruses:

■ be wary of opening any unidentified email attachments which arrive

■ use protective software to inspect any disk or memory stick received from an outside source before opening up any file saved onto it

■ make sure that your protective software is up to date – very often they will update automatically over the internet

If your protective software announces that you have a virus, you should report it at once in your workplace and stop using your computer.

LEGAL REGULATIONS

Any organisation using computer systems of any type must comply with a number of legal requirements.

Businesses inevitably keep records of their customers and suppliers on file – either manually – a card index system, for example – or, more likely, on computer file. This is 'personal data'.

The **Data Protection Act (1998)** which came into force on 1 March 2000 establishes rules for the processing of personal data. The Act follows the guidelines of an EC Directive and brings the UK in line with European legal principles. The Act applies to a filing system of records held on **computer**, eg a computer database of customer names, addresses, telephone numbers, sales details, or a **manual** set of accessible records.

People have the legal right to know what personal details about them are held by an organisation. They can apply in writing for a copy of the personal data held on file by the organisation; they may have to pay a fee.

The Act states that an organisation should not without permission reveal:

■ information about one customer to another customer

■ information about its employees

This obviously applies very directly to data held on a computer accounting system such as Sage 50: customer information such as credit limits and account balances is obviously very sensitive.

Other regulations include the **Health and Safety at Work Act 1974** and **Display Screen Equipment Regulations 1992** which require that employers maintain computer equipment in good and safe condition, making sure that the risk of eyestrain and backstrain to employees is minimised.

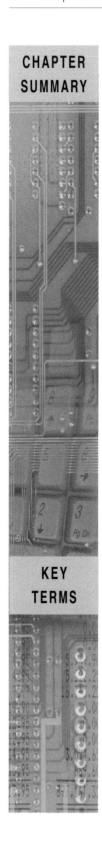

■ A business which has invested in a computer accounting system needs to ensure that both the equipment and the data held on it are well maintained.

■ Starting up a computer system involves a number of visual safety checks – relating to the hardware, plugs and cables – which have to take place before powering up the system

■ Passwords and access rights can be set up on the computer system to restrict access to the data to authorised employees.

■ A number of different dates are involved when logging onto the system: system dates, program dates and financial year dates.

■ Data should be backed up regularly and a back-up routine established. In the case of data corruption, data can be restored from the back-up media.

■ When operating a computer system it is important to know where help can be obtained when things go wrong, eg hardware failure, software failure and corruption of data.

■ It is important to follow the correct close down procedure for a computer system in order to avoid creating problems for the software and hardware.

■ Accounting data kept on a computer is valuable and vulnerable. Outsiders can use it to fraudulently obtain money and information about customers. Employees can log into the system to set up fraudulent money transfers.

■ Accounting data can be protected with virus protection software.

system password — a code word used to allow an employee to 'log on' to access the computer accounting system

software password — a code word used to allow an employee to 'log on' to access a particular computer accounting program, such as Sage 50

access rights — the right of an employee to access specified areas of the computer accounting program

system date — the date allocated by the operating system of the computer – normally the actual date

program date — the date which you can tell the computer accounting software to use as 'today's' date

financial year — the twelve month period used by the business to record its financial transactions

back-up

to copy the computer data onto a separate storage medium in order to ensure that the data is not lost

restore

to copy the back-up data back onto the computer when the original data has been lost or corrupted

corrupt data

data which has become unusable because it will not open, or print, or both

virus

a computer program introduced into the computer system which then disrupts or destroys the operation of the system

Data Protection Act

the law which establishes the regulations for the protection of personal data held by organisations on computer (and paper-based) files

STUDENT ACTIVITIES

2.1   Explain how passwords and access rights to accounting software help protect computer data.

2.2   Explain the difference between a system date and a program date used on a computer accounting program such as Sage.

2.3   Write down a suggested back-up policy for an office which runs a computer accounting system.

2.4   You are running a check on your computer accounting data at the end of the day before carrying out the back-up routine. The message appears on screen that a number of your data files have become corrupted. You normally back-up your data daily at the end of the day. Explain what you would do to rescue your data and bring the computer accounting records up-to-date.

2.5   You hear from a friend working for another business that their computer systems have had a catastrophic crash following infection by a virus which came in over the internet. Describe the measures you could take to safeguard against a similar catastrophe to your own systems.

2.6   Computer accounting data can be very vulnerable to unauthorised access.

(a)   Why could this data be valuable to outsiders and employees?

(b)   Which law protects personal data held by organisations such as businesses?

3 SETTING UP THE COMPANY IN SAGE

chapter introduction

■ Setting up a computer accounting program for a business or other organisation will take some time, but as long as the correct data is entered in the correct format there should be no problem.

■ We will assume here that the organisation setting up the computer accounting program is a business. Sage software always calls a business a 'company' – so we will adopt that term.

■ The chapter introduces a Case Study business – Pronto Supplies Limited – which will be used through this book to show how computer accounting works.

■ There is plenty of help around when you are setting up accounts on the computer. In Sage, for example, there is the user guide, the 'Help' function, and on-screen step-by-step instruction procedures known as 'Wizards'.

■ The data that will have to be input includes:

  - the 'company' details such as name and address, financial year and VAT status

  - the customer details and any sales transactions already carried out

  - the supplier details and any purchases transactions already carried out

  - details of accounts for income and expenses, assets (items owned), liabilities (loans) and capital (money put in by the owner) – this is all contained in the nominal ledger

■ This chapter concentrates on setting up the company details. The other data – customer and supplier details and balances and the nominal ledger – will be covered in the next two chapters.

WHERE ARE YOU STARTING FROM?

If you are reading this book you are likely to be in one of two situations:

1   You are in a real business and looking for guidance in setting up a computer accounting system.

2   You are a student in a training situation and will have the program already set up for you on a training centre network. You will be given exercises to practise the various functions of a computer accounting program.

In the first case – the real business – you will be starting from scratch and will have to go through the whole installation and set-up procedure. This is not at all difficult. The software itself will take you through the various steps.

In the second case – the training centre situation – the computer may already have accounting records on it, possibly another student's work. What you must do here is to remove the data (making sure it is backed up first!) and then start again. This is done using a 'rebuild' procedure. There is more about this on page 177.

The Case Study which follows on the next page – Pronto Supplies Limited – assumes that you are in business setting up computer accounts for the first time using Sage software. It is important for your studies that you know how this is done, even if you may not carry out in the training centre all the procedures explained in the Case Study.

WHY SAGE AND WHICH SAGE?

Osborne Books (the publisher of this book) has chosen Sage software for this book for two very good reasons:

1   Sage software is widely used in business and is recognised as a user-friendly and reliable product.

2   Osborne Books has used Sage itself for over fifteen years and is well used to the way it works.

The Sage software used as a basis for this book is Sage 50 Accounts Professional 2009 (Version 15). The screens displayed in this book are taken from this version by kind permission of Sage (UK) Limited.

screen illustrations

It should be appreciated that some training centres and businesses may be using older and slightly different versions and so some of the screens may look slightly different. This does not matter however: using Sage is like driving different models of car – the controls may be located in slightly different places and the dashboard may not look exactly the same, but the controls are still there and they still do the same thing. So if the screens shown here look unfamiliar, examine them carefully and you will see that they will contain the same (or very similar) Sage icons and functions as the version you are using.

CASE STUDY

PRONTO SUPPLIES LIMITED: SETTING UP THE COMPANY IN SAGE

the business

Pronto Supplies is a limited company run by Tom Cox who has worked as a computer consultant for over ten years. Pronto Supplies provides local businesses and other organisations with computer hardware, software and consumables needed in offices. It also provides consultancy for computer set-ups through its proprietor, Tom Cox. Pronto Supplies has eight employees in total. The business is situated on an industrial estate, at Unit 17 Severnvale Estate, Broadwater Road, Mereford, Wyvern, MR1 6TF.

the accounting system

Pronto Supplies Limited started business on 1 January 2011. The business is registered for VAT (ie it charges VAT on its sales) and after a month of using a manual accounting system Tom has decided to transfer the accounts to Sage 50 software and sign up for a year's telephone technical support. Tom has also decided to put his payroll onto the computer, but this will be run on a separate Sage program.

Tom has chosen Sage 50 because it will enable him to:

■ record the invoices issued to his customers to whom he sells on credit

■ pay his suppliers on the due date

■ keep a record of his bank receipts and payments

■ record his income and expenses, business assets and loans in a nominal ledger

In short he will have an integrated computer accounting package which will enable him to:

■ record all his financial transactions

■ print out reports

■ manage his business finances

■ save time (and money) in running his accounting system

getting started

Tom has decided to use just one machine in the office to run Sage and so he has bought a 'single user' package together with telephone technical support for a year.

He installs the program from his CD and uses the ActiveSetup Wizard to take him through the procedure.

Note

A Wizard is a series of dialogue boxes on the screen which take you step-by-step through a particular procedure. The ActiveSetup Wizard is one of a number of Wizards in Sage. Wizards generally appear automatically on screen when you need to carry out a complicated procedure.

The ActiveSetup Wizard takes Tom through a series of screens by which he can personalise Sage to his business. In the first he chooses to set up a new company as shown below.

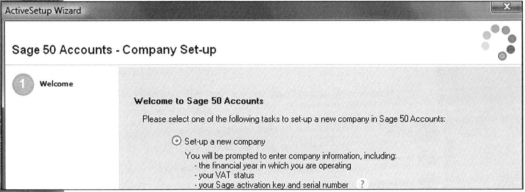

Next he must enter his company details

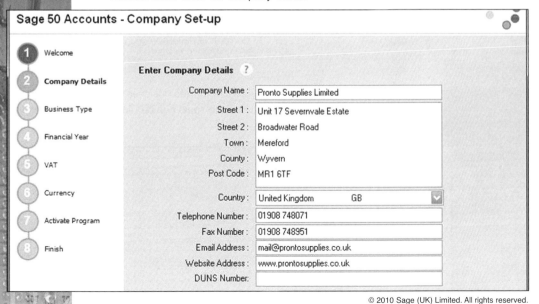

As Pronto Supplies is a fairly standard trading business, in the next screen Tom chooses General (standard) as the type of business. The list of accounts will cover all his business needs such as sales, purchases, bank accounts and expenses.

ActiveSetup Wizard

Sage 50 Accounts - Company Set-up

1 Welcome
2 Company Details
3 **Business Type**
4 Financial Year
5 VAT
6 Currency
7 Activate Program

Select Business Type ?

Select a type of business that most closely matches your own. If your business type is not listed, please select General.

- ⊙ General (standard)
- ○ Accountancy   ○ Hotels
- ○ Agriculture   ○ Legal
- ○ Building   ○ Medical
- ○ Charity   ○ Transport
- ○ Garage   ○ Customised

Preview

Sales (Money In)
Sales Type A
Sales Type B
Sales Type C

Costs (Money Out)
Materials Purchased
Materials Imported
Miscellaneous Purchases

Next he sets up his financial year start date: January 2011

1 Welcome
2 Company Details
3 Business Type
4 **Financial Year**
5 VAT
6 Currency

Select Financial Year ?

Choose when your company financial year begins.

Month January

Year 2011

If you are not sure when your financial year begins, please contact your accountant for guidance before you proceed any further.

The next two screens require Tom to enter the business VAT details and the currency he trades in. Finally he must enter the serial number and activation key provided by Sage to activate the program.

2 Company Details
3 Business Type
4 Financial Year
5 **VAT**
6 Currency
7 Activate Program

Select VAT Details

Is your company VAT registered?

⊙ Yes   ○ No

Enter your VAT registration number 404 7106 52 ?

Is your company using the VAT cash accounting scheme? ?

○ Yes   ⊙ No

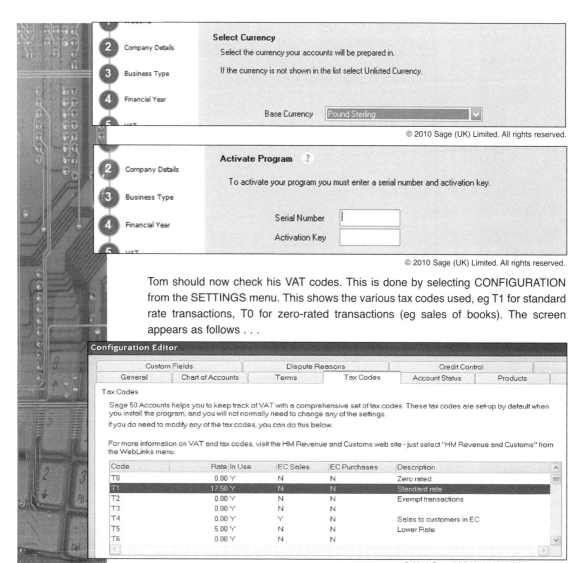

Tom should now check his VAT codes. This is done by selecting CONFIGURATION from the SETTINGS menu. This shows the various tax codes used, eg T1 for standard rate transactions, T0 for zero-rated transactions (eg sales of books). The screen appears as follows . . .

Tom can at any time check and amend if necessary his company details. This is done in COMPANY PREFERENCES which can also be found in the SETTINGS menu. This screen is illustrated on the next page.

There are a number of tabs, including 'Address'. The address entered here will automatically be printed by the program, as required, on business documents such a invoices and credit notes. Tom has the option to enter a different delivery address, but this is unlikely in his case, as all the deliveries from his suppliers will be made to his warehouse at Unit 17 Severnvale Estate. He decides not to bother with this option.

He also does not enter anything into the other tabs as he does not need these facilities at present.

The third tab 'Parameters' provides Tom with a number of options. Most of these he will not have to worry about at the moment.

Tom's COMPANY PREFERENCES screen appears as follows . . .

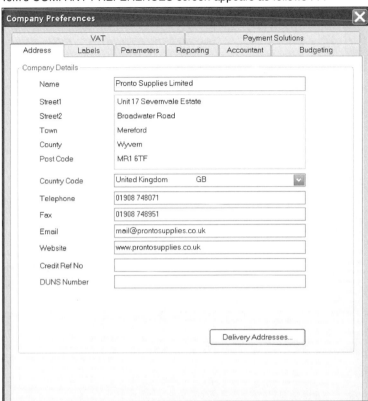

Tom also needs to set up the passwords for members of his staff so that access to the Sage accounts can be restricted to authorised people. Adjustments to passwords and access rights are carried out through the CHANGE PASSWORD and ACCESS RIGHTS in SETTINGS

The screen below shows how Tom creates a password for Ben James, his assistant. Tom subsequently restricts Ben's access to the Bank accounts in ACCESS RIGHTS by clicking on the Details button.

HELP!

Tom now has his business details set up on the computer but he still has to install his account balances and get to know how the system works. Sage provides a number of facilities which help the user when he or she needs information: wizards, a user guide, and an on-screen Help function.

wizards

Wizards, as seen in the Case Study, help the user step-by-step through difficult procedures. We will encounter wizards in later chapters.

user guide

The Sage User Guide is a useful reference source. It can be accessed from within the program and printed if required. Less experienced users may find on-screen guidance more helpful.

on-screen Help

On-screen help can be accessed through either the Help menu or by pressing the F1 function key. It works with three tabs, all of which will enable the user to access information. Look at the diagram below.

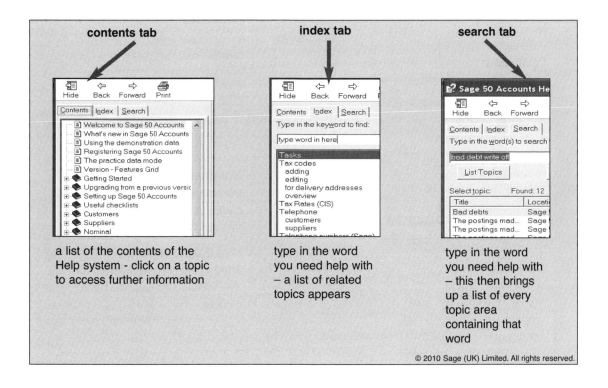

contents tab — a list of the contents of the Help system - click on a topic to access further information

index tab — type in the word you need help with – a list of related topics appears

search tab — type in the word you need help with – this then brings up a list of every topic area containing that word

TRANSFERRING DATA INTO SAGE

When a business first sets up a computer accounting system a substantial amount of data will need to be transferred onto the computer, even if the business is in its first week of trading. A summary of this data is shown in the diagram below.

The images shown in the diagram are the icons on the Sage desktop which represent the different operating areas of the program. As you can see they relate to the ledger structure of a manual book-keeping system.

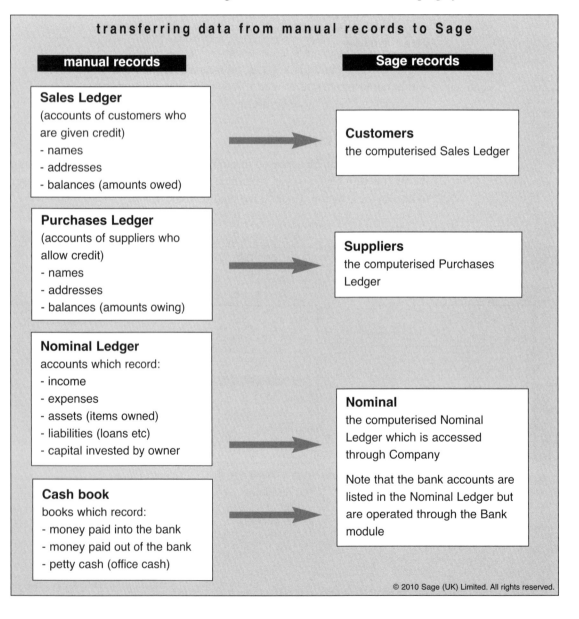

transferring data from manual records to Sage

manual records

Sage records

Sales Ledger
(accounts of customers who are given credit)
- names
- addresses
- balances (amounts owed)

Customers
the computerised Sales Ledger

Purchases Ledger
(accounts of suppliers who allow credit)
- names
- addresses
- balances (amounts owing)

Suppliers
the computerised Purchases Ledger

Nominal Ledger
accounts which record:
- income
- expenses
- assets (items owned)
- liabilities (loans etc)
- capital invested by owner

Nominal
the computerised Nominal Ledger which is accessed through Company

Note that the bank accounts are listed in the Nominal Ledger but are operated through the Bank module

Cash book
books which record:
- money paid into the bank
- money paid out of the bank
- petty cash (office cash)

■ A business setting up a Sage computer accounting program for the first time will have to enter the details of the company on-screen, for example

- the program serial number and Activation Key code

- the start date of the financial year of the business

- the business VAT registration number and VAT Status (where applicable)

- the business name and address

- any passwords that are needed

■ The business will also be required to enter the 'chart of accounts' that it requires – this is the list of Nominal accounts which will automatically be set up on the system.

■ The business can make use of the on-screen Wizard and other 'Help' functions in the set-up process. The index is the most useful of these.

■ The business will need to enter details and balances of its customers, suppliers and its nominal accounts (the other accounts). These are covered in the next two chapters.

Wizard   on-screen dialogue boxes in a Sage program which take you step-by-step through complex procedures

sales ledger   the accounts of customers to whom a business sells on credit   - in Sage this part of the accounting system is known as 'Customers'

purchases ledger the accounts of suppliers from whom a business buys on credit   - in Sage this part of the accounting system is known as 'Suppliers'

nominal ledger   the remaining accounts in the accounting system which are not Customers or Suppliers, eg income, expenses, assets, liabilities – in Sage this is known as 'Nominal'.

chart of accounts the structure of the nominal accounts, which groups accounts into categories such as Sales, Purchases, Overheads . . . and so on

STUDENT ACTIVITIES

3.1   Describe the sources of assistance that are available to Alan Bramley who is setting up a Sage system for the first time.

3.2   Helen Egremont is setting up a Sage system for the first time. What details will have to be input before any account balances can be transferred?

3.3   James Greave has been trading for six months using a manual double-entry book-keeping system. Into what part of a Sage system will the following ledgers be transferred?

(a) Sales Ledger

(b) Purchases Ledger

(c) Nominal Ledger

3.4   Explain briefly what a chart of accounts is.

PRONTO SUPPLIES LIMITED INPUTTING TASK

warning note!
This activity involves you in setting up a new company in Sage and inputting live data into the computer.
Remember to Save your data and keep any printouts as you progress through the tasks.

Task 1

Set the program date as 31 January 2011. Set up the company details of Pronto Supplies Limited in Sage. The details are:

Address/contact	Unit 17 Severnvale Estate, Broadwater Road, Mereford, Wyvern, MR1 6TF.
	Tel 01908 748071, Fax 01908 748951
	Email mail@prontosupplies.co.uk
	www.prontosupplies.co.uk
Financial year start:	January 2011 (if not already input)
VAT Registration number	404 7106 52
Chart of Accounts:	General Business – Standard Accounts

Task 2

Check the business details in the first tab of COMPANY PREFERENCES in SETTINGS.

Now check that the Parameters tab in COMPANY PREFERENCES matches the screen on page 44. Make any amendments if you need to.

chapter introduction

■ The term 'Customers' is a word which in Sage means people to whom a business sells on credit. In other words, the goods or services are supplied straightaway and the customer is allowed to pay at a specified later date – often a month or more later.

■ A business keeps running accounts for the amounts owed by individual customers – much as a bank keeps accounts for its customers. The accounts are maintained by the business in the 'Sales Ledger'.

■ The term 'Suppliers' is a word which in Sage means people from whom a business buys on credit. In other words, the goods or services are supplied straightaway and the business is allowed to pay at a specified later date.

■ A business keeps running accounts for the amounts owed to individual suppliers. The accounts are maintained by the business in the 'Purchases Ledger'.

■ This chapter continues the Pronto Supplies Limited Case Study and shows how the business sets up its Customer and Supplier records on the computer.

■ When the accounts have been set up on the computer the business will need to input the amounts owed by Customers and owing to Suppliers.

■ The next step – dealt with in the next chapter – is to input the Nominal ledger accounts. When this has been done, the set up is complete and the system will be ready for the input of transactions such as sales and purchases.

CASH AND CREDIT SALES

cash and credit – the difference

When businesses such as manufacturers, shops and travel agents sell their products, they will either get their money straightaway, or they will receive the money after an agreed time period. The first type of sale is a **cash sale**, the second is a **credit sale**. These can be defined further as:

cash sale   A sale of a product where the money is received straightaway – this can include payment in cash, or by cheque or by credit card and debit card. The word 'cash' means 'immediate' – it does not mean only notes and coins.

credit sale   A sale of a product where the sale is agreed and the goods or services are supplied but the buyer pays at a later date agreed at the time of the sale.

buying and selling for cash and on credit

Businesses are likely to get involved in cash and credit sales not only when they are selling their products but also when they are buying. Some goods and services will be bought for cash and some on credit. Buying and selling are just two sides of the same operation.

You will see from this that it is the nature of the business that will decide what type of sales and purchases it makes. A supermarket, for example, will sell almost entirely for cash – the cash and cheques and credit/debit card payments come in at the checkouts – and it will buy from its suppliers on credit and pay them later. It should therefore always have money in hand – which is a good situation to be in for a business.

SETTING UP CUSTOMER ACCOUNTS

accounting records for customers

You will first need to learn some accounting terminology.

Customers who buy from a business on credit are known as **debtors** because they owe money to the business.

The amounts owed by customers (debtors) are recorded in individual customer accounts in the **Sales Ledger**. In double-entry terms these customer account balances are **debit balances** (remember debtors = debits).

The total of all the customer (debtor) accounts in the Sales Ledger is recorded in an account known as **Debtors Control Account**. This is the total amount owing by the customers of a business.

accounting records for suppliers

When a business purchases goods and services from its suppliers on credit the suppliers are known as **creditors** because the business owes them money.

The amounts owed to suppliers (creditors) are recorded in individual supplier accounts in the **Purchases Ledger**. In double-entry terms these customer account balances are **credit balances** (remember creditors = credits).

The total of all the supplier (creditor) accounts in the Purchases Ledger is known as **Creditors Control Account**. This is the total amount owing to the suppliers of a business.

All this is summarised in the table set out below.

Customers

- buy from the business

- have individual accounts in the Sales Ledger

- are also known as 'debtors'

- normally have debit balances on their accounts

Suppliers

- sell to the business

- have individual accounts in the Purchases Ledger

- are also known as 'creditors'

- normally have credit balances on their accounts

credit references

A business is only likely to sell to customers on credit (ie receive the money at a later date) if it is reasonably sure that the money will come in. When an account is opened the seller should obtain credit references to make sure the customer can pay. These references can include:

bank reference   can the business meet its financial obligations?

trade references   references from other suppliers to this customer – does the customer have a good history of paying up on time?

credit bureau   a reference from a business (a credit bureau) which specialises in assessing the credit risk of customers

credit limits

When a business is opening a new account it will need to establish a credit limit. A **credit limit** is the maximum amount of credit a seller is willing to grant to a customer. For example if a credit limit of £5,000 is set up by the seller, the customer can owe up to £5,000 at any one time – for example two invoices of £2,500. A well-managed business will keep an eye on situations where a credit limit might be exceeded.

credit terms

The seller will need to establish its **terms** of trading with its customers and the customer will have to agree. The terms are normally set out on the invoice (the invoice is the document issued when the goods or services are sold and supplied). They include:

- **trade discount** given to the customer based on the selling price, for example a customer with a 30% trade discount will pay £70 for goods costing £100, ie £100 minus £30 (30% discount)

- the **payment terms** – the length of credit allowed to the customer, ie the number of days the customer is allowed to wait before paying up – this is commonly 30 days after the invoice date

- **settlement discount** (also known as **cash discount**) sometimes given to a customer who settles up early within a specified number of days, for example a 2.5% reduction for settlement within 7 days

day-to-day customer/supplier information

A business will need information on file relating to its day-to-day dealings with customers and suppliers. For example:

- the name and address of the customer

- telephone, fax and email numbers and website address (if there is one)

- contact names

- credit limit, trade discount, payment terms and any settlement discount agreed

setting up the accounts in Sage

As you will see from the last three pages, there is a great deal of information that has to be input when setting up accounts for customers and suppliers on a computer accounting program such as Sage.

In the Case Study which follows on page 55 we will follow the steps taken by Pronto Supplies Limited in setting up its Customers and Suppliers records.

SETTING UP THE COMPUTER FILES

There are two methods in Sage for setting up new records for customers or suppliers. If, for example, you wanted to set up a new Customers account you could . . .

1   Go to the CUSTOMERS screen and click on NEW. You will be given a Wizard to take you through the procedure.

2   Go to the CUSTOMERS screen and click on RECORD. You will be given blank screens to complete, but with no Wizard guidance.

The Wizard screen is shown below and the second method is illustrated in the Case Study, as the process is very simple.

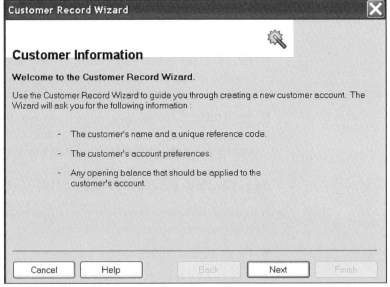

Whether you are using the Wizard or just setting up a new record through RECORD, you will need to have to hand all the customer details you have on file. These are the type of details covered earlier in this chapter.

customer and supplier reference codes

You will see from the Wizard screen shown above that you need to decide on a unique reference code for each customer and supplier account. This code can be letters, numbers, or a mixture of both. If letters are used they are often an abbreviation of the account name. This process, using both letters and numbers, will be illustrated in the Case Study.

customer and supplier record defaults

If you are setting up a number of customer and supplier accounts it is possible that the terms agreed – discounts and payment periods – will be the same for each customer or supplier account. To save you entering these in each and every account (which can take a lot of time!) you can establish a default set of terms which will apply to all accounts. These can be set up from the 'terms' tab of the CONFIGURATION EDITOR in SETTINGS.

It is also important to establish the standard VAT rate to be used in transactions (currently 17.5%) and also the default account number used for sales to customers (usually account number 4000). This is carried out from the 'Record' tab in   CUSTOMER DEFAULTS in SETTINGS. In the illustration below note the default VAT code (T1, 17.5%) and the 'Def N/C' default Sales Account number 4000 ('N/C stands for 'Nominal Code').

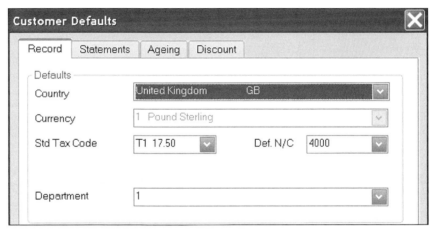

CASE STUDY

PRONTO SUPPLIES LIMITED: SETTING UP CUSTOMERS AND SUPPLIERS IN SAGE

Tom Cox at Pronto Supplies has decided to input his customer and supplier records into the computer first, and will then afterwards input the Nominal balances.

During the month of January Tom had set up accounts for customers and suppliers which at the end of the month (31 January) have balances as follows:

Customers   6 accounts in the Sales Ledger   Total now outstanding £29,534

Suppliers   3 accounts in the Purchases Ledger   Total now outstanding £18,750

Tom has kept the relevant financial documents – sales and purchase invoices and purchase order forms – in two separate files marked 'Credit Sales' and 'Credit Purchases'. The accounts are as follows:

customers

account reference	account name	amount outstanding (£)
JB001	John Butler & Associates	5,500.00
CH001	Charisma Design	2,400.00
CR001	Crowmatic Ltd	3,234.00
DB001	David Boossey	3,400.00
KD001	Kay Denz	6,500.00
LG001	L Garr & Co	8,500.00
Total	(Debtors Control Account)	29,534.00

suppliers

account reference	account name	amount outstanding (£)
DE001	Delco PLC	5,750.00
EL001	Electron Supplies	8,500.00
MA001	MacCity	4,500.00
Total	(Creditors Control Account)	18,750.00

entering the customer defaults

Tom sets his program date to 31 January 2011. He decides that he will save time by setting up his standard terms in the CONFIGURATION EDITOR in SETTINGS:

Payment due days	30 days
Terms of payment	Payment 30 days of invoice

He also checks his default VAT code (T1) and rate (17.5%) and Sales Account number (4000) in CUSTOMER DEFAULTS (reached through SETTINGS):

VAT rate	Standard rate of 17.5% (this is Tax Code T1)
Default nominal code	4000
	(Note that this is his computer hardware Sales Account, which accounts for most of his sales to customers; Tom will later allocate further separate sales account numbers for sales of computer software and computer consultancy services)

Tom decides not to set a default credit limit as this will vary from customer to customer and will be input with the individual customer details.

Note also that as Tom has not long been in business he does not allow **discounts** on his sales nor receive discounts on his purchases. These will be negotiated as time goes on.

entering customer details and opening balances

Tom will now enter the details and the opening balance for each customer. He does this by clicking on RECORD in CUSTOMERS. The first customer to input is John Butler Associates. The information he wants to input (including the invoice issued in January) is as follows:

Account name	John Butler & Associates
Account reference	JB001
Address	24 Shaw Street
	Mereford
	MR4 6KJ
Contact name	John Butler

Telephone 01908 824342, Fax 01908 824295, Email mail@jbutler.co.uk www.jbutler.co.uk

Credit limit £10,000

Invoice reference 10013 for £5,500.00 issued on 05 01 11

Tom inputs the data on the 'Details' screen, checks the data and then Saves.

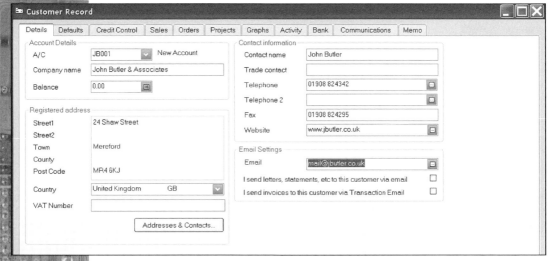

He now has to input the details of the invoice which he had issued on 5 January and which has not yet been paid. He does this by clicking the O/B button which brings up the screen shown on the next page. When prompted to Save the new record, Tom clicks 'Yes'.

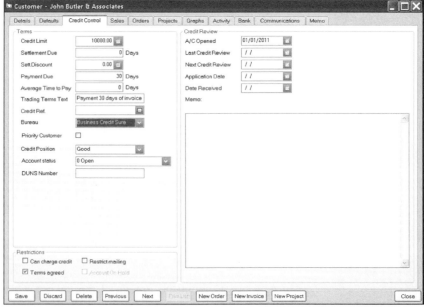

The data Tom inputs into the above screen are:

Ref:	the invoice number
Date:	the date the invoice was issued
Type:	the transaction was the issue of an invoice
Gross:	the total amount of the invoice

Having saved this data, Tom will go to the CREDIT CONTROL screen and input the credit limit, the payment period and the terms, and tick the box marked 'Terms Agreed' and then Save again. Some of these details may already be on screen if Tom has used the CONFIGURATION EDITOR (see page 55).

Tom will now repeat this process with the other five customer records, checking carefully as he goes and saving each record as it is created.

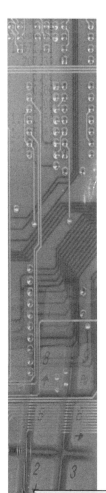

entering supplier details and opening balances

Tom can now carry out the same process for supplier details and opening balances. He will first ensure that the Supplier Defaults in SETTINGS include T1 as the default tax code and 5000 as the default Nominal Account number.

He sets up his Supplier accounts by clicking on RECORD in SUPPLIERS. The first supplier to input is Delco PLC. The information he wants to input (including the invoice issued by the supplier) is as follows:

Account name	Delco PLC
Account reference	DE001
Address	Delco House
	Otto Way
	New Milton
	SR1 6TF
Contact name	Nina Patel

Telephone 01722 295875, Fax 01722 295611, Email sales@delco.co.uk
www.delco.co.uk

Credit limit granted £10,000, payment terms 30 days of invoice date

Invoice reference 4563 for £5,750.00 issued by Delco PLC on 04 01 11

Tom will now input the supplier details and opening balances, starting with Delco PLC. The completed Delco PLC details screen is shown below.

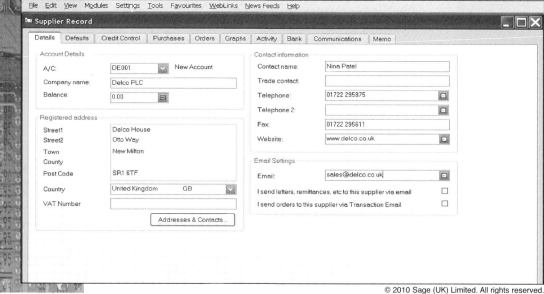

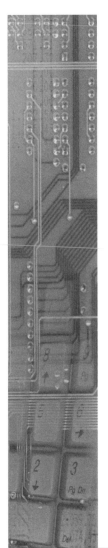

Tom will now input the credit limit and payment terms agreed on the credit control screen of the Supplier record. These are not held as defaults because they may well vary from supplier to supplier. The 'terms agreed' box will also be ticked.

File Edit View Modules Settings Tools Favourites WebLinks News Feeds Help

Supplier - Delco PLC

Details	Defaults	Credit Control	Purchases	Orders	Graphs	Activity	Bank	Communications	Memo

Terms

Credit Limit	10000.00
Settlement Due	0 Days
Sett.Discount	0.00
Payment Due	30 Days
Trading Terms Text	30 days of invoice date
Credit Reference	
Bureau	Business Credit Sure
Priority Supplier	☐
Credit Position	Good
Account status	0 Open
DUNS Number	

Credit Review

A/C Opened	01/01/2011
Last Credit Review	/ /
Next Credit Review	/ /
Application Date	/ /
Date Received	/ /
Memo:	

Tom will now repeat this process with the other supplier records, checking carefully as he goes and saving each record as it is created.

the final checks

Tom will need to ensure that his input is correct and that the customer and supplier accounts are accurate.

Tom will now check the individual account entries by comparing his original paper-based records with reports printed from CUSTOMERS and SUPPLIERS.

The input of customer invoices can be checked from the Day Books: Customer Invoices (Summary) report, which can be printed from the list of reports accessed through the REPORTS icon on the CUSTOMERS menu bar.

Pronto Supplies Limited

Day Books: Customer Invoices (Summary)

Customer From:
Customer To: ZZZZZZZZ

Transaction From: 1
Transaction To: 99,999,999

Tran No.	Items	Tp	Date	A/C Ref	Inv Ref	Details	Net Amount	Tax Amount	Gross Amount
1	1	SI	05/01/2011	JB001	10013	Opening Balance	5,500.00	0.00	5,500.00
3	1	SI	05/01/2011	CH001	10014	Opening Balance	2,400.00	0.00	2,400.00
4	1	SI	09/01/2011	CR001	10015	Opening Balance	3,234.00	0.00	3,234.00
5	1	SI	10/01/2011	DB001	10016	Opening Balance	3,400.00	0.00	3,400.00
6	1	SI	10/01/2011	KD001	10017	Opening Balance	6,500.00	0.00	6,500.00
7	1	SI	17/01/2011	LG001	10019	Opening Balance	8,500.00	0.00	8,500.00
						Totals:	29,534.00	0.00	29,534.00

End of Report

The input of supplier invoices can be checked from the Day Books: Supplier Invoices (Summary) report accessed through REPORTS on the SUPPLIERS menu bar.

Pronto Supplies Limited
Day Books: Supplier Invoices (Summary)

						Supplier From:			
						Supplier To:		ZZZZZZZZ	
Transaction From:	1								
Transaction To:	99,999,999								

Tran No.	Item	Type	Date	A/C Ref	Inv Ref	Details	Net Amount	Tax Amount	Gross Amount
2	1	PI	04/01/2011	DE001	4563	Opening Balance	5,750.00	0.00	5,750.00
8	1	PI	05/01/2011	EL001	8122	Opening Balance	8,500.00	0.00	8,500.00
9	1	PI	09/01/2011	MA001	9252	Opening Balance	4,500.00	0.00	4,500.00
						Totals	18,750.00	0.00	18,750.00

End of Report

Lastly Tom will print out a **trial balance**. He does this by clicking on Company on the vertical toolbar, then Financials in the Links section above and finally the Trial icon on the horizontal toolbar. A trial balance is a list of the account balances of the company. It shows the control (total) accounts as follows.

Debtors control account £29,534 (the total of the customer invoices)

Creditors control account £18,750 (the total of the supplier invoices)

The Suspense Account has been created automatically and shows the arithmetic difference (£10,784) between the two control accounts. It is put in automatically by the system to make the two columns balance.

Pronto Supplies Limited
Period Trial Balance

N/C	Name	Debit	Credit
1100	Debtors Control Account	29,534.00	
2100	Creditors Control Account		18,750.00
9998	Suspense Account		10,784.00
	Totals:	29,534.00	29,534.00

conclusion

The Customer and Supplier records are now installed and their account balances summarised in the two Control 'total' Accounts.

The trial balance is far from complete, however, and Tom's next task will be to input the Nominal Ledger balances – eg income received, expenses paid, loans, items purchased. When these items have all been entered the Trial Balance should 'balance' – the two columns will have the same total and the Suspense Account will disappear. This will be dealt with in the next chapter.

AMENDING RECORDS

As well as setting up customer and supplier records, an organisation operating a computer accounting system will from time-to-time need to amend its records. For example amending records:

■ to take account of changes of address, contact names, terms of supply

■ by indicating that the account is no longer active

■ by deleting the account (if the system allows you to – see next page)

amending records in Sage

The procedures in Sage are very straightforward:

■ select either CUSTOMERS or SUPPLIERS as appropriate

■ highlight the record that needs amending, click Record and go to the

    - DETAILS screen (for customer or supplier details) or

    - CREDIT CONTROL screen (for terms of supply, eg credit limit)

■ make the necessary change on screen

■ SAVE and BACK UP

In the following example, the name of a customer contact at L Garr & Co has been changed from Ted Nigmer to Win Norberry.

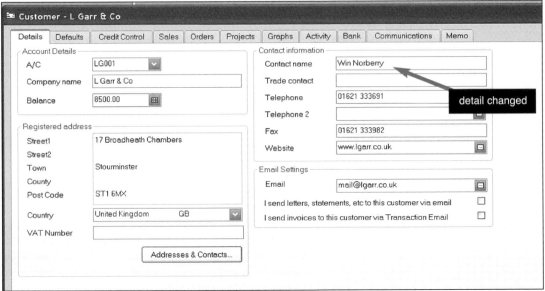

In the example below, the credit limit of £10,000 given to customer John Butler & Associates has been increased to £15,000.

Customer - John Butler & Associates

| Details | Defaults | Credit Control | Sales | Orders | Projects | Graphs | Activity | Bank | Communications | Memo |

Terms

Credit Limit	15000.00
Settlement Due	0	Days
Sett.Discount	0.00
Payment Due	30	Days
Average Time to Pay	0	Days
Trading Terms Text	Payment 30 days of invoice
Credit Ref.	
Bureau	Business Credit Sure
Priority Customer	☐
Credit Position	Good
Account status	0 Open
DUNS Number	

Credit Review

A/C Opened	01/01/2011
Last Credit Review	/ /
Next Credit Review	/ /
Application Date	/ /
Date Received	/ /

Memo:

detail changed

'closing' a customer or supplier account

The question may well arise "What should we do if a customer has ceased trading, or if we no longer use a particular supplier?" The logical answer is to close the account.

Sage does not allow you to **delete** an account when there are transactions recorded on it, even if the balance is nil. Instead you should **amend** the name of the account on the Customer or Supplier Record to something anonymous like 'Closed Account' so that it cannot be used again.

If, on the other hand, the account has no transactions on it (eg it may have been opened and not used), it may be closed by clicking on the Delete button at the bottom of the Details tab of the Record (see below).

CHAPTER SUMMARY

- Businesses buy and sell products either on a cash basis (immediate payment) or on credit (payment made later).

- The accounting records for selling on credit comprise the accounts of customers (debtors) contained in the Sales Ledger.

- The accounting records for buying on credit comprise the accounts of suppliers (creditors) contained in the Purchases Ledger.

- A business will also have to agree the terms of trading with a customer – the credit limit, the level of discounts and the payment period it allows.

- In the Sage accounting system the Sales Ledger is known as 'Customers' and the Purchases Ledger as 'Suppliers'.

- Setting up Customer and Supplier records in Sage involves the input of details such as names, addresses and outstanding financial transactions.

- Records set up in this way should be carefully checked against printed out reports such as the Day Book report and the Trial Balance.

- Customer and Supplier records in Sage can also be amended or deleted (where allowable) as required.

KEY TERMS

cash sale	a sale where payment is immediate
credit sale	a sale where payment follows after an agreed period of time
debtors	customers who owe money to a business
creditors	suppliers who are owed money by a business
debtors control account	the total of the balances of debtors' accounts
creditors control account	the total of the balances of creditors' accounts
credit terms	discounts and extended payment periods allowed to customers who make purchases
defaults	sets of data on the computer which are automatically applied

STUDENT ACTIVITIES

4.1   A cash sale is a sale where the only means of payment is notes and coins. True or false?

4.2   Define:

(a)   a debtor

(b)   a creditor

4.3   What books of the business (ledgers) contain:

(a)   debtors' accounts

(b)   creditors' accounts

4.4   What is shown in:

(a)   debtors control account

(b)   creditors control account

4.5   What is the difference between a trade discount and a settlement discount?

4.6   What report shows the debit and credit balances of the accounts in an accounting system?

4.7   There are two important pieces of information (excluding financial transactions) that are missing from the computer-held customer details shown below.

What are they, and why are they important?

Account name	John Butler & Associates
Address	24 Shaw Street
	Mereford
	MR4 6KJ
Contact name	John Butler

Telephone 01908 824342, Fax 01908 824295, Email mail@jbutler.co.uk
www.jbutler.co.uk

PRONTO SUPPLIES INPUTTING TASKS

warning note!
This activity involves you in setting up Customer and Supplier records in Sage and inputting live data into the computer.
Ensure that you have changed your program date to 31 January 2011 in SETTINGS.

Also check that the Customer and Supplier Defaults are set to Nominal accounts 4000 and 5000 respectively. The default tax code should be T1 (standard rate). The Customer Defaults can also be set up for payment due days as 30 days and terms of payment 30 days of invoice.

Task 1
Enter the customer details into the Customers screens as indicated in the Case Study.
The six customer records are as follows:

> **JB001**   **John Butler & Associates**
> 24 Shaw Street
> Mereford
> MR4 6KJ
> Contact name: John Butler
> Telephone 01908 824342, Fax 01908 824295, Email mail@jbutler.co.uk
> www.jbutler.co.uk
> Credit limit £10,000
> Invoice 10013 issued, 05 01 11, £5,500.00

> **CH001**   **Charisma Design**
> 36 Dingle Road
> Mereford
> MR2 8GF
> Contact name: Lindsay Foster
> Telephone 01908 345287, Fax 01908 345983, Email mail@charisma.co.uk
> www.charisma.co.uk
> Credit limit £5,000
> Invoice 10014 issued, 05 01 11, £2,400.00

CR001   **Crowmatic Ltd**

Unit 12 Severnside Estate

Mereford

MR3 6FD

Contact name: John Crow

Telephone 01908 674237, Fax 01908 674345, Email mail@crowmatic.co.uk

www.crowmatic.co.uk

Credit limit £5,000

Invoice 10015 issued, 09 01 11, £3,234.00

DB001   **David Boossey**

17 Harebell Road

Mereford Green

MR6 4NB

Contact name: David Boossey

Telephone 01908 333981, Fax 01908 333761, Email dboossey@swoopwing.com

Credit limit £5,000

Invoice 10016 issued, 10 01 11, £3,400.00

KD001   **Kay Denz**

The Stables

Martley Hillside

MR6 4FV

Contact name: Kay Denz

Telephone 01908 624945, Fax 01908 624945, Email kdenz@centra.com

Credit limit £10,000

Invoice 10017 issued,10 01 11 , £6,500.00

LG001   **L Garr & Co**

17 Broadheath Chambers

Stourminster

ST1 6MX

Contact name: Ted Nigmer

Telephone 01621 333691, Fax 01621 333982, Email mail@lgarr.co.uk

www.lgarr.co.uk

Credit limit £15,000

Invoice 10019 issued, 17 01 11, £8,500.00

Task 2

Enter the supplier details into the Suppliers screens as indicated in the Case Study.

The three supplier records are as follows:

DE001   **Delco PLC**

Delco House

Otto Way

New Milton

SR1 6TF

Contact name: Nina Patel

Telephone 01722 295875, Fax 01722 295611, Email sales@delco.co.uk

www.delco.co.uk

Credit limit £10,000, payment period 30 days.

Invoice 4563 issued, 04 01 11, £5,750.00

EL001   **Electron Supplies**

17 Maxim Way

Manchester

M1 5TF

Contact name: Jon Summers

Telephone 0161 6282151, Fax 0161 628161, Email sales@electronsupplies.co.uk

www.electronsupplies.co.uk

Credit limit £15,000, payment period 30 days.

Invoice 8122 issued 05 01 11, £8,500.00

MA001   **MacCity**

Unit 15 Elmwood Trading Estate

RoughWay

RM2 9TG

Contact name: Josh Masters

Telephone 01899 949233, Fax 01899 949331, Email sales@maccity.co.uk

www.maccity.co.uk

Credit limit £10,000, payment period 30 days.

Invoice 9252 issued 09 01 11, £4,500.00

Task 3

Print out a Day Books: Customer Invoices (Summary) report for the new Customer accounts and check and agree the amounts you have input. Check it against the printout on page 243.

Task 4

Print out a Day Books: Supplier Invoices (Summary) report for the new Supplier accounts and check and agree the amounts you have input. Check it against the printout on page 243.

Task 5

Print out a Trial Balance for January 2011 and check that the Debtors and Creditors Control account balances agree with the figures on page 61 and the totals shown on the Day Book reports produced in Tasks 3 and 4.

Task 6

At the end of January Ted Nigmer, who is your named contact at L Garr & Co, retires. He has been replaced by Win Norberry. You are asked to amend the customer details as appropriate.

Task 7

At the end of January, Tom of Pronto Supplies has had discussions with a good customer, J Butler Associates, and has agreed to amend their credit limit to £15,000. You are asked to amend the customer record as appropriate.

Task 8

Tom asks you how you would delete a customer or supplier record on the Sage system if you ceased to deal with the customer or supplier. What would be your reply?

Would your reply be any different if the account had not been used at all, and had no transactions on it?

Reminder! Have you made a back-up?

SETTING UP THE NOMINAL LEDGER

■ In the last two chapters we have set up the company in Sage and entered details of Customers and Suppliers. All that remains to be done is to set up the Nominal Ledger on the computer.

■ The Nominal Ledger contains all the other accounts in the accounting system:

- income accounts, including Sales

- purchases accounts for goods that the company trades in

- expenses and overheads accounts

- asset accounts (for items the business owns)

- liability accounts (for items the business owes)

- capital accounts (the investment of the business owner)

■ The Nominal Ledger lists the bank accounts of the business, but they are operated through a separate BANK module, just as in a manual accounting system the bank accounts are recorded in a Cash Book, kept separately from the Nominal Ledger accounts.

■ The accounts in the nominal ledger are set up in Sage using the structure of a 'Chart of Accounts' provided by the program. This allocates suitable reference numbers to the various accounts which are grouped in categories (eg expenses, assets, liabilities) so that the computer program knows where to find them in the system and can then provide suitable reports to management.

■ One of the reports produced by the computer is the Trial Balance, which lists the nominal account balances in two balancing columns. When the balances of all the nominal accounts have been entered on the computer, the two columns should balance and the Suspense Account (which records any difference) should disappear.

NOMINAL ACCOUNTS

nominal accounts

An account in an accounting system records financial transactions and provides a running balance of what is left in the account at the end of each day. The **nominal ledger** accounts in any accounting system are the accounts which are not Customer accounts (sales ledger) or Supplier accounts (purchases ledger). The nominal accounts record:

- income - eg sales, rent received
- expenses - eg wages, advertising
- assets - items that a business owns or amounts that it is owed
- liabilities - money that a business owes, eg loans or creditors
- capital - money invested by the owner(s) and profits made

bank accounts

In a manual accounting system the bank accounts are kept in a separate Cash Book and are not strictly speaking part of the Nominal Ledger. In Sage the bank accounts of the business are *listed* in NOMINAL, but they are *operated* through a separate BANK module.

the default Nominal accounts

When Tom in the Case Study set up his company he chose the set of nominal accounts automatically provided by the Sage program.

If you click on the COMPANY button in the Sage opening screen the accounts are to be found in the NOMINAL opening screen (see below). You can scroll down this screen to see the whole list (summarised on the next page).

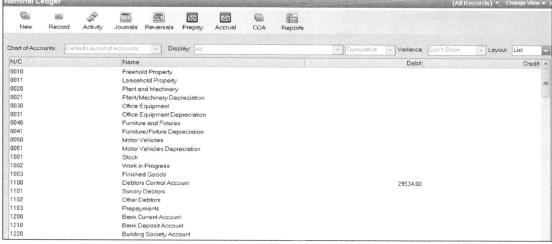

Nominal Account List

0010	Freehold Property
0011	Leasehold Property
0020	Plant and Machinery
0021	Plant/Machinery Depreciation
0030	Office Equipment
0031	Office Equipment Depreciation
0040	Furniture and Fixtures
0041	Furniture/Fixture Depreciation
0050	Motor Vehicles
0051	Motor Vehicles Depreciation
1001	Stock
1002	Work in Progress
1003	Finished Goods
1100	Debtors Control Account
1101	Sundry Debtors
1102	Other Debtors
1103	Prepayments
1200	Bank Current Account
1210	Bank Deposit Account
1220	Building Society Account
1230	Petty Cash
1240	Company Credit Card
1250	Credit Card Receipts
2100	Creditors Control Account
2101	Sundry Creditors
2102	Other Creditors
2109	Accruals
2200	Sales Tax Control Account
2201	Purchase Tax Control Account
2202	VAT Liability
2204	Manual Adjustments
2210	P.A.Y.E.
2211	National Insurance
2220	Net Wages
2230	Pension Fund
2300	Loans
2310	Hire Purchase
2320	Corporation Tax
2330	Mortgages
3000	Ordinary Shares
3010	Preference Shares
3100	Reserves
3101	Undistributed Reserves
3200	Profit and Loss Account
4000	Sales Type A
4001	Sales Type B
4002	Sales Type C

4009	Discounts Allowed
4100	Sales Type D
4101	Sales Type E
4200	Sales of Assets
4400	Credit Charges (Late Payments)
4900	Miscellaneous Income
4901	Royalties Received
4902	Commissions Received
4903	Insurance Claims
4904	Rent Income
4905	Distribution and Carriage
5000	Materials Purchased
5001	Materials Imported
5002	Miscellaneous Purchases
5003	Packaging
5009	Discounts Taken
5100	Carriage
5101	Import Duty
5102	Transport Insurance
5200	Opening Stock
5201	Closing Stock
6000	Productive Labour
6001	Cost of Sales Labour
6002	Sub-Contractors
6100	Sales Commissions
6200	Sales Promotions
6201	Advertising
6202	Gifts and Samples
6203	P.R.(Literature & Brochures)
6900	Miscellaneous Expenses
7000	Gross Wages
7001	Directors Salaries
7002	Directors Remuneration
7003	Staff Salaries
7004	Wages-Regular
7005	Wages-Casual
7006	Employers N.I.
7007	Employers Pensions
7008	Recruitment Expenses
7009	Adjustments
7010	SSP Reclaimed
7011	SMP Reclaimed
7100	Rent
7102	Water Rates
7103	General Rates
7104	Premises Insurance
7200	Electricity
7201	Gas
7202	Oil
7203	Other Heating Costs
7300	Fuel and Oil
7301	Repairs and Servicing

7302	Licences
7303	Vehicle Insurance
7304	Miscellaneous Motor Expenses
7350	Scale Charges
7400	Travelling
7401	Car Hire
7402	Hotels
7403	U.K. Entertainment
7404	Overseas Entertainment
7405	Overseas Travelling
7406	Subsistence
7500	Printing
7501	Postage and Carriage
7502	Telephone
7503	Telex/Telegram/Facsimile
7504	Office Stationery
7505	Books etc.
7600	Legal Fees
7601	Audit and Accountancy Fees
7602	Consultancy Fees
7603	Professional Fees
7700	Equipment Hire
7701	Office Machine Maintenance
7800	Repairs and Renewals
7801	Cleaning
7802	Laundry
7803	Premises Expenses
7900	Bank Interest Paid
7901	Bank Charges
7902	Currency Charges
7903	Loan Interest Paid
7904	H.P. Interest
7905	Credit Charges
7906	Exchange Rate Variance
8000	Depreciation
8001	Plant/Machinery Depreciation
8002	Furniture/Fitting Depreciation
8003	Vehicle Depreciation
8004	Office Equipment Depreciation
8100	Bad Debt Write Off
8102	Bad Debt Provision
8200	Donations
8201	Subscriptions
8202	Clothing Costs
8203	Training Costs
8204	Insurance
8205	Refreshments
9998	Suspense Account
9999	Mispostings Account

CHART OF ACCOUNTS

If you look at the nominal account list you will see that a four digit code is given to each nominal account in the nominal ledger. These account number codes range from 0010 to 9999. Tom is very unlikely to use all these accounts and may even want to change some.

What is important, however, is that Tom – or any user of Sage – must appreciate that these accounts are organised into categories by account number. These categories are set out in the **chart of accounts.** They can be accessed in the Nominal Ledger by clicking on the COA (chart of accounts) icon and then EDIT . . .

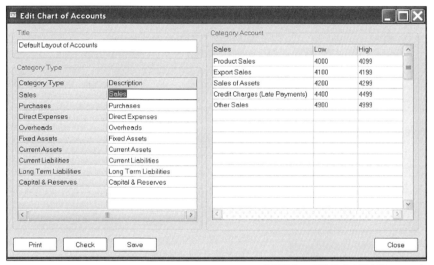

The left hand panel shows the **categories** of account, eg Sales, Purchases. If you click on a category you will see the ranges of accounts and account numbers covered by that category displayed in the right-hand panel.

In this case the Sales category has been selected and the types of Sales listed on the right. This panel tells you that all Product Sales should have an account number between 4000 and 4099. When you set up the Customer records in the last chapter you chose 4000 as the default number (see page 55) for sales to customers.

But if you wanted to categorise customer sales (by area or type of product, for example) you could choose to have three accounts running for Product Sales: 4000 Sales Type A, 4001 Sales Type B, 4002 Sales Type C.

reports from Nominal

The Sage Nominal accounts are used as the basis for a number of computer-generated management reports telling the owner about subjects such as the profit and the value of the business. If accounts get into the wrong category, the reports will also be wrong.

a summary of categories

It may be that a new business will adopt all the default nominal accounts (see list on page 72) because it does not need any others, but if a new account has to be set up it is critical that the new account is in the right category. The business owner will therefore need to understand what the categories mean and what they include.

The nominal categories and account number ranges are:

Sales	4000 - 4999	income from sales of goods or services
Purchases	5000 - 5299	items bought bought to produce goods to sell
Direct Expenses	6000 - 6999	expenses directly related to producing goods
Overheads	7000 - 8299	expenses the business has to pay anyway

*These are used to produce the **profit and loss statement** which shows what profit (or loss) the business has made.*

Fixed Assets	0010 - 0059	items bought to keep in the business long-term
Current Assets	1000 - 1250	items owned by the business in the short-term
Current Liabilities	2100 - 2299	items owed by the business in the short-term
Long Term Liabilities	2300 - 2399	items owed by the business in the long-term
Capital & Reserves	3000 - 3299	the financial investment of the owner(s)

*These are used to produce the **balance sheet** which gives an idea of the value of the business and shows the owner what is represented by the capital investment (the money put in by the owner).*

We will now put this theory into practice with a continuation of the Pronto Supplies Limited Case Study.

CASE STUDY

PRONTO SUPPLIES LIMITED: SETTING UP THE NOMINAL ACCOUNTS

Pronto Supplies Limited was set up in January 2011 and during that month operated a **manual** book-keeping system using hand-written double-entry ledger accounts.

It was a busy month for Tom Cox . . .

financing Tom paid £75,000 into the bank as ordinary share capital to start up the limited company business.

Tom also raised a £35,000 business loan from the bank.

assets The finance raised enabled Tom to buy:

office computers	£35,000
office equipment	£15,000
furniture for the office	£25,000

purchases Tom bought in a substantial amount of stock during January for £69,100.

All of this stock was for resale by Pronto Supplies Limited.

sales Tom divided his sales into three types:

Computer hardware sales
Computer software sales
Computer consultancy

overheads Tom also had to pay fixed expenses including:

Wages	£16,230
Advertising	£12,400
Rent	£4,500
Rates	£450
Electricity	£150
Telephone	£275
Stationery	£175

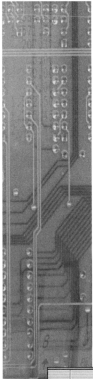

Pronto Supplies Trial Balance

Tom at the end of January listed all the balances of his accounts in two columns, using a spreadsheet. This is his **trial balance** and will form the basis of the entries to the Sage system. The columns are headed up Debit (Dr) and Credit (Cr) and they have the same total. In double-entry book-keeping each debit entry in the accounts is mirrored by a credit entry. (Refer to Chapter 14 if you are not sure about this). If the book-keeping is correct, the total of debits should be the same as the total of the credits. The spreadsheet is shown below. Note that:

- **debits** = assets and expenses   **credits** = liabilities, capital and income

- the control (total) account for debtors shows the total amount owed by all Tom's customers; it is a debit balance because it is money owed to the business

- the control (total) account for creditors shows the total amount owed by Tom to his suppliers: it is a credit balance because it is money owed by the business

- Tom is registered with HM Revenue & Customs for Value Added Tax (VAT). This means that he has to quote his registration number on all his documents and also

    - charge VAT on his sales – this is due to HM Revenue & Customs and so is a credit balance - Sales tax control account

    - reclaim VAT on what he has bought – this is due from HM Revenue & Customs and so is a debit balance - Purchase tax control account

	A	B	C	D	E
1	**TRIAL BALANCE**	Dr	Cr		
2					
3	Plant and machinery	35000			
4	Office equipment	15000			
5	Furniture and fixtures	25000			
6	Debtors control account	29534			
7	Bank current account	14656			
8	Creditors control account		18750		
9	Sales tax control account		17920		
10	Purchase tax control account	26600			
11	Loans		35000		
12	Ordinary Shares		75000		
13	Computer hardware sales		85000		
14	Computer software sales		15000		
15	Computer consultancy sales		2400		
16	Materials purchased	6900			
17	Advertising	1200			
18	Gross wages	16230			
19	Rent	4500			
20	General rates	450			
21	Electricity	150			
22	Telephone	275			
23	Stationery	175			
24					
25	Total	249070	249070		
26					

inputting the accounts into Sage Nominal

The date is 31 January 2011.

Tom uses his trial balance as the source document for inputting his nominal account balances. The procedure he adopts is:

1   He clicks on the Company button on the vertical toolbar and examines the nominal accounts list which appears on the Nominal Ledger screen. He allocates the accounts in his existing books with computer account numbers as follows:

Plant and machinery (computers)	0020
Office equipment (photocopiers, phones etc)	0030
Furniture and fixtures	0040
Debtors control account	1100
Bank current account	1200
Creditors control account	2100
Sales tax control account	2200
Purchase tax control account	2201
Loans	2300
Ordinary Shares	3000
Sales type A (hardware)	4000
Sales type B (software)	4001
Sales type C (consultancy)	4002
Materials purchased	5000
Advertising	6201
Gross wages	7000
Rent	7100
General rates	7103
Electricity	7200
Telephone	7502
Stationery	7504

2   Tom scrolls down the screen and clicks on all the accounts that he is going to need – they then show as selected.

But – importantly – he does not click on the following two accounts:

Debtors Control Account - the total of the Customers' accounts

Creditors Control Account - the total of the Suppliers' accounts

This is because he has already input the debtors' (Customers') and creditors' (Suppliers') balances (see the last chapter). If he inputs these totals now they will be entered into the computer twice and cause havoc with the accounting records!

The NOMINAL screen is shown at the top of the next page.

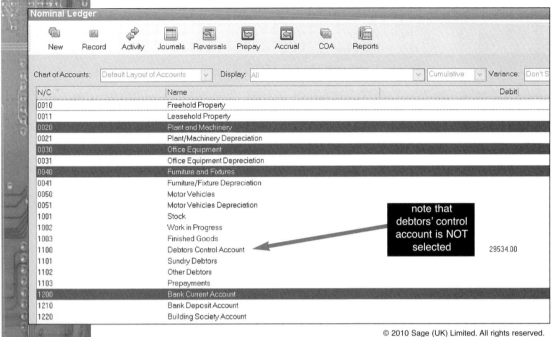

3 Tom is now ready to input the balances of these accounts. To do this he will

- Select the RECORD icon which will bring up a RECORD window.

- Click on O/B on the balance box which asks him to enter the date (31/01/2011) and the balance which must go in the correct box: debits on the left, credits on the right. He should ignore the 'ref' box. The first account entry will look like this;

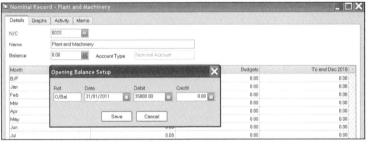

This record should then be saved.

Tom should repeat this for all the selected accounts (using the Next button to move to the next one), making sure that he is saving all the data as he goes along.

checking the input – the trial balance

Tom needs to check that what he has input is accurate. He needs to check his original list of balances – his trial balance (see page 76) – against the computer trial balance.

The trial balance is produced through FINANCIALS by clicking on the TRIAL icon. The printout produced is shown below.

Pronto Supplies Limited
Period Trial Balance

To Period: Month 1, January 2011

N/C	Name	Debit	Credit
0020	Plant and Machinery	35,000.00	
0030	Office Equipment	15,000.00	
0040	Furniture and Fixtures	25,000.00	
1100	Debtors Control Account	29,534.00	
1200	Bank Current Account	14,656.00	
2100	Creditors Control Account		18,750.00
2200	Sales Tax Control Account		17,920.00
2201	Purchase Tax Control Account	26,600.00	
2300	Loans		35,000.00
3000	Ordinary Shares		75,000.00
4000	Sales Type A		85,000.00
4001	Sales Type B		15,000.00
4002	Sales Type C		2,400.00
5000	Materials Purchased	69,100.00	
6201	Advertising	12,400.00	
7000	Gross Wages	16,230.00	
7100	Rent	4,500.00	
7103	General Rates	450.00	
7200	Electricity	150.00	
7502	Telephone	275.00	
7504	Office Stationery	175.00	
	Totals:	249,070.00	249,070.00

End of Report

Is the input accurate? Yes, because all the figures agree with the original trial balance figures and they are all in the correct column. The totals also agree.

You will see that the Suspense Account which the system created in the last chapter (see page 61) has now disappeared because the total of the debits now equals the total of the credits, as on Tom's spreadsheet shown on page 76.

Tom is now ready to input February's transactions – new sales invoices, new purchase invoices and payments in and out of the bank. These will be dealt with in the chapters that follow.

CHANGING NOMINAL ACCOUNT NAMES

It is possible to change the names of accounts in the Nominal Ledger if they do not fit in with the nature of your business. If, for example, you run a travel agency your Nominal account names may be very different from the names used by an insurance broker.

The important point to remember is that if you change your account names they must fit in with the categories in the Chart of Accounts. You should not, for example, include an Office Rent Paid Account in the Purchases category. Much of this should be common sense.

adding new nominal accounts

Accounts can be added to the Nominal Ledger. Again, care should be taken to ensure that any new account fits into the Chart of Accounts structure (see page 73).

In the Case Study continuation below, Tom changes the names of his Sales accounts to reflect more accurately what is going on in his business. Tom also plans to offer a computer helpline to customers and so decides to add this to his sales accounts

CASE STUDY

PRONTO SUPPLIES LIMITED: CHANGING NOMINAL ACCOUNT NAMES

Tom looks at his Trial Balance (see page 79) and realises that his Sales Accounts are named 'Type A' and 'Type B' and Type C'. This does not really tell him much about what he is actually selling, so he decides that he will change the names as follows:

account number	old name	new name
4000	Sales Type A	Computer hardware sales
4001	Sales Type B	Computer software sales
4002	Sales Type C	Computer consultancy

He selects the three accounts in the NOMINAL list screen, goes to RECORD in NOMINAL and overwrites the old name in the name box for each account and Saves. The amended screen for Account 4000 (Computer hardware sales) is shown below.

To add a new nominal account, Tom clicks Record and types 4003 into the N/C box. Sage recognises this as a New Account. Tom enters 'Computer helpline' in the account name box. There is no opening balance so Tom saves the new record. The new account now appears in the nominal list.

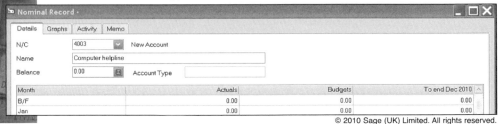

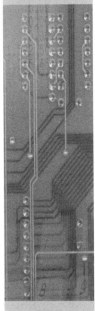

CHAPTER SUMMARY

■ When a business sets up its accounts on a Sage computer accounting package it will normally set up its Customer and Supplier records first.

■ The next stage will be for the business to set up its nominal accounts, adopting the default list of accounts supplied by Sage in its 'chart of accounts' structure.

■ If the business has already started trading it should input all its nominal account balances (except for the Debtors and Creditors control accounts).

■ The input balances should be checked carefully against the source figures. The Sage program can produce a trial balance which will show the balances that have been input.

■ Account names can be changed and new accounts added to suit the nature of the business – but it is important that the type of account should be consistent with the appropriate category in the 'chart of accounts'.

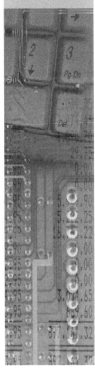

KEY TERMS

nominal ledger the remaining accounts in the accounting system which are not Customers or Suppliers, eg income, expenses, assets, liabilities – in Sage this is known as 'Nominal'

chart of accounts the structure of the nominal accounts, which groups accounts into categories such as Sales, Purchases, Overheads . . . and so on

categories subdivisions of the chart of accounts (eg Sales, Purchases) each of which is allocated a range of account numbers by the computer

trial balance a list of the accounts of a business divided into two columns:

debits – mostly assets and expenses

credits – mostly income and liabilities

The two columns should have the same total, reflecting the workings of the double-entry book-keeping system

STUDENT
ACTIVITIES

5.1   Explain briefly what a chart of accounts is.

5.2   List the categories of account in a chart of accounts and write a sentence for each category, explaining what type of account that category includes.

5.3   You are transferring the manual accounting records of a company into a Sage system. The account names listed below are included in those used in the manual system. Refer to the nominal account list on page 72 and the categories of account numbers on page 74.

(a)   What account numbers will you allocate to these accounts?

(b)   In what categories in the chart of accounts will these accounts appear?

Complete the table below (or draw up your own table).

account name	account number	category
Freehold Property		
Office Equipment		
Motor Vehicles		
Materials Purchased		
Bank current account		
Creditors Control		
Directors Salaries		
Electricity		
Ordinary Shares		

PRONTO SUPPLIES INPUTTING TASKS

warning note!
This activity involves inputting live data into the computer.
Remember to Save your data and keep your printouts as you progress through the tasks.

Task 1

Make sure the program date is set to 31 January 2011.

Open up the Nominal ledger and select accounts in the computer nominal ledger list screen for the accounts included on the spreadsheet trial balance (see page 76).

But do *not* select Debtors Control Account or Creditors Control Account as they already have balances on them.

Task 2

Enter the balances from the spreadsheet trial balance (see page 76) into the appropriate nominal accounts as opening balances – but do not input the debtors control account and the creditors control account.

Make sure that debits are entered as debits and credits as credits.

Task 3

Print out a trial balance for January 2011 from the computer and check it against the trial balance on page 79, or have it checked by your tutor. The suspense account should have disappeared.

Task 4

Change the names of the three sales accounts you have chosen as follows:

number	old name	new name
4000	Sales Type A	Computer hardware sales
4001	Sales Type B	Computer software sales
4002	Sales Type C	Computer consultancy

Task 5

Add new account number 4003 Computer helpline to the Nominal list.

Reminder! Have you made a back-up?

chapter introduction

- n   *A business that sells on credit will invoice the goods or services supplied and then receive payment at a later date.*

- n   *The invoice is an important document because it sets out the details of the goods or services supplied, the amount owing, and the date by which payment should be made.*

- n   *It is therefore essential that details of the invoice are entered in the computer accounting records so that the sale can be recorded and the amount owed by the customer logged into the accounting system.*

- n   *Some Sage computer accounting programs contain an invoicing function which will enable the business to input and print out invoices on a printer linked to the computer. Other more basic programs do not actually print out the invoice but require the business to enter details of each invoice.*

- n   *In this chapter we look at the more basic programs which require invoice details to be entered but which do not print out the invoices. If you are working with a program that will print out invoices, the principles are just the same and you should relate them to the way your program works.*

- n   *A business that sells on credit may have to issue a refund for some or all of the goods or services supplied. They may be faulty or the sale may be cancelled. As payment has not yet been made, the 'refund' takes the form of a deduction from the amount owing. The document that the seller issues in this case is a credit note.*

- n   *A credit note is dealt with by a computer accounting program in much the same way as an invoice: some programs will print out credit notes, some more basic programs do not print them out but require the details to be input. This chapter deals with the input of credit note details into the computer accounting records.*

- n   *This chapter continues the Pronto Supplies Case Study and shows how details of invoices and credit notes are entered into the computer accounting records.*

- n   *The next chapter looks at how the invoices and credit notes issued by suppliers are dealt with by a computer accounting program.*

BACKGROUND TO FINANCIAL DOCUMENTS

When a business sells goods or services it will use a number of different financial documents. A single sales transaction involves both seller and buyer. In this chapter we look at the situation from the point of view of the seller of the goods or services. Documents which are often used in the selling process for goods include:

n   **purchase order** which the seller receives from the buyer

n   **delivery note** which goes with the goods from the seller to the buyer

n   **invoice** which lists the goods and tells the buyer what is owed

n   **credit note** which is sent to the buyer if any refund is due

n   **statement** sent by the seller to remind the buyer what is owed

n   **remittance advice** sent by the buyer with the **cheque** to make payment

Study the diagram below which shows how the documents 'flow' between buyer and seller.

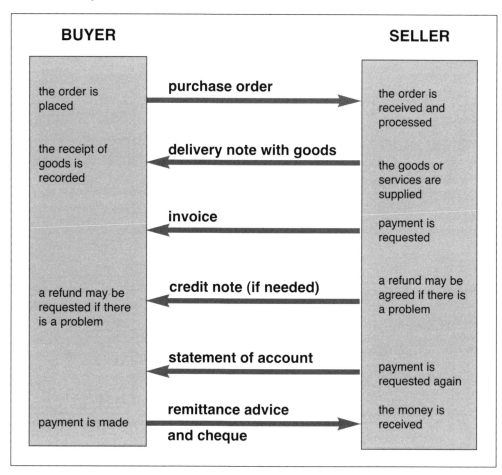

INVOICE

The main document we will deal with in this chapter is the **invoice** which is sent by the seller to the buyer to state what is owing and when it has to be paid. An invoice is illustrated below and explained on the next page.

INVOICE

DELCO PLC

Delco House, Otto Way, New Milton SR1 6TF
Tel 01722 295875 Fax 01722 295611 Email sales@delco.co..uk
VAT Reg GB 0745 4672 76

invoice to

Pronto Supplies Limited Unit 17 Severnvale Estate Broadwater Road Mereford MR1 6TF

invoice no	12309
account	3993
your reference	47609
date	02 10 11

product code	description	quantity	price	unit	total	discount %	net
Z324	Zap storage disks	10	40.00	box of 10	400.00	0.00	400.00

terms
30 days

goods total	400.00
VAT	70.00
TOTAL	470.00

The invoice here has been issued by Delco PLC for some Zap computer disks ordered by Pronto Supplies on a purchase order.

The reference number quoted here is the order number on Pronto Supplies' original purchase order.

The date here is the date on which the goods have been sent. It is known as the 'invoice date'.

The date is important for calculating when the invoice is due to be paid. In this case the 'terms' (see the bottom left-hand corner of the invoice) are 30 days. This means the invoice is due to be paid within 30 days of the invoice date.

The arithmetic and details in this line must be checked very carefully by Pronto Supplies to make sure that they pay the correct amount:

- *product code* – this is the catalogue number for the disks which Pronto put on the original purchase order
- *description* – this describes the goods ordered – the disks
- *quantity* – this should be the same as the quantity on the purchase order
- *price* – this is the price of each unit shown in the next column
- *unit* is the way in which the unit is counted up and charged for, eg units (single items), or 10s, boxes (as here)
- *total* is the price multiplied by the number of units
- *discount %* is the percentage allowance (known as trade discount) given to customers who regularly deal with the supplier, ie they receive a certain percentage (eg 10%) deducted from their bill
- *net* is the amount due to the seller after deduction of trade discount, and before VAT is added on

The Goods Total is the total of the column above it. It is the final amount due to the seller before VAT is added on.

Value Added Tax (VAT) is calculated and added on – here it is 17.5% of the Goods Total, ie £400.00 x $\frac{17.5}{100}$ = £70.00

The VAT is then added to the Goods Total to produce the actual amount owing:
£400.00 + £70.00 = £470.00

The 'terms' explain the conditions on which the goods are supplied. Here '30 days' mean that Pronto has to pay within 30 days of 2 October.

CREDIT NOTE

The other document we will deal with in this chapter is the **credit note**.

The **credit note** is issued when some form of refund has to be given to the buyer of goods or services. As payment has not yet been made the credit note allows the buyer to deduct an amount from the invoice when settlement is finally made.

Note that it is never acceptable practice to change the amounts on an invoice; a credit note is always required.

The credit note illustrated below has been issued by Delco PLC because one of the boxes of Zap computer disks ordered by Pronto Supplies was faulty. Pronto Supplies has returned the box, asking for a reduction in the amount owing.

Study the document below and read the notes which follow.

CREDIT NOTE

DELCO PLC

Delco House, Otto Way, New Milton SR1 6TF
Tel 01722 295875 Fax 01722 295611 Email sales@delco.co..uk
VAT Reg GB 0745 4672 76

to

Pronto Supplies Limited
Unit 17 Severnvale Estate
Broadwater Road
Mereford
MR1 6TF

credit note no	12157
account	3993
your reference	47609
our invoice	12309
date/tax point	10 10 11

product code	description	quantity	price	unit	total	discount %	net
Z324	Zap storage disks	1	40.00	box	40.00	0.00	40.00

Reason for credit
1 box of Zap disks received faulty and returned.

GOODS TOTAL	40.00
VAT	7.00
TOTAL	47.00

notes on the credit note

You will see from the credit note on the previous page that the credit note total is £47. This can be deducted from the invoice total (see page 86) of £470. In other words, Pronto Supplies now owes £470 minus £47 = £423.

Note in particular from the credit note opposite:

n   The format of the credit note is very much the same as the invoice.

n   The reference quoted is Pronto Supplies' purchase order number.

n   The columns (eg 'product code') are identical to those used on the invoice and work in exactly the same way.

n   VAT is also included – it has to be refunded because the goods have not now been supplied.

n   If there was any discount this should also be refunded – but there is no discount here.

n   The reason for the credit note (the 'reason for credit') is stated at the bottom of the document. Here it is a box of faulty disks that has been returned to Delco PLC by Pronto Supplies.

INVOICES, CREDIT NOTES AND SAGE

the book-keeping background

The totals of invoices and credit notes have to be entered into the accounting records of a business. They record the sales and refunds made to customers who have bought on credit – the **debtors** of the business (known in Sage as Customers). The amounts from these documents combine to provide the total of the **Sales Ledger**, which is the section of the accounting records which contains all the debtor (Customer) balances. This is recorded in the **Debtors Control Account** which tells the business how much in total is owing from customers who have bought on credit.

methods of recording invoices and credit notes

When a business uses a computer accounting program such as Sage, it will have to make sure that the details of each invoice and credit note issued are entered into the computer accounting records. Businesses using Sage accounting programs have two alternatives: batch entry and computer printed invoices.

batch entry

The business produces the invoices independently of the computer program (for example, it may write them out) and then enters the invoice details into the computer accounting program on a **batch invoice** screen. A 'batch' is simply a group of items (eg a 'batch' of cakes in the oven). The term is used in this context to describe a group of invoices which are all input at one time. This may not be the day that each invoice is produced – it may be the end of the week, or even the month.

It is normal practice to add up the totals of all the actual invoices that are being input – the 'batch total' – and check this total against the invoice total calculated by the computer from the actual input. This will pick up any errors.

A batch invoice entry screen with four invoices input is shown below.

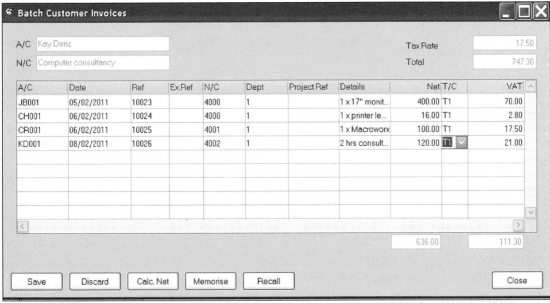

notes on the data entry columns:

n 'A/C' column contains the customer account reference

n 'Date' is the date on which each invoice was issued

n 'Ref' column is the invoice number (note that they are consecutive)

n 'Ex.Ref' is optional – it could be used for the purchase order number

n 'N/C' column is the nominal account code which specifies which type of sale is involved

n 'Dept' is 1 by default and is not used here

n 'Project ref' is optional and is not used here

n 'Details' describes the goods that have been sold

- n 'Net' is the amount of the invoice before VAT is added on
- n 'T/C' is the tax code which sets up the VAT rate that applies – here T1 refers to Standard Rate VAT, and is the default rate set up in Customer Preferences in SETTINGS.
- n 'VAT' is calculated automatically

When the operator has completed the input and checked the batch totals with the computer totals, the batched invoices can be saved.

computer printed invoices

Most versions of Sage include an invoicing function which requires the business to input the details of each invoice on screen. The computer system will then print out the invoices on the office printer – exactly as input. The invoices can either be for stock or for a service provided. If the invoice is for stock, 'product' records with product codes will normally have to be set up in Sage, and the product code used each time stock is invoiced.

Service invoices do not require a product code, because no stock is involved in the transaction. A service invoice input screen is shown below.

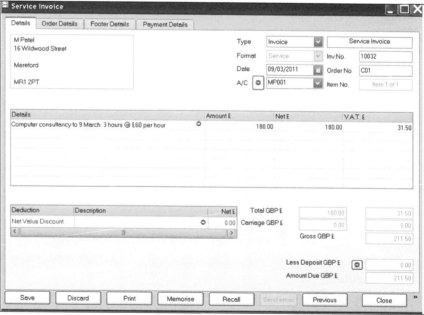

important note: treatment of invoicing in this book

In this book we will initially concentrate on the batch entry method of recording invoices and credit notes. It is far simpler to operate and is common to all versions of Sage. If your system can print out its own invoices and you want to use this facility in the exercises that follow, turn to Chapter 13 (pages 194 to 195) which will explain how to do this – even without having to set up product codes.

PRONTO SUPPLIES LIMITED:
PROCESSING SALES INVOICES AND CREDIT NOTES

Tom Cox runs Pronto Supplies Limited which provides computer hardware, software and consultancy services. At the end of January he input his Nominal accounts and his Customer and Supplier details and balances into his Sage accounting program. He has set up four Sales Accounts in his Nominal Ledger:

Computer hardware sales	Account number 4000
Computer software sales	Account number 4001
Computer consultancy	Account number 4002
Computer helpline	Account number 4003

It is now February 9, the end of the first full trading week. Tom needs to input

- the sales invoices he has issued to his customers
- the credit notes he has issued to his customers

He has the documents on file and has collected them in two batches . . .

SALES INVOICES ISSUED

invoice	name	date	details	net amount	VAT
10023	John Butler & Associates	5/02/11	1 x 17" monitor	400.00	70.00
10024	Charisma Design	6/02/11	1 x printer lead	16.00	2.80
10025	Crowmatic Ltd	6/02/11	1 x MacroWorx software	100.00	17.50
10026	Kay Denz	8/02/11	2 hours consultancy	120.00	21.00
Subtotals				636.00	111.30
Batch total					747.30

CREDIT NOTES ISSUED

credit note	name	date	details	net amount	VAT
551	David Boosey	6/02/11	Software returned	200.00	35.00
552	L Garr & Co	6/02/11	Disks returned (hardware)	40.00	7.00
Subtotals				240.00	42.00
Batch total					282.00

batch invoice entry

Tom will start by opening up the CUSTOMERS screen in Sage and clicking on the INVOICE icon. This will show the screen shown on the next page. He will then

- identify the account references for each of the four customers
- enter each invoice on a new line

- take the data from the invoice: date, invoice no ('Ref'), product details and amounts
- enter the appropriate Sales account number ('N/C') for the type of sale
- enter the T1 tax code for standard rate VAT and check that the VAT amount calculated on screen is the same as on the invoice

When the input is complete Tom should check his original batch totals (Net, VAT and Total) against the computer totals. Once he is happy that his input is correct he should SAVE.

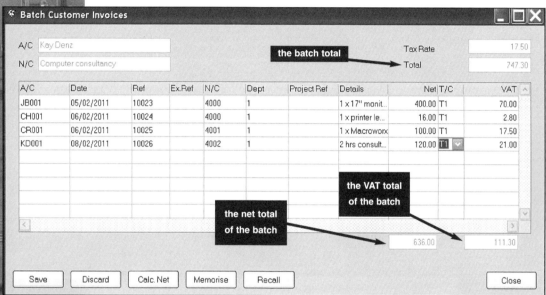

checking the invoices are on the system

As a further check Tom could print out a Day Book Report. This can be obtained through the REPORTS icon on the CUSTOMERS menu bar. The title of the report is 'Day Books: Customer Invoices (Detailed)'. The report appears as follows:

Pronto Supplies Limited
Day Books: Customer Invoices (Detailed)

| Date From: | 05/02/2011 | | | | | | | Customer From: | | |
| Date To: | 08/02/2011 | | | | | | | Customer To: | ZZZZZZZZ | |

Transaction From: 1 N/C From:
Transaction To: 99,999,999 N/C To: 99999999

Dept From: 0
Dept To: 999

Tran No.	Type	Date	A/C Ref	N/C	Inv Ref	Dept.	Details	Net Amount	Tax Amount	T/C	Gross Amount	V	B
48	SI	05/02/2011	JB001	4000	10023	1	1 x 17" monitor	400.00	70.00	T1	470.00	N	-
49	SI	06/02/2011	CH001	4000	10024	1	1 x printer lead	16.00	2.80	T1	18.80	N	-
50	SI	06/02/2011	CR001	4001	10025	1	1 x Macroworx	100.00	17.50	T1	117.50	N	-
51	SI	08/02/2011	KD001	4002	10026	1	2 hrs consultancy	120.00	21.00	T1	141.00	N	-
							Totals:	636.00	111.30		747.30		

batch credit note entry

Tom will input the details from the two credit notes in much the same way as he processed the invoices. He will start by opening up the CUSTOMERS screen in Sage and clicking on the CREDIT icon. This will show the screen shown below. He will then identify the account references for each of the two customers and the Sales account numbers and input the credit note details as shown on the screen. When the input is complete Tom should check his original batch totals (Net, VAT and Total) against the computer totals. Once he is happy that his input is correct he should SAVE.

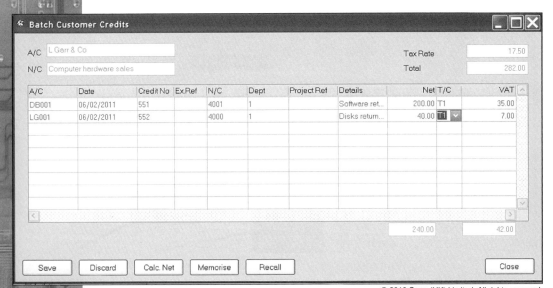

A/C	Date	Credit No	Ex.Ref	N/C	Dept	Project Ref	Details	Net	T/C	VAT
DB001	06/02/2011	551		4001	1		Software ret...	200.00	T1	35.00
LG001	06/02/2011	552		4000	1		Disks return...	40.00	T1	7.00

A/C L Garr & Co Tax Rate 17.50
N/C Computer hardware sales Total 282.00

240.00 42.00

Save Discard Calc. Net Memorise Recall Close

checking the credit notes are on the system

As a further check Tom could print out a Day Book Report for Credit notes. This can be obtained through the REPORTS icon on the CUSTOMERS toolbar. The title of the report is 'Day Books: Customer Credits (Detailed)'.

The report appears as follows:

Pronto Supplies Limited

Day Books: Customer Credits (Detailed)

Date From:	06/02/2011
Date To:	06/02/2011
Transaction From:	1
Transaction To:	99,999,999
Dept From:	0
Dept To:	999

Customer From:	
Customer To:	ZZZZZZZZ
N/C From:	
N/C To:	99999999

Tran No.	Type	Date	A/C Ref	N/C	Inv Ref	Dept.	Details	Net Amount	Tax Amount	T/C	Gross Amount	V	B
52	SC	06/02/2011	DB001	4001	551	1	Software returned	200.00	35.00	T1	235.00	N	-
53	SC	06/02/2011	LG001	4000	552	1	Disks returned (hardware)	40.00	7.00	T1	47.00	N	-
							Totals:	240.00	42.00		282.00		

CHAPTER SUMMARY

- When a business sells on credit it will issue an invoice to the buyer. This sets out the amount owing and the date by which it has to be paid.

- When a business has to make a refund to a customer to whom it sells on credit it will issue a credit note to the customer. This sets out the amount by which the amount owing is reduced.

- Sales invoices and credit notes are part of the 'flow of documents' which occurs when a sale is made on credit. The full list is purchase order, delivery note, invoice, credit note, statement, remittance advice and cheque. Not all of these will be used all of the time.

- The details of invoices and credit notes must be entered into the accounting records of a business. If a computer program is used the details will be input on screen.

- Computer accounting programs will either print out the invoices after input, or will need to have the details of existing invoices input, commonly in batches.

- It is essential to check the details of invoices and credit notes which have been input. This can be done by printing out a daybook report.

KEY TERMS

credit sale	a sale made where payment is due at a later date
debtors	customers who owe money to a business
sales ledger	the part of the accounting system where the debtors' accounts are kept – it records the amounts that are owed to the business
purchase order	the financial document which requests the supply of goods or services and specifies exactly what is required
invoice	the financial document which sets out the details of the goods sold or services provided, the amount owing and the date by which the amount is due
credit note	the financial document – normally issued when goods are returned – which reduces the amount owing by the customer
batch	a group of documents, eg invoices or credit notes
batch entry	the input of a number of documents in a group

STUDENT ACTIVITIES

6.1 Place the following documents in the order in which they are likely to be used in a transaction in which goods are sold on credit.

statement

invoice

purchase order

delivery note

cheque

credit note

6.2 A delivery note will always be used in a sale made on credit. True or false?

6.3 A credit note will always be used in a sale made on credit. True or false?

6.4 List two important pieces of information that the invoice will provide to the purchaser of goods or services.

6.5 Give a definition of the 'debtors' of a business.

6.6 Where in the accounting records of a business will the debtor balances be found?

6.7 What are the two ways in which computer accounting programs deal with the recording of invoices and credit notes?

6.8 What arithmetic checks should be made when inputting details of invoices and credit notes into a computer accounting system?

6.9 What details would you expect to enter when inputting details of each invoice into a computer accounting system?

6.10 What difference does the tax code make when inputting details of an invoice or credit note into a computer accounting system?

PRONTO SUPPLIES INPUTTING TASKS

warning note!

This activity involves inputting live data into the computer.

Remember to Save your data and keep your printouts as you progress through the tasks.

Task 1

Making sure that you have set the program date to 9 February 2011, enter the following invoice details into the computer. Check your totals before saving and print out a Day Books: Customer Invoices (Detailed) Report to confirm the data that you have saved. Check this report against the report on page 93.

SALES INVOICES ISSUED					
invoice	name	date	details	net amount	VAT
10023	John Butler & Associates	5/02/11	1 x 17" monitor	400.00	70.00
10024	Charisma Design	6/02/11	1 x printer lead	16.00	2.80
10025	Crowmatic Ltd	6/02/11	1 x MacroWorx software	100.00	17.50
10026	Kay Denz	8/02/11	2 hours consultancy	120.00	21.00
Subtotals				636.00	111.30
Batch total					747.30

Task 2

Enter the following credit note details into the computer. Check your totals before saving and print out a Day Books: Customer Credits (Detailed) Report. Check this report against the report on page 94.

CREDIT NOTES ISSUED					
credit note	name	date	details	net amount	VAT
551	David Boosey	6/02/11	Software returned	200.00	35.00
552	L Garr & Co	6/02/11	Disks returned (hardware)	40.00	7.00
Subtotals				240.00	42.00
Batch total					282.00

Task 3

It is now a week later and the date is now 16 February 2011. Change your program date setting. You have a further batch of invoices to process. Enter the details into the computer. Check your totals before saving and print out a Day Books (Detailed) Report (12 to 16 Feb) and check it against the report on page 244.

account	invoice date	number	details	net	VAT
John Butler & Associates	12/02/11	10027	2 hours consultancy	120.00	21.00
David Boossey	13/02/11	10028	1 x EF102 printer	600.00	105.00
L Garr & Co	16/02/11	10029	2 x Zap drive	180.00	31.50
Kay Denz	16/02/11	10030	1 x Fileperfect software	264.00	46.20
Charisma Design	16/02/11	10031	1 x 15" monitor	320.00	56.00
				1,484.00	259.70

Task 4

You also on the same date have two credit notes to process. Enter the details shown below into the computer. Check your totals before saving and print out a Day Books (Detailed) Report (12 to 13 Feb) to confirm the data that you have saved. Check your printout against the report on page 245.

Finally, print out a Trial Balance and check it against the the Trial Balance on page 245.

account	date	reference	details	net	VAT
Kay Denz	12/02/11	553	1 x printer lead	16.00	2.80
Crowmatic Ltd	13/02/11	554	Zap disks (hardware)	20.00	3.50
				36.00	6.30

Reminder! Have you made a backup?

chapter introduction

■   *This chapter should be read in conjunction with the last chapter 'Selling to customers on credit' as it represents 'the other side of the coin' – the invoice and the credit note as they are dealt with by the purchaser.*

■   *A business purchaser that buys on credit will receive an invoice for the goods or services supplied and will then have to pay at a later date.*

■   *Details of invoices and any credit notes received are entered by the purchaser into the account of the supplier in the computer accounting records. In this way the credit purchase and any credit due are recorded and the total amount owing by the purchaser logged into the accounting system.*

■   *This chapter continues the Pronto Supplies Case Study and shows how details of invoices and credit notes received are entered into supplier accounts in the computer accounting records.*

INVOICES AND CREDIT NOTES

Make sure that you are familiar with the two types of financial document we will be dealing with – the invoice and the credit note. Read the descriptions below and remind yourself of the 'flow of documents' by studying the diagram on the opposite page.

invoice

The main document we will deal with in this chapter is the **invoice** which is sent by the seller to the buyer to state the amount that is owing and the date by which it has to be paid. See page 86 for an illustration.

credit note

The **credit note** is issued by the seller when some form of refund has to be given to the buyer of goods or services. As payment has not yet been made the credit note allows the buyer to deduct an amount from the invoice when settlement is finally made. See page 88 for an illustration.

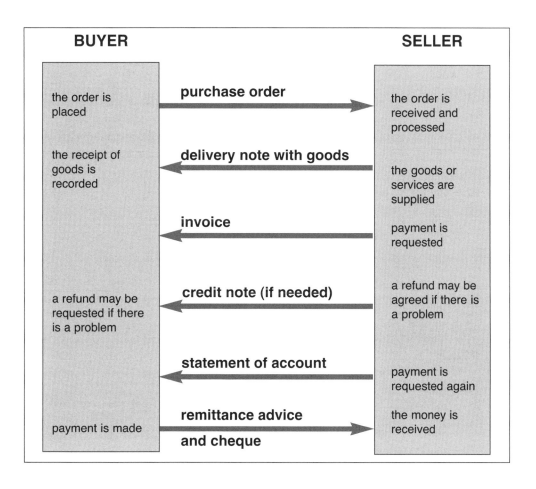

THE BOOK-KEEPING BACKGROUND

Details of invoices and credit notes have to be entered into the accounting records of a business that buys on credit. They record the sales and refunds made by suppliers who have sold on credit – the **creditors** of the business, known in Sage as 'Suppliers'.

The amounts from these documents combine to provide the total of the **Purchases Ledger**, which is the section of the accounting records which contains all the supplier accounts and their balances. The total of the **Purchases Ledger** (recorded in the **Creditors Control Account**) tells the business how much in total it owes to suppliers.

The documents received from the suppliers – invoices and credit notes – are recorded in the computer accounting system on the **batch** basis illustrated in the Case Study in the last chapter. The important point about receiving documents from a seller is that they have to be checked very carefully before input – is the buyer being overcharged, for example?

PURCHASES AND EXPENSES AND CAPITAL ITEMS

One point that is very important to bear in mind is the difference between **purchases** and **expenses** and **capital items**, as it affects the nominal account codes used when inputting invoices and credit notes on the computer. Look at the Pronto Supplies account list (with account numbers) shown below.

N/C	Name
0020	Plant and Machinery
0030	Office Equipment
0040	Furniture and Fixtures
1100	Debtors Control Account
1200	Bank Current Account
2100	Creditors Control Account
2200	Sales Tax Control Account
2201	Purchase Tax Control Account
2300	Loans
3000	Ordinary Shares
4000	Computer hardware sales
4001	Computer software sales
4002	Computer consultancy
4003	Computer helpline
5000	Materials Purchased
6201	Advertising
7000	Gross Wages
7100	Rent
7103	General Rates
7200	Electricity
7502	Telephone
7504	Office Stationery

Purchases are items a business buys which it expects to turn into a product or sell as part of its day-to-day business. For example:

- a business that makes cheese will buy milk to make the cheese
- a supermarket will buy food and consumer goods to sell to the public

All these items are bought because they will be sold or turned into a product that will be sold. In Sage these purchases will be recorded in a **purchases account**, normally 5000, or a number in that category. In the list shown above Pronto Supplies uses account 5000 for 'Materials Purchased'.

Expenses, on the other hand, are items which the business pays for which form part of the business running expenses (overheads), eg rent and electricity. They all have separate nominal account numbers.

Capital items are 'one off' items that the business buys and intends to keep for a number of years, for example office equipment and furniture. These categories of asset all also have separate nominal account numbers.

conclusion

The important point here is that all of these items may be bought on credit and will have to be entered into the computer accounting records, **but with the correct nominal account number.**

CASE STUDY

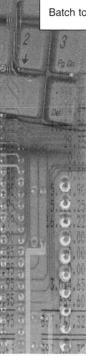

PRONTO SUPPLIES LIMITED: PROCESSING PURCHASES INVOICES AND CREDIT NOTES

It is February 16 2011. Tom has a number of supplier invoices and supplier credit notes to enter into the computer accounting system.

He has the documents on file and has collected them in two batches.

PURCHASES INVOICES RECEIVED

invoice	name	date	details	net amount	VAT
11365	Delco PLC	9/02/11	Desktop computers	3,600.00	630.00
8576	Electron Supplies	9/02/11	Peripherals	2,000.00	350.00
2947	MacCity	12/02/11	Powerbooks	3,680.00	644.00
Subtotals				9,280.00	1624.00
Batch total					10,904.00

CREDIT NOTES RECEIVED

credit note	name	date	details	net amount	VAT
7223	Delco PLC	6/02/11	1 x Computer	480.00	84.00
552	MacCity	8/02/11	1 x optical mouse	38.00	6.65
Subtotals				518.00	90.65
Batch total					608.65

batch invoice entry

Tom will start by opening up the SUPPLIERS screen in Sage and clicking on the INVOICE icon. This will show the screen shown on the next page. He will then

- identify the account references for each of the three customers
- enter each invoice on a new line
- take the data from the invoice: date, invoice no ('Ref'), product details and amounts
- ignore the Dept (2 by default), Project Ref and Cost Code columns
- enter the Materials Purchased account number 5000 under 'N/C'
- enter the T1 tax code for standard rate VAT and check that the VAT amount calculated on screen is the same as on the invoice – if there is a difference it should be queried (there could, for example, be a calculation mistake on the original invoice or a 'rounding' difference might occur)*

When the input is complete Tom should check his batch totals (Net, VAT and Total) against the computer totals. Once he is happy that his input is correct he should SAVE.

* Sometimes the VAT on the document will vary by a penny from the VAT on the screen. This is because Sage 'rounds' VAT <u>up or down</u> to the nearest penny, whereas the VAT authorities require that VAT is rounded <u>down</u> to the nearest penny. These one penny differences can be altered on the input screen to tally with the document VAT amount.

The batch suppliers' invoice screen will appear like this:

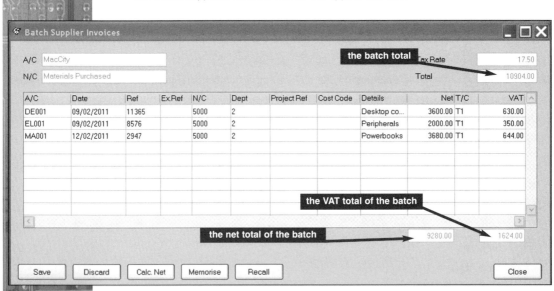

checking the invoices are on the system

As a further check Tom could print out a Day Book Report. This can be obtained through the REPORTS icon on the SUPPLIER menu bar. The title of the report is 'Day Books: Supplier Invoices (Detailed)'. The report appears as follows:

Pronto Supplies Limited
Day Books: Supplier Invoices (Detailed)

Date From:	09/02/2011							Supplier From:				
Date To:	12/02/2011							Supplier To:	ZZZZZZZZ			
Transaction From:	1							N/C From:				
Transaction To:	99,999,999							N/C To:	99999999			
Dept From:	0											
Dept To:	999											

Tran No.	Type	Date	A/C Ref	N/C	Inv Ref	Dept	Details	Net Amount	Tax Amount	T/C	Gross Amount	V	B
61	PI	09/02/2011	DE001	5000	11365	2	Desktop computers	3,600.00	630.00	T1	4,230.00	N	-
62	PI	09/02/2011	EL001	5000	8576	2	Peripherals	2,000.00	350.00	T1	2,350.00	N	-
63	PI	12/02/2011	MA001	5000	2947	2	Powerbooks	3,680.00	644.00	T1	4,324.00	N	-
							Totals	9,280.00	1,624.00		10,904.00		

batch credit note entry

Tom will input the details from the two credit notes in much the same way as he processed the invoices. He will open up the SUPPLIERS screen in Sage and click on the CREDIT icon. This will show the screen shown on the next page. He will then identify the account references for each of the two customers and input the credit note details as shown on the screen. He will use the Materials Purchased account number 5000. When the input is complete he should again check his original totals (Net, VAT and Batch total) against the computer totals. Once he is happy that his input is correct he should SAVE.

The batch suppliers' credit note screen will appear like this:

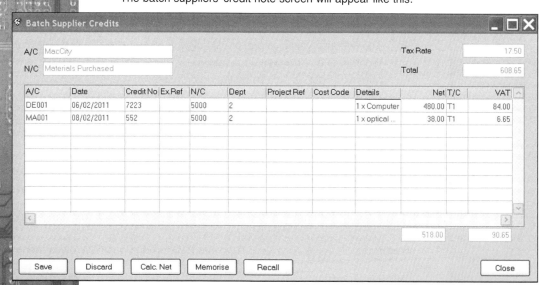

checking the credit notes are on the system

As a further check Tom could print out a Day Book Report for Supplier Credit notes. This can be obtained through the REPORTS icon on the SUPPLIERS toolbar. The title of the report is 'Day Books: Supplier Credits (Detailed)'. The report appears as follows:

Pronto Supplies Limited
Day Books: Supplier Credits (Detailed)

Date From:	06/02/2011					**Supplier From:**	
Date To:	08/02/2011					**Supplier To:**	ZZZZZZZZ
Transaction From:	1					**N/C From:**	
Transaction To:	99,999,999					**N/C To:**	99999999
Dept From:	0						
Dept To:	999						

Tran No.	Type	Date	A/C Ref	N/C	Inv Ref	Dept	Details	Net Amount	Tax Amount	T/C	Gross Amount	V	B
64	PC	06/02/2011	DE001	5000	7223	2	1 x Computer	480.00	84.00	T1	564.00	N	-
65	PC	08/02/2011	MA001	5000	552	2	1 x optical mouse	38.00	6.65	T1	44.65	N	-
							Totals	518.00	90.65		608.65		

what next?

Tom has now entered into his computer:

- his company details and nominal accounts and balances
- customer and supplier details
- customer and supplier invoices
- customer and supplier credit notes

The next chapter shows how he enters details of payments made to suppliers and payments received from customers. The 'flow of documents' will be complete.

CHAPTER SUMMARY

- When a business buys on credit it will receive invoices and possibly credit notes from its suppliers as part of the 'flow of documents'.

- The details of invoices and credit notes must be entered into the accounting records of a business. If a computer program is used the details are normally input on screen on the batch basis.

- In the case of supplier invoices and credit notes it is important that the correct Nominal account number is used to describe whether the transaction relates to purchases, expenses or capital items.

- It is essential to check the details of invoices and credit notes before input and the details of input by printing out, for example, a day book report.

KEY TERMS

credit sale	a sale made where payment is due at a later date
creditors	suppliers to whom the business owes money
purchases ledger	the part of the accounting system where the suppliers' accounts are kept
purchases	items bought which will be turned into a product or be sold as part of day-to-day-trading
expenses	payments made which relate to the running of the business – also known as overheads
capital items	items bought which the business intends to keep
batch	a group of documents, eg invoices or credit notes

STUDENT ACTIVITIES

7.1 Define the term 'creditors'.

7.2 In what section of the accounting system are supplier balances kept? What information does this provide for the owner of the business?

7.3 What is the difference between purchases, expenses and capital items? Why is it important to identify these types of transaction before entering a supplier invoice on the computer?

7.4 Write a list of instructions for a person entering supplier invoices into a batch screen on a computer accounting program. Explain what data is entered in each of the columns and what checks should be made before and after input.

PRONTO SUPPLIES INPUTTING TASKS

Task 1

Set the program date to 16 February 2011. Enter the following invoice details into the computer. Check your totals before saving and print out a Day Books: Supplier Invoice (Detailed) Report. Check this against the report on page 102.

PURCHASES INVOICES RECEIVED					
invoice	name	date	details	net amount	VAT
11365	Delco PLC	9/02/11	Desktop computers	3,600.00	630.00
8576	Electron Supplies	9/02/11	Peripherals	2,000.00	350.00
2947	MacCity	12/02/11	Powerbooks	3,680.00	644.00
Subtotals				9,280.00	1624.00
Batch total					10,904.00

Task 2

Enter the following credit note details into the computer. Check your totals before saving and print out a Day Books: Supplier Credits (Detailed) Report. Check this against the report on page 103.

CREDIT NOTES RECEIVED					
credit note	name	date	details	net amount	VAT
7223	Delco PLC	6/02/11	1 x Computer	480.00	84.00
552	MacCity	8/02/11	1 x optical mouse	38.00	6.65
Subtotals				518.00	90.65
Batch total					608.65

Task 3

On the same day (16 February) Tom receives two further supplier invoices in the post. He wants them to be input straightaway while the computer is up and running. He checks all the documentation and finds that the invoices are both correct. You are to input them, taking care to use the correct nominal code (see the codes listed on page 100). The computer and printer purchased are not for resale to customers but are to be used permanently as office equipment at Pronto Supplies.

When the input is complete the totals should be checked and a Day Book (Detailed) Report printed, showing just the last two invoices. Note that showing a range of selected invoices can be achieved by limiting the date range in the report selection criteria. Then print out a Trial Balance.

Check with the Day Book Report and Trial Balance shown on page 246.

invoice	name	date	details	net amount	VAT
11377	Delco PLC	14/02/11	Desktop computer	400.00	70.00
8603	Electron Supplies	14/02/11	Laser Printer	360.00	63.00
Subtotals				760.00	133.00
Batch total					893.00

Reminder! Have you made a back-up?

8 CUSTOMER AND SUPPLIER PAYMENTS

chapter introduction

■ So far in this book we have set up accounts for customers and suppliers and entered details of financial documents. But we have not covered the way in which the accounting system records the payment of money by customers to the business or by the business to suppliers.

■ The bank account is central to any accounting system as the payment of money is vital to all business transactions.

■ The bank account will be used not only for payments by customers and to suppliers (credit transactions), but also for transactions for which settlement is made straightaway (cash transactions), for example payment of telephone bills and wages.

■ A computer accounting system may maintain more than one 'bank' account in its Nominal Ledger. For example, it may also keep a petty cash account for purchases made from the office petty cash tin and a credit card account for purchases made with its company credit card.

■ This chapter concentrates on the use of the bank account for credit transactions, ie when a business receives payment of its customers' invoices and when it makes payments of its suppliers' invoices.

The 'cash' transactions mentioned above are covered in detail in the next two chapters.

THE BANK ACCOUNTS IN COMPUTER ACCOUNTING

The bank accounts and all the functions associated with them are found in Sage by clicking on the BANK button on the vertical toolbar.

The BANK screen then appears as shown on the next page.

Study the screen below and read the notes that follow. The most important icons are explained by the text with the arrows.

types of bank account

The accounts listed above come from the default list in the chart of accounts (see page 72 if you need reminding about this). The business does not have to adopt all the accounts listed here, but may use some of them if it needs them:

- **bank current account** records all payments in and out of the bank 'cheque' account used for everyday purposes – it is the most commonly used account

- **bank deposit account** and **Building Society account** can be used if the business maintains interest-paying accounts for savings and money that is not needed in the short term

- **petty cash account** can be used if the business keeps a petty cash tin in the office for small business purchases such as stationery and stamps

- **company credit card account** can be used if the business issues credit cards to its employees to enable them to pay for expenses

- **credit card receipts account** can be used if the business receives a significant number of credit or debit card payments from its customers

cash or credit payments?

The number of icons on the menu bar record payments which are either:

- **cash payments** – ie made straightaway without the need for invoices or credit notes
- **credit payments** – ie made in settlement of invoices

The problem is, which is which? The rule is:

= **cash payments** (not involving credit customers or suppliers)

= **credit payments** (payments from customers and to suppliers in settlement of accounts)

bank account details

It must be stressed that if a Sage computer account number is listed on the BANK screen it does not *have* to be used. It is there so that it can be used if the business needs it. The Bank Current Account (here number 1200), for example, is always going to be used, assuming businesses always have bank current accounts!

When a business is setting up its bank accounts it should click on RECORD on the BANK screen to produce the bank account DETAILS screen . . .

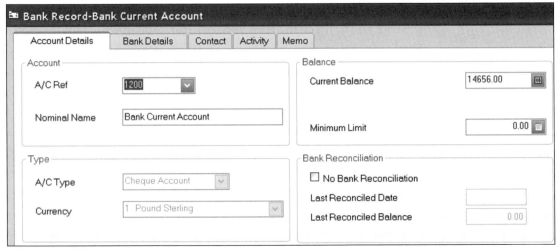

This screen enables the business to input details of the account, the bank and bank contact and to see the activity on the account.

RECORDING PAYMENTS FROM CUSTOMERS

how do payments arrive?

When a payment arrives from a customer who has bought on credit it will normally arrive at the business in one of two ways:

- A cheque and **remittance advice**. A remittance advice is a document stating what the payment relates to – eg which invoices and credit notes.

- A **BACS payment.** A BACS (Bankers Automated Clearing Services) payment is a payment sent directly between the banks' computers and does not involve a cheque. Information relating to the BACS payment may be received in the form of a BACS remittance advice or from the business bank statement.

Examples of cheque and BACS remittance advices are shown below:

TO	**REMITTANCE ADVICE**	FROM
Pronto Supplies Ltd Unit 17 Severnvale Estate Broadwater Road Mereford MR1 6TF		**Compsync** **4 Friar Street** **Broadfield** **BR1 3RF** Tel 01908 761234 Fax 01908 761987 VAT REG GB 0745 8383 56

Account PS765   6 November 2011

date	your reference	our reference	payment amount
01 10 11	INVOICE 787923	47609	277.30
10 10 11	CREDIT NOTE 12157	47609	(27.73)
		CHEQUE TOTAL	249.57

BACS REMITTANCE ADVICE

FROM: Excelsior Services
17 Gatley Way
Bristol BS1 9GH

TO
Pronto Supplies Ltd
Unit 17 Severnvale Estate, Broadwater Rd, Mereford MR1 6TF   06 12 11

Your ref	Our ref		Amount
13982	3323	BACS TRANSFER	465.00
		TOTAL	465.00

THIS HAS BEEN PAID BY BACS CREDIT TRANSFER DIRECTLY INTO YOUR BANK ACCOUNT AT ALBION BANK NO 11719881 SORT CODE 90 47 17

customer payments and the accounting system

An incoming payment from a customer settling one or more invoices (less any credit notes) needs to be recorded in the accounting system:

- the balance in the bank account will increase (a debit in double-entry)
- the balance in the customer's account (and the Debtors Control Account) will decrease because the customer will owe less (a credit in double-entry accounting)

In computer accounting the payment is input once and the two entries will be automatically made from the same screen.

the practicalities

The business will normally input a number of payments at one time on a regular basis, eg every week, using the remittance advice and/or the bank statement as the source document.

The appropriate bank account should first be selected on the BANK screen and then the CUSTOMER icon selected to access the Customer Receipt input screen:

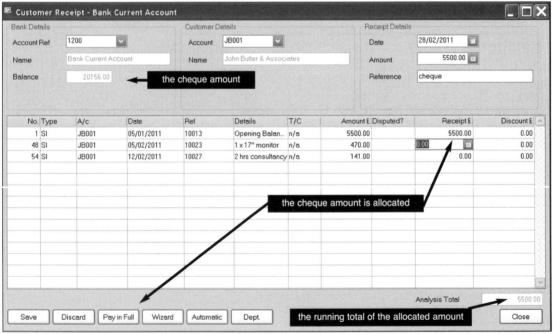

processing the payments received

The procedure for recording the customer payment on this screen is to:

- input the customer account reference – this will bring up on screen the account name and all the outstanding amounts due on invoices

- input a reference if required – for example you might type 'cheque' or 'BACS' or the numerical reference relating to the payment

- input the amount of the payment in the Amount box

- click on the 'Receipt' box of the invoice that is being paid

- click on the 'Pay in Full' button at the bottom

- if cash/settlement discount has been deducted from the payment, enter the net amount received in the Receipt box and the discount taken in the Discount box (see pages 198-199 for a full explanation of this discount)

- if there is more than one invoice being paid click on the items being paid as appropriate; the Analysis Total box at the bottom will show a running total of the money allocated

- if there is a long list of invoices and a payment to cover them, click on 'Automatic' at the bottom and the computer will allocate the payment down the invoice list until it runs out

- if a credit note (code 'SC') has been taken account of in the net payment, this should be dealt with first - see page 115 for a full explanation

- check that what you have done is correct and SAVE; details to check are:
  - customer, amount, invoices being paid and amount received
  - the amounts in the Amount box and the Analysis Total box should be the same (but see next point)

- if the amount received by way of payment is greater than the amount allocated to outstanding invoices the extra payment will show as a 'Payment on Account' after you have saved

- if the amount received by way of payment is less than the amount of the invoice(s) it is settling, the amount received will be allocated to the appropriate invoice(s) and the unpaid amount will show as outstanding on the Customer's account

- you should print out a Day Books: Customer Receipts (Summary) for these transactions from REPORTS in BANK to check that the total of the cheques (or BACS payments) received equals the total input

RECORDING PAYMENTS TO SUPPLIERS

what documents are involved?

A business often pays its suppliers after it receives a **statement** setting out the amounts due from invoices and any deductions made following the issue of credit notes. This is not a hard and fast rule, however, and it is quite in order to pay individual invoices as and when they are received.

Payment may be made by cheque, although payments are increasingly processed electronically by BACS transfer between the banks' computers. Payment is normally made in full, but occasionally a part payment may be made. A typical payment cheque, together with a completed counterfoil (cheque stub) is shown below.

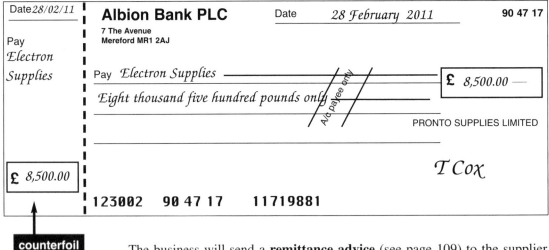

The business will send a **remittance advice** (see page 109) to the supplier with the cheque, or, if a BACS payment is being made, on its own.

supplier payments and the accounting system

Payment to a supplier settling one or more invoices (less any credit notes) needs to be recorded in the accounting system:

- the balance in the bank account will decrease (a credit in double-entry)
- the balance in the supplier's account (and the Creditors Control Account) will decrease because the supplier will be owed less (a debit in double-entry accounting)

In computer accounting the payment is input once and the two entries will be automatically made from the same screen.

processing the payments

As with customer receipts, the business will normally input a number of payments at one time on a regular basis, for example just after the cheques have been written out, or the BACS payment instructions prepared.

The payments are input in Sage from the SUPPLIER icon on the BANK screen – after the appropriate bank account has been selected.

The procedure for recording the supplier payment is to:

- input the supplier reference in the box next to the word 'Payee' on the 'cheque' – this will bring up on screen the account name and all the outstanding amounts due on invoices

- input the cheque number on the cheque and alter the date if the cheque date is different

- input the amount of the payment in the amount box on the cheque; if it is a part payment the same procedure will be followed

- click on the Payment box of the invoice that is being paid – here it is the first one – and click on the 'Pay in full' icon at the bottom; if there is more than one invoice being paid click on the items being paid as appropriate; any part payment will be allocated to the appropriate invoice(s) in the same way

- check that what you have done is correct (ie supplier, amount, invoices being paid) and SAVE (refer to page 114 if you wish to print out a remittance advice)

- print out a Day Books: Supplier Payments (Summary) from REPORTS in BANK to check that the total of the cheques (or BACS payments) issued equals the total input on the computer

Note that when processing supplier payments you may, as with customer payments, have to adjust for credit notes, overpayments and underpayments. These are covered in detail on pages 115-116. The treatment of cash/settlement discount is dealt with on pages 198-199.

A supplier payment screen is shown below.

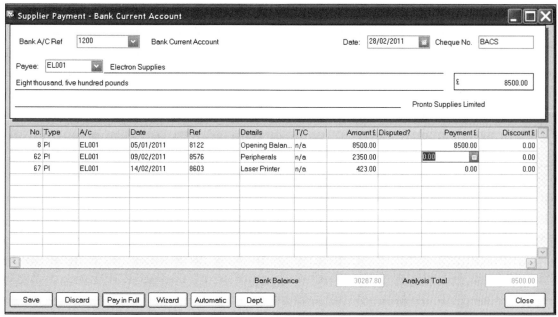

printing remittance advices and cheques

Remittance advices and cheques may be printed once a payment has been processed in Sage.

To print a remittance advice, click on Remittance on the Bank toolbar. Select the transaction or transactions for which the remittance advice is required, click Print and then choose one of the remittance options and click Run.

To print cheques (with remittance advice attached), click on Cheques on the Bank toolbar. Pre-printed cheques to use with Sage must be specially ordered.

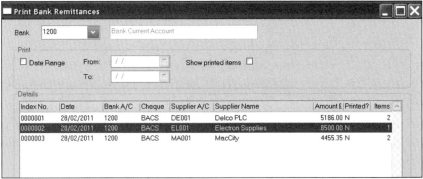

An extract from the printed remittance advice is shown below.

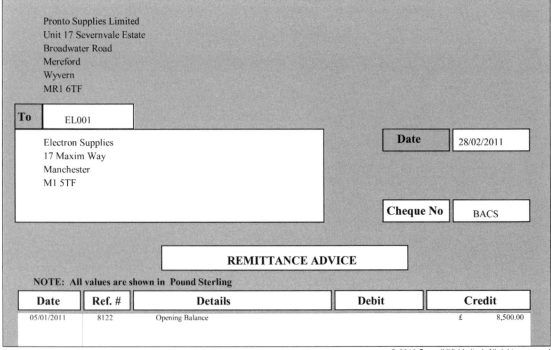

DEALING WITH CREDIT NOTES

When inputting payments from customers and to suppliers in a program like Sage, you may encounter the situation where the amount received (or paid out) is not the same as the amount of the invoice being settled.

For example, if a customer is issued with an invoice for £1,000 and then issued with a credit note for £100 because some of the goods are faulty, the customer will only owe – and pay – £900. The computer screen, however, will show this £900 as two separate lines: an invoice for £1,000 and a credit note for £100. If the £900 cheque received is allocated against the £1,000, the computer will think a balance of £100 still needs to be paid against this invoice, even though the account balance is nil.

the solution

The credit note needs to be allocated to the balance of the invoice. This is done by:

- clicking on the Receipt box on the credit note line
- clicking on 'Pay in Full' so that the analysis total shows a minus amount
- clicking on the Receipt box on the invoice line and then 'Pay in Full' so that the analysis box shows the payment amount

This procedure can be carried out during or after the payments received routine. In the example below a credit note for £235 is being set off against an invoice for £3,400, the amount received being £3,165.

Note that the procedure for allocating supplier credit notes to supplier invoices works on exactly the same principle.

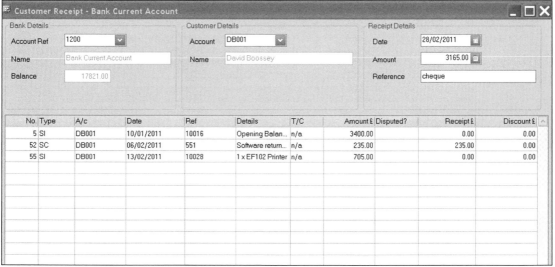

DEALING WITH PAYMENTS THAT ARE TOO HIGH OR TOO LOW

Sometimes a customer will send an amount which does not tally with the amount that appears on the customer's statement and the amount on the computer records. For example:

- the customer sends a part payment of an invoice because he or she is short of money, or thinks a credit note is due
- the customer sends too much money, ignoring a credit note that has been issued

the solution – underpayment

The amount that has been received is allocated against the relevant invoice. The amount that is still owing will show on the computer records.

the solution – overpayment

The amount that has been received is allocated against all the relevant invoices. The extra amount that is received will show as a 'Payment on Account' which will be available to allocate against future invoices.

In the example below, D Boossey paid his account with a cheque for £4,105 at the end of the month. He unfortunately did not make an adjustment for a credit note for £235 he had received and so he overpaid by this amount. Note the 'payment on account' on the second screen which shows how his account appears following the payment.

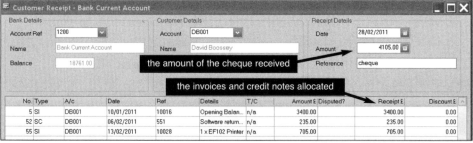

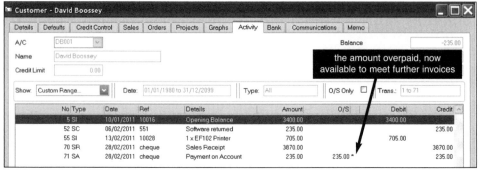

set-off payments/contra entries

Where a business trades with another as both a customer and a supplier, the two parties may agree to settle their respective accounts using set-off rather than making payments to each other. In Sage this is referred to as 'contra entry'.

In the example below, Pronto Supplies trades with Charisma Design as both a customer and a supplier. They agree to set off the amount owed to Charisma Design (£1,175.00) against the amount owing to them.

The contra entry screen is found in the Tools menu at the top of the screen.

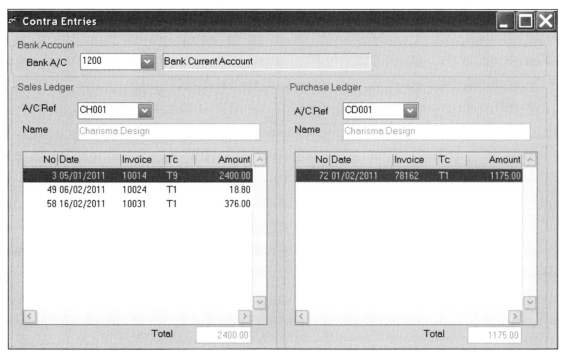

As the two accounts involved do not have the same balance, a warning screen alerts the user and suggests a possible solution. The answer in this case is Yes.

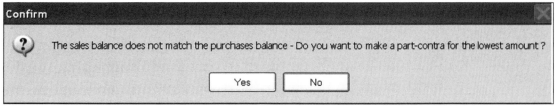

We will now look at the way in which Tom Cox's business, Pronto Supplies Limited, inputs its payments from customers and payments to suppliers on the computer.

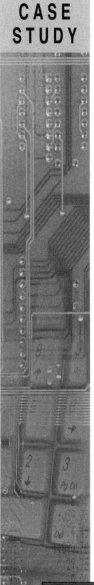

CASE STUDY

PRONTO SUPPLIES LIMITED: PROCESSING PAYMENTS FROM CUSTOMERS AND TO SUPPLIERS

It is February 28 2011. Tom has received a number of payments (with remittance advices) from his customers in settlement of their accounts.

Tom also has a list of supplier invoices to pay, the money being due at the end of the month.

receipts from customers

The list of payments received is shown below.

John Butler & Associates	£5,500.00	Cheque
Charisma Design	£2,418.80	Cheque
Crowmatic Limited	£3,234.00	BACS
David Boossey	£3,165.00	Cheque
Kay Denz	£6,500.00	BACS
L Garr & Co	£8,500.00	BACS
Total of payments received	£29,317.80	

Tom notes the following:

- The cheque from Charisma Design includes payment of an invoice for £18.80 issued on 6 February
- The cheque from David Boossey includes an adjustment made for a credit note issued on 6 February

These payments are entered into the computer accounting system under CUSTOMERS in the BANK section as shown on the screen below. This illustrates the John Butler & Associates cheque being input.

When entering the cheque received from David Boossey, Tom takes account of the credit note by clicking first in the Receipt box on the credit note line and then 'Pay in Full', before allocating the amount to the line of the amount originally due.

Tom then prints out a report 'Day Books: Customer Receipts (Summary)' which shows the transactions he has processed. This is shown on the next page. He checks the total on the report against the batch total of the payments (or remittance advices) he has received.

Customer Receipt - Bank Current Account

Bank Details

Account Ref	1200
Name	Bank Current Account
Balance	20156.00

Customer Details

Account	JB001
Name	John Butler & Associates

Receipt Details

Date	28/02/2011
Amount	5500.00
Reference	cheque

No.	Type	A/c	Date	Ref	Details	T/C	Amount £	Disputed?	Receipt £	Discount £
1	SI	JB001	05/01/2011	10013	Opening Balan...	n/a	5500.00		5500.00	0.00
48	SI	JB001	05/02/2011	10023	1 x 17" monitor	n/a	470.00		0.00	0.00
54	SI	JB001	12/02/2011	10027	2 hrs consultancy	n/a	141.00		0.00	0.00

Pronto Supplies Limited

Day Books: Customer Receipts (Summary)

Date From:	28/02/2011							Bank From:	1200	
DateTo:	28/02/2011							Bank To:	1200	

Transaction From:	1	Customer From :
Transaction To:	99,999,999	Customer To: ZZZZZZZZ

Bank   1200   Currency   Pound Sterling

No	Type	Date	Account	Ref	Details	Net £	Tax £	Gross £ B	Bank Rec.
70	SR	28/02/2011	JB001	cheque	Sales Receipt	5,500.00	0.00	5,500.00 N	
71	SR	28/02/2011	CH001	cheque	Sales Receipt	2,418.80	0.00	2,418.80 N	
72	SR	28/02/2011	CR001	BACS	Sales Receipt	3,234.00	0.00	3,234.00 N	
73	SR	28/02/2011	DB001	cheque	Sales Receipt	3,165.00	0.00	3,165.00 N	
74	SR	28/02/2011	KD001	BACS	Sales Receipt	6,500.00	0.00	6,500.00 N	
75	SR	28/02/2011	LG001	BACS	Sales Receipt	8,500.00	0.00	8,500.00 N	
					Totals £	29,317.80	0.00	29,317.80	

payments to suppliers

Tom has made a list of the amounts he owes to his suppliers for goods sent to Pronto Supplies Limited in January.

The documents he has for this are his original purchase orders, invoices received and any credit notes issued by his suppliers.

The data is now ready for input. The details are:

Delco PLC	£5,186.00	BACS
Electron Supplies	£8,500.00	BACS
MacCity	£4,455.35	BACS
Total of payments made	£18,141.35	

Tom notes that the payments from Delco PLC and MacCity include adjustments for credit notes issued.

These payments are entered into the computer accounting system under SUPPLIERS in the BANK section as shown below. Tom will also print out remittance advices to send out.

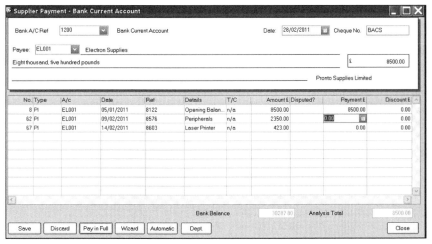

Tom then prints out a report Day Books: Supplier Payments (Summary) which shows the transactions he has processed. He checks the total on the report against the total of the payments he has issued.

Pronto Supplies Limited
Day Books: Supplier Payments (Summary)

Date From:	28/02/2011								Bank From:	1200	
DateTo:	28/02/2011								Bank To:	1200	
Transaction From:	1								Supplier From:		
Transaction To:	99,999,999								Supplier To:	ZZZZZZZ	

Bank	1200			Currency	Pound Sterling						
No	Type	Date	Supplier	Ref	Details	Net £	Tax £	Gross £ B	Bank Rec. Date
76	PP	28/02/2011	DE001	BACS	Purchase Payment	5,186.00	0.00	5,186.00 N	
77	PP	28/02/2011	EL001	BACS	Purchase Payment	8,500.00	0.00	8,500.00 N	
78	PP	28/02/2011	MA001	BACS	Purchase Payment	4,455.35	0.00	4,455.35 N	
					Totals £	18,141.35	0.00	18,141.35	

CHAPTER SUMMARY

- The bank account is a central account in the operation of any business as so many transactions pass through it.

- A business can set up not only the bank current account in the computer accounting system, but also a number of other 'money' accounts. These, which include petty cash account and credit card accounts, enable the business to keep track of the processing of money in a variety of forms.

- Payments received from customers who have bought on credit can be processed through the computer accounting system. The accounting system is adjusted in each case by an increase in the bank current account and a reduction of the customer's account balance in the Sales Ledger.

- Payments to suppliers from whom the business has bought on credit can also be processed on the computer and remittance advices printed if required. The accounting entries in this case are a decrease in the bank current account and a reduction in the supplier's account balance in the Purchases Ledger.

- The payment amount in each case (customer or supplier) will relate to invoices and any credit notes issued. Any overpayment or underpayment will be logged on the relevant Sage account.

- Sometimes the customer or supplier payment amount will be reduced because settlement (cash) discount has been deducted. Any discount of this type will be entered in a discount column in Sage.

- It is essential to check the input of payments from customers and to suppliers by obtaining a printout such as a Day Book Report from the computer.

- Set-off or contra entries may be used to settle accounts between businesses that owe each other money

KEY TERMS

current account	the 'everyday' bank account which handles routine receipts and payments
cash payments	payments made straightaway
credit payments	payments made at a later date following the issue of an invoice to a customer or by a supplier
remittance advice	a document that tells a business that a payment is being made

STUDENT ACTIVITIES

8.1 What do the icons Payment, Supplier, Receipt and Customer represent on a BANK menu bar?

8.2 Why is it helpful if a business receives a remittance advice when payment is made direct to its bank account from a customer settling an invoice or account?

8.3 What entries to the accounting system will be made when a business receives a payment from a credit customer and makes a payment to a supplier?

8.4 What printout from a computer accounting system lists payments made to suppliers on any particular day? Why is it important that a report like this is extracted? What might happen if a business decided not to obtain this printout?

PRONTO SUPPLIES INPUTTING TASKS

Task 1

Set the program date to 28 February 2011. Enter the following customer payments into BANK (CUSTOMERS). Check your total before saving and print out a Day Books: Customer Receipts (Summary) Report to confirm the accuracy of your input (see page 247).

Note:

■ the cheque from Charisma Design also includes payment of an invoice issued on 6 February

■ the cheque from David Boossey includes an adjustment made for a credit note, which will have to be allocated as described in the Case Study (see page 118)

John Butler & Associates	£5,500.00	Cheque
Charisma Design	£2,418.80	Cheque
Crowmatic Limited	£3,234.00	BACS
David Boossey	£3,165.00	Cheque
Kay Denz	£6,500.00	BACS
L Garr & Co	£8,500.00	BACS
Total of payments received	£29,317.80	

Task 2

Enter into the computer the three BACS payments listed below that Tom is paying to suppliers.

In the case of Delco PLC and MacCity, ensure that you adjust the account for credit notes issued.

Check your total before saving and print out a Day Books: Supplier Payments (Summary) Report to confirm the accuracy of your input (see page 247).

If you are able to, print out remittance advices.

Delco PLC	£5,186.00
Electron Supplies	£8,500.00
MacCity	£4,455.35
Total of payments made	£18,141.35

Task 3

Print out a Trial Balance for Pronto Supplies as at 28 February 2011 from the FINANCIALS module and check it against the Trial Balance on page 248.

Compare this new Trial Balance with the Trial Balance produced at the end of the last chapter.

Explain the changes you can see in the Bank Account balance, Debtors Control Account and Creditors Control Account. What has happened in the accounting system? Keep your printout with your answer.

- The last chapter explained how payments settling invoices are recorded in a computer accounting system. These payments received from customers and made to suppliers settle up 'credit sales' where invoices are issued when the sale is made and payment is made later.

- A business will also process a substantial number of varied 'cash payments' where the money is transferred at the same time as the transaction. Note that 'cash' does not just mean notes and coins in this context; it means immediate payment.

  Example of these payments (and receipts) include:

  • money received from sales – over the counter sales or online sales

  • money spent on purchases – buying stock and material for use in the business

  • running expenses paid – wages, power bills, rent

  • items bought for permanent use in the business – fixed assets not bought on credit

  • loans made to the business

  • money (capital) put into the business by the owner(s)

- A computer accounting system will record these 'cash' items in a different way from the 'credit' items seen in the last chapter. In a Sage system they are processed through the PAYMENT or RECEIPT icons on the BANK menu bar.

- The transactions mentioned so far involve payments which are made straight through the bank current account. A business may also use other funds for making payments and receiving money. These are covered in the next chapter.

THE BANK ACCOUNTS

The last chapter started by looking at the different bank accounts that a Sage system will allow a business to set up. Whereas the last chapter concentrated on the use of the Bank Current Account for payments made on credit, this chapter examines the way in which cash payments (immediate payments) are recorded in the Bank Current Account of a computer accounting system.

The BANK screen shown below (the default accounts screen) explains the icons that you will be using in this chapter.

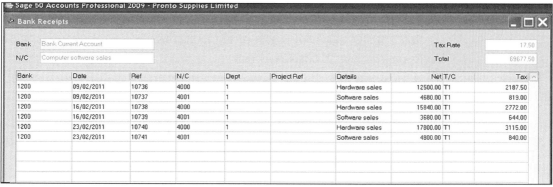

CASH RECEIPTS

Cash sales made by a business are usually sales made at a checkout or through an online shop. 'Cash' here means 'immediate payment.'

Receipts from cash sales can be made by cash, cheque or debit or credit card. The important point here is that the business should ensure the money is paid into the bank current account as soon as possible, so that it can be used to meet payments the business may have made or may have to make.

The input screen for cash sales is reached from the RECEIPT icon on the BANK menu bar. It looks like this:

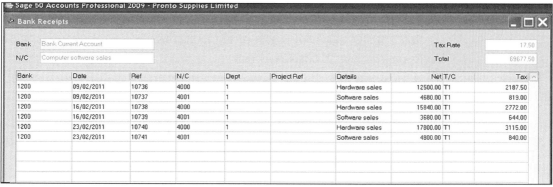

inputting bank receipts

Cash sales paid straight into the bank may be input from the bank paying-in slips recorded in the business cash book or from a sales listing sheet. These receipts are known in Sage as Bank Receipts and are input as follows:

- input the computer bank account number
- enter the date (usually the date the money is paid into the bank)
- enter a reference (this can be the reference number of the paying-in slip)
- input the appropriate nominal code (N/C) for the type of sales involved
- enter a description of the payment (eg 'hardware sales') under 'Details'
- enter the net amount of the sales (ie the sales amount excluding VAT) and then click on T1 if the goods are standard rated for VAT – the computer will then automatically calculate the VAT amount for you and show it in the right-hand column
- check that the VAT amount shown agrees with your figure and change it on screen if it does not – there may be a rounding difference
- check the input details and totals and then SAVE

a note on VAT

The rates of VAT (**tax codes**) that you are most likely to come across are:

T1	standard rate (17.5% at the time of writing)
T2	exempt from VAT – eg postage stamps, insurance
T0	zero-rated, ie VAT could be charged but it is zero at the moment – eg books, food and some children's clothes
T9	transactions not involving VAT

If you only have a VAT inclusive figure and do not know what the VAT amount is, enter the total figure in the 'Net' column and click on 'Calc.Net' at the bottom of the screen. The computer then automatically calculates and shows the net amount and the VAT.

other cash receipts

You can also enter other cash (= not credit) receipts using the same Bank Receipts screen. Examples include:

- money invested by the owner(s) of the business – capital
- loans and grants from outside bodies
- income from other sources such as rent received, bank interest or commission received

This money is likely to be received in the form of a cheque or bank transfer and will need to be recorded as such.

CASH PAYMENTS

Most credit payments made by businesses, as we saw in the last chapter, are to suppliers for goods and services provided and paid for on invoice. But businesses also have to make payments on a day-to-day cash basis (immediate payment) for running costs and expenses such as wages, telephone bills, owner drawings and sundry (miscellaneous) expenses. Cash payments may also be made to suppliers where no credit terms have been agreed.

These payments are input from the screen reached by clicking on the PAYMENT icon on the BANK menu bar. Study the example shown below: a telephone bill and wages have been paid from the Bank Current Account.

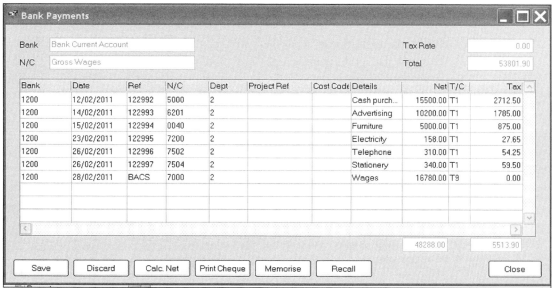

inputting cash payments

Cash payments can be input from the handwritten business **cash book** (if one is used), or from the cheques issued and bills being paid (which should show any VAT element). The procedure for inputting is:

- input the computer bank account number
- enter the date (the date the payment is made)
- enter a reference (normally the cheque number or 'BACS' if the payment is a BACS payment)
- input the appropriate nominal code (N/C) for the type of payment involved
- enter a brief description of the nature of the payment (eg 'Telephone') under 'Details'

■ enter the net amount of the payment (ie the amount excluding VAT) and then click on T1 if the product is standard rated for VAT – the computer will then automatically calculate the VAT amount for you and show it in the right-hand column

■ check that the VAT amount shown agrees with your figure and change it on screen if it does not – there may be a rounding difference

a note on VAT

The VAT rates used here are:

T1	the telephone bill is standard rated
T9	wages do not involve VAT

The code for a zero-rated item would have been T0. The code for a VAT exempt item would have been T2.

If you do not know what the VAT amount is included in a payment figure, enter the total figure in the 'Net' column and click on 'Calc.Net' at the bottom of the screen. The computer will then automatically calculate the VAT and adjust the Net figure accordingly.

checking the input data

It is important to check your input for each item against the source data for the input. You will see that the screen on the previous page has running total boxes below the Net and Tax columns. There is also a Total (Net plus Tax) box at the top. These boxes will all update as you enter the transactions.

If you are entering the data for a number of transactions you should add up the three 'batch' totals (Net, VAT and Total) and check them against the screen figures in the total boxes when you have finished your data entry.

As a final check you should print out a Day Book report (see extract below) from Reports in BANK and check the entries against your handwritten records (your cash book, for example).

Pronto Supplies Limited
Day Books: Bank Payments (Detailed)

Bank:	1200		Currency:	Pound Sterling									
No	Type	N/C	Date	Ref	Details	Dept	Net £	Tax £ T/C	Gross £ V B
85	BP	5000	12/02/2011	122992	Cash purchases	2	15,500.00	2,712.50 T1	18,212.50 N N
86	BP	6201	14/02/2011	122993	Advertising	2	10,200.00	1,785.00 T1	11,985.00 N N
87	BP	0040	15/02/2011	122994	Furniture	2	5,000.00	875.00 T1	5,875.00 N N
88	BP	7200	23/02/2011	122995	Electricity	2	158.00	27.65 T1	185.65 N N
89	BP	7502	26/02/2011	122996	Telephone	2	310.00	54.25 T1	364.25 N N
90	BP	7504	26/02/2011	122997	Stationery	2	340.00	59.50 T1	399.50 N N
91	BP	7000	28/02/2011	BACS	Wages	2	16,780.00	0.00 T9	16,780.00 - N
						Totals £	48,288.00	5,513.90	53,801.90

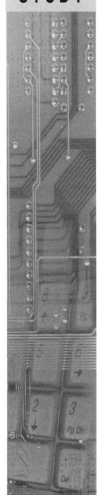

CASE STUDY

PRONTO SUPPLIES LIMITED: CASH RECEIPTS AND PAYMENTS

It is February 28 2011 and Tom has completed and checked his input of customer receipts and supplier payments (see pages 118 to 119).

He now has to input the various cash receipts and payments received and made during the month.

cash receipts

Pronto Supplies Limited paid takings of cash sales into the bank current account three times during the month. The amounts recorded in the cash book are shown below. The reference quoted is the paying-in slip reference.

Date	Details	Net amount (£)	VAT (£)	ref.
9 Feb 2011	Hardware sales	12,500.00	2187.50	10736
9 Feb 2011	Software sales	4,680.00	819.00	10737
16 Feb 2011	Hardware sales	15,840.00	2,772.00	10738
16 Feb 2011	Software sales	3,680.00	644.00	10739
23 Feb 2011	Hardware sales	17,800.00	3,115.00	10740
23 Feb 2011	Software sales	4,800.00	840.00	10741
	Totals	59,300.00	10,377.50	

These sales receipts are entered into the computer accounting system on the RECEIPTS screen reached from the BANK menu bar. Note that the Bank Current Account and the appropriate nominal sales code (N/C) are used each time.

Tom can use some helpful features when inputting. When in a line and wanting to copy the box above (eg the bank account number or the date) he presses F6; when wanting to raise the number in the box by one (eg reference number) he presses Shift F6.

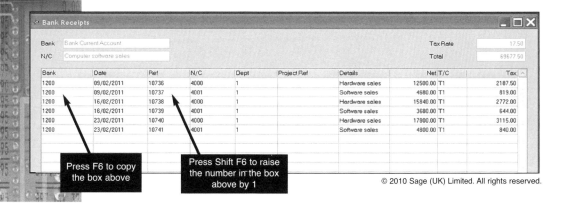

Press F6 to copy the box above

Press Shift F6 to raise the number in the box above by 1

Tom then checks his listing totals against the on-screen totals for accuracy and clicks SAVE. He then prints out a report Day Books: Bank Receipts (Detailed) as a paper-based record of the transactions he has processed. This is shown below. He again checks the totals on the report against the totals on his original listing.

Pronto Supplies Limited
Day Books: Bank Receipts (Detailed)

| Date From: | 09/02/2011 |
| DateTo: | 23/02/2011 |

| Transaction From: | 1 | | | | | | | N/C From: | |
| Transaction To: | 99,999,999 | | | | | | | N/C To: | 99999999 |

| Dept From: | 0 |
| Dept To: | 999 |

| Bank: | 1200 | | Currency: | Pound Sterling |

No	Type	N/C	Date	Ref	Details	Dept	Net £	Tax £	T/C	Gross £	V	B
79	BR	4000	09/02/2011	10736	Hardware sales	1	12,500.00	2,187.50	T1	14,687.50	N	N
80	BR	4001	09/02/2011	10737	Software sales	1	4,680.00	819.00	T1	5,499.00	N	N
81	BR	4000	16/02/2011	10738	Hardware sales	1	15,840.00	2,772.00	T1	18,612.00	N	N
82	BR	4001	16/02/2011	10739	Software sales	1	3,680.00	644.00	T1	4,324.00	N	N
83	BR	4000	23/02/2011	10740	Hardware sales	1	17,800.00	3,115.00	T1	20,915.00	N	N
84	BR	4001	23/02/2011	10741	Software sales	1	4,800.00	840.00	T1	5,640.00	N	N
						Totals £	59,300.00	10,377.50		69,677.50		

cash payments

Tom sees from the company cash book that Pronto Supplies Limited has made a number of cheque 'cash' payments during the month for a variety of purposes. They are listed below. They include:

- normal day-to-day running expenses paid by cheque on a cash basis
- the purchase of furniture for £5,000 (a fixed asset) on 15 February

Date	Details	Net amount (£)	VAT (£)	chq no
12 Feb 2011	Cash purchases	15,500.00	2,712.50	122992
14 Feb 2011	Advertising	10,200.00	1,785.00	122993
15 Feb 2011	Furniture	5,000.00	875.00	122994
23 Feb 2011	Electricity	158.00	27.65	122995
26 Feb 2011	Telephone	310.00	54.25	122996
26 Feb 2011	Stationery	340.00	59.50	122997
28 Feb 2011	Wages	16,780.00	no VAT	BACS
	Totals	48,288.00	5,513.90	

These payments are entered into the computer accounting system on the PAYMENTS screen reached from the BANK menu bar. Note that the Bank Current Account and the appropriate nominal code (N/C) is used each time. The reference in each case is the relevant cheque number or BACS.

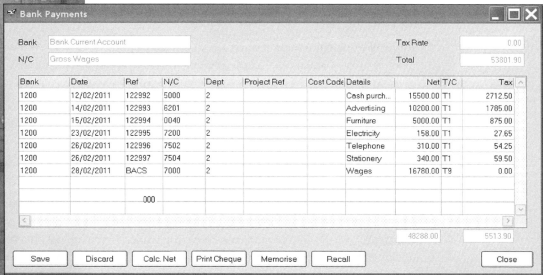

If Tom wants to insert or delete lines when entering data, he can press F7 to insert a blank line between two lines already entered, or F8 to delete a line already entered.

Tom then checks his listing totals against the on-screen totals for accuracy and clicks SAVE. He prints out a report Day Books: Bank Payments (Detailed) as a record of the transactions he has processed. This is shown below. He compares the totals on the report against the totals on his original listing as a final check of input accuracy.

Pronto Supplies Limited
Day Books: Bank Payments (Detailed)

Date From: 12/02/2011
DateTo: 28/02/2011

Transaction From:	1				N/C From:	
Transaction To:	99,999,999				N/C To:	99999999

Dept From: 0
Dept To: 999

Bank: 1200   Currency: Pound Sterling

No	Type	N/C	Date	Ref	Details	Dept	Net £	Tax £ T/C	Gross £ V B	Bank Date
85	BP	5000	12/02/2011	122992	Cash purchases	2	15,500.00	2,712.50 T1	18,212.50 N N	
86	BP	6201	14/02/2011	122993	Advertising	2	10,200.00	1,785.00 T1	11,985.00 N N	
87	BP	0040	15/02/2011	122994	Furniture	2	5,000.00	875.00 T1	5,875.00 N N	
88	BP	7200	23/02/2011	122995	Electricity	2	158.00	27.65 T1	185.65 N N	
89	BP	7502	26/02/2011	122996	Telephone	2	310.00	54.25 T1	364.25 N N	
90	BP	7504	26/02/2011	122997	Stationery	2	340.00	59.50 T1	399.50 N N	
91	BP	7000	28/02/2011	BACS	Wages	2	16,780.00	0.00 T9	16,780.00 - N	
						Totals £	48,288.00	5,513.90	53,801.90	

RECEIPTS AND PAYMENTS AND THE ACCOUNTING SYSTEM

It is important to appreciate how the cash receipts and payments in this chapter relate to the accounting system of a business, particularly if you are also studying double-entry book-keeping.

Remember that transactions involve debits and credits and that the debit amount always equals the credit amount. Because of the VAT included in many sales and purchases, these transactions may involve three entries:

- the amount posted to the bank account (the full amount)
- the 'net' amount (the amount before VAT is added on) posted to the sales account or purchases (or expense) account
- any VAT involved in the transaction being posted to Sales or Purchases VAT account

The whole cash payment system is summarised in the linked diagram below. This shows how the money comes into and out of the bank account and illustrates how the double-entry book-keeping works. If you are not studying double-entry, just concentrate on the types of receipts and payments and study how they are input.

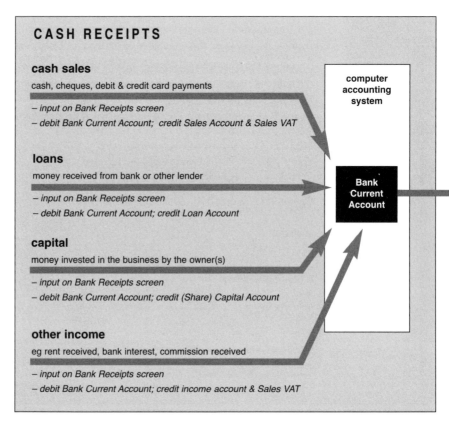

CASH RECEIPTS

cash sales
cash, cheques, debit & credit card payments
– input on Bank Receipts screen
– debit Bank Current Account; credit Sales Account & Sales VAT

loans
money received from bank or other lender
– input on Bank Receipts screen
– debit Bank Current Account; credit Loan Account

capital
money invested in the business by the owner(s)
– input on Bank Receipts screen
– debit Bank Current Account; credit (Share) Capital Account

other income
eg rent received, bank interest, commission received
– input on Bank Receipts screen
– debit Bank Current Account; credit income account & Sales VAT

computer accounting system

Bank Current Account

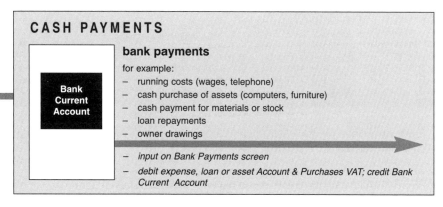

CASH PAYMENTS

bank payments

for example:
- running costs (wages, telephone)
- cash purchase of assets (computers, furniture)
- cash payment for materials or stock
- loan repayments
- owner drawings

- *input on Bank Payments screen*
- *debit expense, loan or asset Account & Purchases VAT; credit Bank Current Account*

CHAPTER SUMMARY

■ Cash payments are payments which are immediate, unlike credit payments which are made at a later date.

■ Cash receipts and payments include payment by cash, cheques, debit and credit cards and BACS

■ Businesses receive cash payments from a variety of sources: cash sales, loans, capital introduced by the owner(s) and other income such as rent of property, bank interest and commission received.

■ Businesses make cash payments for day-to-day running costs, purchases where no credit is given, loan repayments and owner drawings

■ A computer accounting program will record cash payments coming in – ie cash receipts – by adding the money to the bank account and by adjusting the appropriate other account (eg sales, loan, capital, income account) and the Sales VAT account (if there is any VAT involved).

■ A computer accounting program will record cash payments going out – ie cash payments – by deducting the money from the bank account and by adjusting the appropriate other account (eg expense, asset purchase) and the Purchases VAT account (if there is any VAT involved).

KEY TERMS

cash sales — sales made where payment is immediate

current account — the 'everyday' bank account which handles routine receipts and payments

tax codes — a term used by Sage to refer to the rate of VAT which is applied to transactions; T1 refers to standard rate, T0 to the zero rate, T2 to VAT exempt items and T9 to transactions which do not involve VAT

cash book — the manual record which records money paid in and out of the bank account

9.1 From which icon on the BANK menu bar will the screen needed for recording a cash sale from a customer be reached? RECEIPT or CUSTOMER?

9.2 From which icon on the BANK menu bar will the screen needed for recording a cash purchase from a supplier be reached? PAYMENT or SUPPLIER?

9.3 Complete the sentences below using the following computer account names:

■ Bank   ■ Purchases   ■ Sales   ■ Purchases VAT   ■ Sales VAT

(a) A business makes a cash sale for £117.50, which is made up of £100 net and £17.50 VAT. The postings to the computer accounts will be:

£117.50 to .... account

£100.00 to .... account

£17.50 to .... account

(b) A business makes a cash purchase for £940, which is made up of £800 net and £140 VAT. The postings to the computer accounts will be:

£140.00 to .... account

£940.00 to .... account

£800.00 to .... account

9.4 Businesses from time-to-time pay into the bank cash payments which are not received from cash sales. Give three examples of this type of cash receipt.

PRONTO SUPPLIES INPUTTING TASKS

Task 1

Set the program date to 28 February 2011. Enter the following bank receipts into the computer. Check your totals before saving and print out a Day Books: Bank Receipts (Detailed) Report (date range 9 Feb to 23 Feb) to confirm the accuracy of your input (see page 130).

Date	Details	Net amount (£)	VAT (£)	ref.
9 Feb 2011	Hardware sales	12,500.00	2187.50	10736
9 Feb 2011	Software sales	4,680.00	819.00	10737
16 Feb 2011	Hardware sales	15,840.00	2,772.00	10738
16 Feb 2011	Software sales	3,680.00	644.00	10739
23 Feb 2011	Hardware sales	17,800.00	3,115.00	10740
23 Feb 2011	Software sales	4,800.00	840.00	10741
	Totals	59,300.00	10,377.50	

Task 2

Keeping the program date as 28 February 2011, enter the following cash payments into the computer. Take care over the nominal accounts that you chose and the VAT Tax codes used. T1 is the standard rate code, T2 is for exempt items and T9 is the code for transactions which do not involve VAT.

Check your totals before saving and print out a Day Books: Bank Payments (Detailed) Report, using an appropriate date range to confirm the accuracy of your input (see page 249).

Date	Details	Net amount (£)	VAT (£)	chq no
12 Feb 2011	Cash purchases*	15,500.00	2,712.50	122992
14 Feb 2011	Advertising	10,200.00	1,785.00	122993
15 Feb 2011	Furniture	5,000.00	875.00	122994
23 Feb 2011	Electricity	158.00	27.65	122995
26 Feb 2011	Telephone	310.00	54.25	122996
26 Feb 2011	Stationery	340.00	59.50	122997
28 Feb 2011	Wages	16,780.00	no VAT	BACS
	Totals	48,288.00	5,513.90	

*use 'Materials Purchased' account for this transaction, as the purchases are for stock

Task 3

Keep the program date as 28 February 2011.

Tom has won £5,000 on a Premium Bond. He decides to pay the cheque into the business as extra issued share capital under reference 10742, Code T9.

On 28 February he also spends £4,000 plus VAT on a new colour printer for his office, using cheque number 122998 for the cash purchase.

Make the necessary entries into the computer accounts (the nominal accounts used will be Ordinary Shares and Office Equipment).

Task 4

Print out a Trial Balance as at 28 February 2011 to check the accuracy of your input to date. Note particularly the increases in Share Capital and Office Equipment Accounts. Check with the Trial Balance on page 249.

Reminder! Have you made a back-up?

■ *The last chapter explained how cash payments made directly in and out of the bank current account are recorded in a computer accounting system. 'Cash payment' here means 'immediate payment'. It can involve cash, cheques, payments by debit and credit card and BACS.*

■ *The computer program also enables a business to set up accounts on the system which record funds of money held by the business. These funds are classified by Sage as 'Bank' accounts, but the money is not held at the bank – it is held by the business and managed by the business. These accounts cover both cash payments and cash receipts.*

■ *The 'Bank' accounts – which allow payments to be made – include:*

  - petty cash account – a cash fund held under lock and key in the office, used for making small purchases and payments

  - credit card account – company credit cards issued to employees which enable the employees to pay expenses and for the business to be billed by the credit card company

  The money for these accounts will come from the bank current account and be recorded in Sage by a Bank Transfer.

■ *If a business – a shop for example – receives cash payments and then holds them on the premises for a length of time before paying them into the bank, it may decide to open a Cash Account to record the takings.*

  When the money is eventually paid into the bank, the business will record a Bank Transfer from Cash Account in Sage to show the money being paid into the bank.

■ *Businesses will from time-to-time need to record regular payments made in and out of the bank current account. Examples include standing orders and direct debits for outgoing payments of insurance premiums and business rates and incoming receipts of rent from tenants.*

  In Sage the Recurring Entries facility enables the business to set up the payments so that they can be recorded automatically each month in the accounts on the click of a button.

THE BANK ACCOUNTS IN COMPUTER ACCOUNTING

The bank accounts and all the functions associated with them are found in Sage by clicking on the BANK button in the vertical toolbar.

The accounts listed come from the default list in the chart of accounts. The business does not have to adopt all the accounts, but may use some of them if it needs them. It can also set up new accounts within the appropriate account number range by clicking on NEW on the menu bar and using the new account Wizard. A summary of the Sage bank accounts is on page 107.

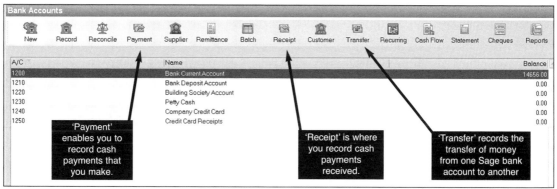

when is a bank account not a bank account?

The first three types of account shown on the above screen are actually maintained at the bank or building society. They are true 'bank' accounts. The last three accounts – petty cash and credit card payment and receipts accounts – are not kept at the bank but within the business. They are the accounts Sage uses to record money funds within the business which originally came from the bank or will be paid into the bank.

transfers between accounts

A TRANSFER facility on the BANK menu bar records movements between the 'bank' accounts. The screen below shows a business paying a company credit card bill with a cheque for £1,276.85. The money comes out of the current account and wipes out all the payments made with the card and recorded on the Company Credit Card Account (see page 143).

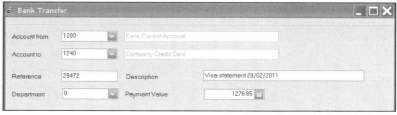

OPENING UP A PETTY CASH ACCOUNT

what is a petty cash payment?

Petty cash is a float of cash – notes and coins – kept in an office, normally in a locked tin. It provides employees with the cash to make small purchases for the business, eg stationery, postage stamps and business taxi fares.

The petty cash is topped up with cash periodically. Some businesses operate an 'imprest' system, where the cash is topped up to a set limit, £100 for example. The amount of the top up will be the amount that has been spent: for example if £80 has been spent, the top up will be £80, restoring the imprest to £100.

The document used is the petty cash voucher (see below). When a payment is made, a petty cash voucher is completed and the appropriate evidence of payment is attached, for example:

- a till receipt from a shop or a Post Office receipt for stamps
- a rail or bus ticket or a receipt from a taxi firm

The cash can be paid out (or refunded) when the voucher is completed and authorised.

petty cash voucher		Number	*807*	
		date	*15 May 2011*	
description				**amount**
			£	p
Envelopes			6	*00*
	VAT		*1*	*05*
Receipt obtained			7	*05*
signature	*T Harris*			
authorised	*R Patel*			

petty cash and the accounting system

Petty cash is a fund of money kept in the business in the same way as the bank current account is a fund of money kept in the bank. A 'bank' account will be set up for petty cash which will handle all the transactions:

- payments of cash into petty cash from the bank current account
- payments out of petty cash to pay for small expense items

payments into petty cash

The Sage computer system has a default Petty Cash Account which it classes as a bank account, although, of course, the money is not in the bank. The computer sees it as a 'money fund'.

When cash is needed to top up the petty cash, the business will cash a cheque at the bank and then put the money in the cash tin. The computer program requires the business to input the transaction as a TRANSFER from the BANK menu bar. In the screen below, the business has cashed a £100 cheque at the bank (using cheque 122991) to provide the cash.

payments out of petty cash

Payments out of Petty Cash Account are handled in exactly the same way on the computer as payments out of Bank Current Account. The PAYMENTS screen is reached through the BANK menu bar. The details are then input from the petty cash vouchers or the petty cash book in which they are recorded.

The screen below shows the input of the petty cash voucher for stationery shown on the opposite page.

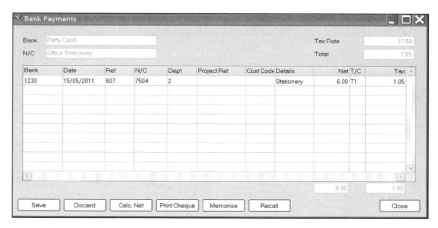

Points to remember are:

- the bank account number used is the Petty Cash Account number
- the reference is the petty cash voucher number
- petty cash vouchers and their receipts will not always show the VAT amount – the VAT and net amount can be calculated on the computer by inputting the full amount under 'Net' and then clicking on 'Calc.Net' at the bottom of the screen (using T1 code to denote standard rate VAT)
- when the details have been checked you should SAVE
- the details can also be checked against a Cash Payments Day Book printout if required (accessed through Reports in BANK)

CASE STUDY

PRONTO SUPPLIES LIMITED:
SETTING UP THE PETTY CASH SYSTEM

At the beginning of February Tom Cox set up a petty cash system at Pronto Supplies Limited. The situation at 28 February is as follows:

- Tom notes that he cashed cheque no 122991 for £100 at the bank on 1 February.

- The £100 cash was transferred to the petty cash tin on 1 February.

- The tin contains three vouchers for payments made during the month – these are shown below and on the next page. They are ready for entry in the petty cash book as part of the month-end routine.

  Voucher PC101 shows the VAT included in the total (standard rate: T1)

  Voucher PC102 does not have any VAT in it (postage stamps are exempt:T2)

  Voucher PC103 does not show the VAT included in the total (standard rate: T1) because it was not shown on the original receipt.

petty cash voucher		Number *PC101*
	date	*7 Feb 2011*

description		amount	
		£	p
Copy paper		36	00
	VAT	6	30
Receipt obtained		42	30

signature   *Nick Vellope*

authorised   *Tom Cox*

petty cash voucher		Number *PC102*
	date	*14 Feb 2011*

description		amount	
		£	p
Postage stamps		25	00
	VAT		
Receipt obtained		25	00

signature .... *R Patel* ....

authorised .... *Tom Cox* ....

petty cash voucher		Number *PC103*
	date	*20 Feb 2011*

description		amount	
		£	p
Envelopes			
Receipt obtained (VAT included but not shown separately)	VAT		
		18	80

signature .... *B Radish* ....

authorised .... *Tom Cox* ....

the transfer to petty cash

Tom Cox first inputs the £100 transfer from the Bank Current Account to the Petty Cash Account. The screen is illustrated below. Note the use of the cheque number as the reference.

inputting the vouchers

The petty cash payments are entered into the computer accounting system on the PAYMENTS screen reached from the BANK menu bar.

Note that the bank Petty Cash Account number and the appropriate nominal code (N/C) is used each time.

The postage stamps nominal code was taken from the default nominal list.

The reference in each case is the relevant petty cash voucher number.

Postage stamps are VAT exempt. The VAT on the third petty cash voucher was not on the receipt but has been calculated on-screen by inputting the total amount of £18.80 in the 'Net' column and clicking on 'Calc.Net' at the bottom of the screen:

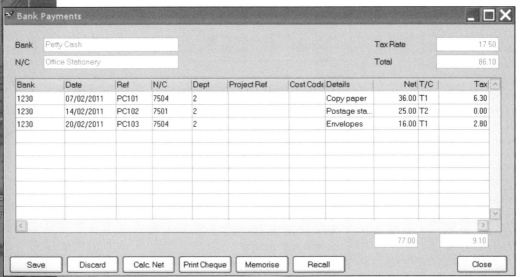

© 2010 Sage (UK) Limited. All rights reserved.

Tom then checks the batch total with the total of the vouchers and when he is happy that all the details are correct he will SAVE. The Day Book report will now show the petty cash payments. Note that the transaction code is 'CP' (second column from the left). This stands for 'Cash Payment'. This distinguishes the petty cash payments from payments from the bank current account (input through the same screen). These payments have the code 'BP' which stands for 'Bank Payment'.

Pronto Supplies Limited

Day Books: Cash Payments (Detailed)

| Date From: | 07/02/2011 | | | | | | | | | | Bank From: | 1230 | | |
| Date To: | 20/02/2011 | | | | | | | | | | Bank To: | 1230 | | |

| Transaction From: | 1 | | | | | | | | N/C From: | |
| Transaction To: | 99,999,999 | | | | | | | | N/C To: | 99999999 |

| Dept From: | 0 |
| Dept To: | 999 |

| Bank: | 1230 | | Currency: | Pound Sterling | | | | | | | | | | | Bank Rec. |
No	Type	N/C	Date	Ref	Details	Dept	Net £	Tax	£ T/C	Gross £	V	B	Date
96	CP	7504	07/02/2011	PC101	Copy paper	2	36.00	6.30	T1	42.30	N	N	
97	CP	7501	14/02/2011	PC102	Postage stamps	2	25.00	0.00	T2	25.00	N	N	
98	CP	7504	20/02/2011	PC103	Envelopes	2	16.00	2.80	T1	18.80	N	N	
						Totals £	77.00	9.10		86.10			

© 2010 Sage (UK) Limited. All rights reserved.

CARD ACCOUNTS

use of company credit cards

Credit cards are often issued by an employer for use by their employees when they are out on business – for example a sales representative who needs to buy fuel for the company car and to take a client out to lunch. All expenses are billed to the company on the credit card statement and are checked by the management to make sure that the expenses are valid claims.

company credit card payments in the accounts

The business with a computer accounting system can make use of the credit card account in the BANK function. This will be used to record all payments in Sage using the BANK PAYMENT screen seen earlier in this chapter, but inputting the payments to the Company Credit Card Account.

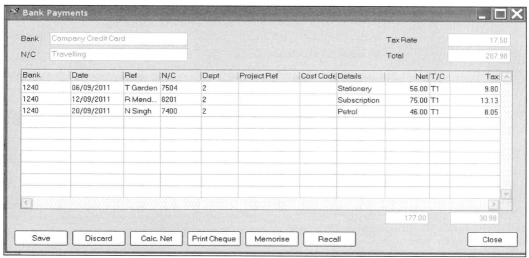

When the business pays the credit card bill the total amount will be input on the TRANSFER screen in the same way as the petty cash can be topped up to the imprest amount (see page 137).

credit/debit card receipt accounts

A business using computer accounting might also open up an account in BANK to record credit and debit card receipts. Totals will then be transferred to the current account in Sage (1200). Alternatively, these receipts can be entered directly into the current account. Totals should be reconciled with the advices from the card merchant.

USING A CASH RECEIPTS ACCOUNT

We have seen so far that cash receipts – for example the cash and cheques takings from a shop – are best paid into the bank current account as soon as possible. This reduces the risk of theft and means that the business has the use of the money earlier rather than later.

There may be a case, however, where a business keeps its cash takings on the premises for some time before paying in. This could happen when a week's takings of a shop, for example, are paid in the following Monday. The business here could open up a special Cash Receipts Account in BANK to record the money fund kept on the premises. The procedure would be:

- open up a Cash Receipts Account in BANK as a 'Cash' Account

- enter the totals of daily takings in RECEIPTS from the BANK menu – the totals could be taken from the various till listings or a summary

- using TRANSFER from the BANK menu, record the amounts as and when they are paid into the bank current account – the source document is the paying-in slip and the transfer is made from Cash Receipts Account to Bank Current Account

The RECEIPT and TRANSFER screens are shown below and on the next page.

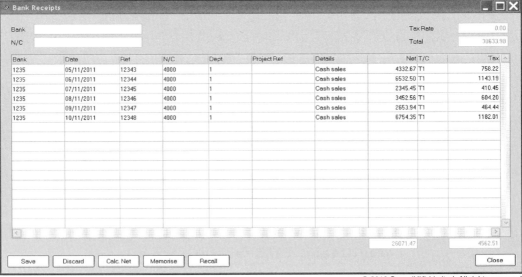

Here the takings for a week's trading (Monday to Saturday) by a shop are recorded on the BANK RECEIPTS screen. The money will be paid in on the following Monday and is held securely on the shop premises.

Bank Transfer		
Account from	1235	Cash Receipts
Account to	1200	Bank Current Account
Reference	511/1011	Description	From cash receipts to bank
Department	0	Payment Value	30633.98
Date	12/11/2011		

Here the shop takings for the week are being paid into the bank on a paying-in slip on Monday. The amount is transferred from Cash Receipts Account to Bank Current Account. The balance on the Cash Receipts Account should then revert to nil as all the money will have left the premises.

RECURRING PAYMENTS AND RECEIPTS

Recurring entries are payments or transfers which are made monthly or weekly or at other intervals. Businesses, for example

- *receive* recurring payments, for example rent from an office owned
- *make* recurring payments, for example loan repayments, insurance premiums, rent and rates paid

These payments are often made direct from the bank account of the payer to the bank account of the recipient ('beneficiary') by direct debit or standing order using the computer transfer BACS system.

Payments due are often recorded on a document called a 'Standing order/Direct debit schedule'. If a business operates a manual accounting system these payments will be written individually in the cash book each time they are made or received – a laborious and time-consuming process. A business using a computer accounting system such as Sage can automate this procedure.

setting up recurring entries in Sage

The RECURRING ENTRIES routine is reached from the RECURRING icon on the BANK menu bar.

The RECURRING ENTRIES screen shows any existing entries already set up. If there are none, the screen will be blank.

To add a recurring entry, the Add button at the bottom of the screen should be clicked.

Now study the Case Study on the next two pages.

PRONTO SUPPLIES LIMITED:
SETTING UP RECURRING ENTRIES

setting up a recurring payment

Tom has set up a maintenance contract for his Xerax 566 colour printer/copier. He has to pay £19.80 plus VAT every month for the next 12 months and has completed a direct debit form so that the money can be taken directly from Pronto's bank current account.

The RECURRING ENTRIES routine is reached from the RECURRING icon on the BANK menu bar.

The RECURRING ENTRIES screen is blank because there are no existing recurring entries.To add a recurring entry, Tom clicks the Add button at the bottom of the screen and then inputs the details as follows:

Note the following:

- Tom indicates that the entry is a Bank/Cash/Credit Card Payment

- he inputs the bank account and nominal account to be used (which is already set up on the Chart of Accounts)

- the Transaction Reference entered is 'DD' (which stands for Direct Debit)

- the Transaction Details explain what the payment is for

- the Posting Frequency is every 15th of the month

- the number of Total Required Postings is 12

- the Net Amount and VAT (tax) code T1 are entered to generate the VAT amount

setting up a recurring receipt

Pronto Supplies receives from the tenant of a small office at 10A High Street regular monthly rent payments of £456. Tom charges VAT on these payments. The payment is made by standing order to the bank current account.

Tom clicks the Add button at the bottom of the RECURRING ENTRIES and then inputs the details as follows:

Note the following:

■ Tom indicates that the entry is a Bank/Cash/Credit Card Receipt

■ he inputs the bank account and nominal account to be used (which is already set up on the Chart of Accounts)

■ the Transaction Reference is 'STO' (which stands for Standing Order)

■ the Transaction Details explain what the payment is for

■ the Posting Frequency is every 15th of the month and is 'perpetual' – ie until further notice

■ the Net Amount and VAT (tax) code T1 are entered to generate the VAT amount

Tom returns to the RECURRING ENTRIES screen, which shows the two payments:

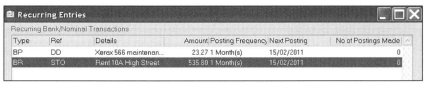

Tom can process all the payments up to the current date by clicking on the Process button. The program will only allow him to process each payment and receipt once in each month.

CHAPTER SUMMARY

- Businesses can set up accounts on a computer accounting program for funds of money held by the business. These accounts are classified as 'bank' accounts, but the money is not held at the bank. The money for these accounts will come from the bank or will be paid into the bank and recorded in Sage by a Bank Transfer.

- Payment 'Bank' accounts – in addition to the ordinary Bank Current Account include:
  - Petty Cash Account – a cash fund held under lock and key in the office, used for making small purchases and payments
  - Credit Card Account – records payments by employees on company credit cards

  These two accounts will be 'topped up' regularly by a transfer from the bank current account.

- 'Bank' accounts for receiving payments may also be set up, for example a Cash Receipts account or a Card Receipts account. These record money received from sales and held in the business. When the money is paid into the bank current account a Bank Transfer will be made on the computer.

- Businesses use Recurring Entries on the computer accounting system to record regular payments made in and out of the bank current account. These include standing orders and direct debits for outgoing payments and incoming receipts. The Recurring Entries facility enables the business to set up the payments so that they can be recorded automatically each month in the accounts on the click of a button.

KEY TERMS

petty cash	a float of cash kept in the office for making small purchases
petty cash account	an account used to record payments of small cash purchases from the office petty cash fund
petty cash voucher	the document which records and authorises a payment out of petty cash
company credit card account	an account used to record payments made on credit cards issued to employees to cover business expenses
cash receipts account	an account used to record cash receipts made by a business where the money is kept for a time by the business before it is paid into the bank
recurring entry	a bank payment or receipt which occurs on a regular basis and which is automated within the computer accounting program
Standing order/Direct debit schedule	a document which lists recurring payments and receipts with their due dates

STUDENT ACTIVITIES

10.1 Which of the following accounts held in the 'Bank' section of the computer is not actually held by the bank of the business?

■ Petty Cash Account   ■ Cash Receipts Account   ■ Bank Current Account

■ Company Credit Card Account

10.2 What entries to the computer accounts are made when the Petty Cash system is operated? State which screens are used.

(a)   for payments into Petty Cash

(b)   for payments out of Petty Cash

10.3 You are getting some petty cash vouchers ready for input and notice some points which you think might cause problems:

(a)   A petty cash voucher for postage stamps does not have any VAT shown on it.

(b)   A petty cash voucher for stationery does not have any VAT shown on it.

(c)   A petty cash voucher does not have an authorisation signature on it.

Write down what you think should be done in these three situations.

10.4 R R Printers Limited is setting up a company credit card scheme whereby its sales reps can use company credit cards for business expenses.

(a)   How should the credit card scheme be set up in the company's computer accounting system? How would the scheme work?

(b)   What advantages are there for the business and the sales reps in such a scheme?

10.5 If a shop kept the cash and cheques taken from sales on the premises and only paid into the bank at the end of every week, it might set up a Cash Receipts Account on the computer.

(a)   Describe the entries the business would make to the Cash Receipts Account.

(b)   Write down two disadvantages to the business of keeping money on the premises.

10.6 Describe the circumstances in which a business might set up Recurring Entries on the computer.

PRONTO SUPPLIES INPUTTING TASKS

Task 1

Set the program date as 28 February 2011.

On 1 February Tom cashed cheque 122991 for £100 at his bank to set up a petty cash system.

Carry out a bank transfer from Bank Current Account to Petty Cash Account for this amount.

Task 2

Keep the program date as 28 February 2011.

Tom has just authorised two more petty cash vouchers (shown below). Input these together with the three petty cash vouchers on pages 140 to 141 into Bank Payments, taking particular care with the VAT element on each one (postages are VAT exempt and packaging - nominal code 5003 - is standard-rated). Print out a Day Books: Cash Payments (Detailed) Report to confirm the accuracy of your input of the five vouchers (see p250). Hint: remember to select the Petty Cash Bank account on screen before running the report.

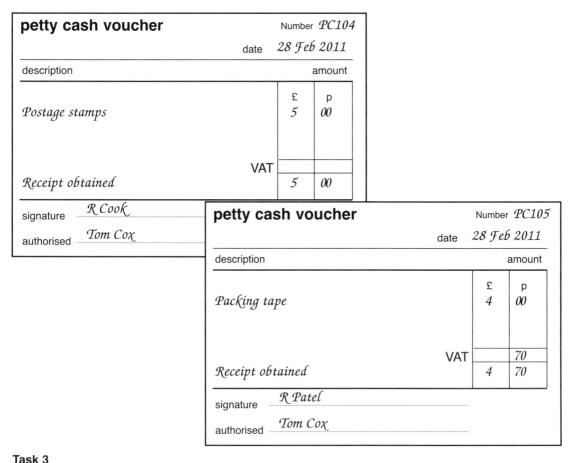

Task 3

Keep the program date as 28 February 2011.

Create an account for Cash Receipts within BANK using the number 1235. Call the account Cash Receipts Account and designate it a 'cash' account. No bank reconciliation is required at present.

Tom sees that he has three days' of cash takings in the office safe and so decides to enter these in the Cash Receipts Account. Take care over selecting the correct Sales account number. The details are:

Date	Details	Net amount (£)	VAT (£)	ref.
26 Feb 2011	Hardware sales	5,000.00	875.00	10743
26 Feb 2011	Software sales	480.00	84.00	10743
27 Feb 2011	Hardware sales	1,200.00	210.00	10744
27 Feb 2011	Software sales	890.00	155.75	10744
28 Feb 2011	Hardware sales	600.00	105.00	10745
28 Feb 2011	Software sales	120.00	21.00	10745
	Totals	8,290.00	1,450.75	

Enter these transactions, check the totals, SAVE and print out a Cash Receipts (Detailed) Day Book. Check with the printout on page 250.

Task 4

Keep the program date as 28 February 2011.

Create recurring entries for the payments and receipts on the schedule below. You will need to ensure that your Nominal List includes the following accounts.

You will need to ensure that your Nominal list includes the following accounts:

   7701 Office Machine Maintenance; 4904 Rent Income; 7100 Rent (paid out); 7103 General Rates

When the recurring entries have been set up, process them for February.

Note that the Sage program will remind you to process recurring entries when they are due by posting a message on the screen. You can then decide whether or not to process them.

Pronto Supplies Standing Order and Direct Debit Schedule						
Start date	Type	To/from	Details	Value	Frequency	Total payments
15 02 11	DD payment	Xerax Machines	Maintenance	£19.80 plus VAT	Monthly	12
15 02 11	STO receipt	F Morton	Rent 10A High St	£456.00 plus VAT	Monthly	Perpetual
16 02 11	DD payment	Broadwater Properties	Rent paid	£4500.00 plus VAT	Monthly	Perpetual
19 02 11	STO payment	Wyvern DC	Rates	£350.00 (VAT exempt)	Monthly	2

Task 5

Keep the program date as 28 February 2011. Print out from FINANCIALS the following reports:

(a)   an Audit Trail (summary version) of all the transactions on the computer so far (see page 251)

(b)   a Trial Balance as at 28 February 2011 (this can be checked against the Trial Balance on page 253)

Check with your tutor that all your input to date is accurate. These reports will be dealt with in the next chapter. Corrections of errors will be dealt with in Chapter 12.

Reminder! Have you made a back-up?

11 REPORTS AND ROUTINES

chapter introduction

- *One of the major advantages of running a computer accounting system is that it will provide the business manager and administrative staff with a wide range of reports – on demand.*

- *These reports are produced regularly – sometimes at the end of the month – to enable the business to check the accuracy of its records and to ensure that customer and supplier payments are being made on time.*

- *The reports that can be produced to help with checking the accuracy of the records include:*
  - *the trial balance – a full list of the Nominal account balances*
  - *the audit trail – a full numbered list of the transactions input on the computer in order of input*

- *The reports that can be produced to help with dealing with customers and suppliers include:*
  - *'aged' analyses – separate lists of customers and suppliers which show what payments are due and when*
  - *activity reports – lists of transactions on individual accounts*
  - *account lists – lists of customers and suppliers with telephone numbers*
  - *label lists – names and addresses of customers and suppliers – suitable for mailing labels*
  - *customer statements – sent to each sales ledger customer, listing transactions and telling the customer the amount that is due*

- *A further regular checking routine is the bank reconciliation statement which agrees the bank statement with the accounting records of the business.*

- *The end of the month is also a good time to process recurring entries and other regular account transfers.*

- *The business in the Case Study – Pronto Supplies Limited – has reached the end of February and so will be used in this chapter to illustrate the various reports and routines and their uses.*

- *Retention of records legislation governs how long businesses must keep accounting records*

THE IMPORTANCE OF INFORMATION

information for management

The accounting system of any business – whether hand-written or computer-based – contains important information for management and provides an accurate basis for decision-making. The advantage of using a computer accounting system is that this information is available instantly.

The **trial balance** is a list of the Nominal account balances at a set date – which is often the last day of the month. The figures are set out in balancing debit and credit columns to prove the accuracy of the book-keeping entries. If the column totals are not the same in a manual system, there is likely to be one or more errors in the double-entry book-keeping. Computerised trial balances will normally balance.

The trial balance figures show how much money there is in the bank and provides management with details about sales and expense accounts.

Activity on individual nominal accounts, eg sales, can be printed using a **nominal activity** report.

information for finance and administrative staff

The computer accounting program also enables finance and administrative staff to extract useful information, for example:

- The **audit trail** is a full list of the transactions input into the computer, presented in order of input. Accounts staff will use the audit trail to check the accuracy of the input and trace any discrepancies and errors.

- The analysis of customer accounts (the **aged debtor analysis**) tells credit control staff which customers need chasing for payment and which debts may need writing off. The computer can also print letters to customers chasing overdue accounts.

- The analysis of supplier accounts (the **aged creditor analysis**) tells accounts staff which bills and invoices need paying and when.

- The computer will also produce **activity reports** on individual customer and supplier accounts; these list all the transactions on each individual account and are useful to bring up on screen when a customer telephones in with a query.

- Computer-produced **account lists** set out the names, account codes and telephone numbers of customers and suppliers. These are useful to sales and accounts staff when contacting customers and suppliers and when coding invoices and credit notes.

- The computer will also produce the names and addresses of customers and suppliers on **labels**, which is useful when doing a promotional mailing or a change of address notification.

We will now illustrate these procedures with a continuation of the Case Study.

PRONTO SUPPLIES LIMITED: END-OF-MONTH REPORTS

It is 28 February 2011. Tom Cox has completed the input into his computer accounting system during the course of the month Looking back he can see that he has:

- set up the company details and the Nominal ledger balances
- entered customer and supplier records and balances
- input customer and supplier invoices and credit notes processed during February
- input payments received from customers and sent to suppliers during February
- input cash receipts and payments for February
- set up a petty cash system and recurring entries for standing orders and direct debits

trial balance

Tom first extracts his Trial Balance as at the end of February. He does this by clicking on TRIAL on the FINANCIALS menu bar. His printout is shown below.

Pronto Supplies Limited
Period Trial Balance

To Period: Month 2, February 2011

N/C	Name	Debit	Credit
0020	Plant and Machinery	35,000.00	
0030	Office Equipment	19,760.00	
0040	Furniture and Fixtures	30,000.00	
1100	Debtors Control Account	2,382.90	
1200	Bank Current Account	36,783.08	
1230	Petty Cash	4.20	
1235	Cash Receipts	9,740.75	
2100	Creditors Control Account		11,797.00
2200	Sales Tax Control Account		30,150.75
2201	Purchase Tax Control Account	35,281.02	
2300	Loans		35,000.00
3000	Ordinary Shares		80,000.00
4000	Computer hardware sales		139,380.00
4001	Computer software sales		29,814.00
4002	Computer consultancy		2,640.00
4904	Rent Income		456.00
5000	Materials Purchased	93,362.00	
5003	Packaging	4.00	
6201	Advertising	22,600.00	
7000	Gross Wages	33,010.00	
7100	Rent	9,000.00	
7103	General Rates	800.00	
7200	Electricity	308.00	
7501	Postage and Carriage	30.00	
7502	Telephone	585.00	
7504	Office Stationery	567.00	
7701	Office Machine Maintenance	19.80	
	Totals:	329,237.75	329,237.75

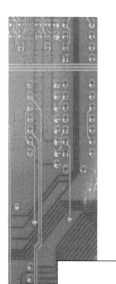

The trial balance shows the balances of the Nominal accounts. The debit column on the left equals the credit column on the right because in double entry book-keeping the total of debit entries should always equal the total of credit entries.

If in a manual accounting system the two columns totals were not the same, there could be one or more errors in the book-keeping entries. In a computer-based system the totals should always be the same because the computer generates equal debits and credits from every entry. If Tom's column totals were not the same it would mean that the computer data had become corrupted, which could be a major problem.

audit trail

As a further check (and also to satisfy his accountants) Tom prints out an audit trail which shows each transaction entered into the computer in order of input. This is done from the AUDIT icon on the FINANCIALS menu bar. An extract from a Summary Audit Trail is shown below. This should provide Tom with all the information he needs.

Pronto Supplies Limited
Audit Trail (Summary)

| | | Customer From: |
| | | Customer To: |

| Transaction From: | 1 | Supplier From: |
| Transaction To: | 99,999,999 | Supplier To: |

| Dept From: | 0 | N/C From: |
| Dept To: | 999 | N/C To: |

| Exclude Deleted Tran: | No |

No	Type	Date	A/C	N/C	Dept	Ref	Details	Net	Tax	T/C	Pd	Paid	V	B	Bank Rec. Date
1	SI	05/01/2011	JB001	9998	0	10013	Opening Balance	5,500.00	0.00	T9	Y	5,500.00	-	-	
2	PI	04/01/2011	DE001	9998	0	4563	Opening Balance	5,750.00	0.00	T9	Y	5,750.00	-	-	
3	SI	05/01/2011	CH001	9998	0	10014	Opening Balance	2,400.00	0.00	T9	Y	2,400.00	-	-	
4	SI	09/01/2011	CR001	9998	0	10015	Opening Balance	3,234.00	0.00	T9	Y	3,234.00	-	-	
5	SI	10/01/2011	DB001	9998	0	10016	Opening Balance	3,400.00	0.00	T9	Y	3,400.00	-	-	
6	SI	10/01/2011	KD001	9998	0	10017	Opening Balance	6,500.00	0.00	T9	Y	6,500.00	-	-	
7	SI	17/01/2011	LG001	9998	0	10019	Opening Balance	8,500.00	0.00	T9	Y	8,500.00	-	-	
8	PI	05/01/2011	EL001	9998	0	8122	Opening Balance	8,500.00	0.00	T9	Y	8,500.00	-	-	
9	PI	09/01/2011	MA001	9998	0	9252	Opening Balance	4,500.00	0.00	T9	Y	4,500.00	-	-	
10	JD	31/01/2011	0020	0020	0	O/Bal	Opening Balance	35,000.00	0.00	T9	Y	35,000.00	-	-	
11	JC	31/01/2011	9998	9998	0	O/Bal	Opening Balance	35,000.00	0.00	T9	Y	35,000.00	-	-	
12	JD	31/01/2011	0030	0030	0	O/Bal	Opening Balance	15,000.00	0.00	T9	Y	15,000.00	-	-	
13	JC	31/01/2011	9998	9998	0	O/Bal	Opening Balance	15,000.00	0.00	T9	Y	15,000.00	-	-	
14	JD	31/01/2011	0040	0040	0	O/Bal	Opening Balance	25,000.00	0.00	T9	Y	25,000.00	-	-	
15	JC	31/01/2011	9998	9998	0	O/Bal	Opening Balance	25,000.00	0.00	T9	Y	25,000.00	-	-	
16	JD	31/01/2011	1200	1200	0	O/Bal	Opening Balance	14,656.00	0.00	T9	Y	14,656.00	-	-	15/04/2010
17	JC	31/01/2011	9998	9998	0	O/Bal	Opening Balance	14,656.00	0.00	T9	Y	14,656.00	-	-	
18	JC	31/01/2011	2200	2200	0	O/Bal	Opening Balance	17,920.00	0.00	T9	Y	17,920.00	-	-	
19	JD	31/01/2011	9998	9998	0	O/Bal	Opening Balance	17,920.00	0.00	T9	Y	17,920.00	-	-	
20	JD	31/01/2011	2201	2201	0	O/Bal	Opening Balance	26,600.00	0.00	T9	Y	26,600.00	-	-	
21	JC	31/01/2011	9998	9998	0	O/Bal	Opening Balance	26,600.00	0.00	T9	Y	26,600.00	-	-	
22	JC	31/01/2011	2300	2300	0	O/Bal	Opening Balance	35,000.00	0.00	T9	Y	35,000.00	-	-	
23	JD	31/01/2011	9998	9998	0	O/Bal	Opening Balance	35,000.00	0.00	T9	Y	35,000.00	-	-	
24	JC	31/01/2011	3000	3000	0	O/Bal	Opening Balance	75,000.00	0.00	T9	Y	75,000.00	-	-	
25	JD	31/01/2011	9998	9998	0	O/Bal	Opening Balance	75,000.00	0.00	T9	Y	75,000.00	-	-	
26	JC	31/01/2011	4000	4000	0	O/Bal	Opening Balance	85,000.00	0.00	T9	Y	85,000.00	-	-	
27	JD	31/01/2011	9998	9998	0	O/Bal	Opening Balance	85,000.00	0.00	T9	Y	85,000.00	-	-	
28	JC	31/01/2011	4001	4001	0	O/Bal	Opening Balance	15,000.00	0.00	T9	Y	15,000.00	-	-	
29	JD	31/01/2011	9998	9998	0	O/Bal	Opening Balance	15,000.00	0.00	T9	Y	15,000.00	-	-	
30	JC	31/01/2011	4002	4002	0	O/Bal	Opening Balance	2,400.00	0.00	T9	Y	2,400.00	-	-	
31	JD	31/01/2011	9998	9998	0	O/Bal	Opening Balance	2,400.00	0.00	T9	Y	2,400.00	-	-	
32	JD	31/01/2011	5000	5000	0	O/Bal	Opening Balance	69,100.00	0.00	T9	Y	69,100.00	-	-	
33	JC	31/01/2011	9998	9998	0	O/Bal	Opening Balance	69,100.00	0.00	T9	Y	69,100.00	-	-	
34	JD	31/01/2011	6201	6201	0	O/Bal	Opening Balance	12,400.00	0.00	T9	Y	12,400.00	-	-	
35	JC	31/01/2011	9998	9998	0	O/Bal	Opening Balance	12,400.00	0.00	T9	Y	12,400.00	-	-	
36	JD	31/01/2011	7000	7000	0	O/Bal	Opening Balance	16,230.00	0.00	T9	Y	16,230.00	-	-	
37	JC	31/01/2011	9998	9998	0	O/Bal	Opening Balance	16,230.00	0.00	T9	Y	16,230.00	-	-	
38	JD	31/01/2011	7100	7100	0	O/Bal	Opening Balance	4,500.00	0.00	T9	Y	4,500.00	-	-	
39	JC	31/01/2011	9998	9998	0	O/Bal	Opening Balance	4,500.00	0.00	T9	Y	4,500.00	-	-	

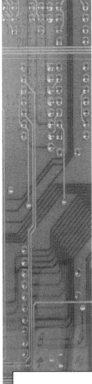

Every transaction input into the computer (within the time period stipulated) is shown on the audit trail. The columns of the audit trail show, from the left . . .

■ the unique number allocated by the computer to the transaction

■ the nature of the transaction, for example SI = sales invoice, PI = purchase invoice

■ the date of the transaction (which is not necessarily the date of input)

■ the account into which the item is entered

■ the Nominal account code relating to the transaction

■ the Department reference, normally only used in larger organisations

■ the transaction reference (eg invoice or cheque number) input at the time

■ the description of the transaction

■ the net amount, any VAT, VAT tax code and the gross ('paid') amount

Tom will need to keep the audit trail for future reference in case any errors or discrepancies come to light. His accountants may also need to see it if they have to verify his accounts.

nominal activity

Tom can check his monthly sales for each sales code. He selects code 4000 (Computer hardware sales) in the Nominal Ledger screen and then clicks on Reports. In Nominal Activity Reports he chooses Nominal Activity and enters the date range of 1-28 February. The report, shown below, shows total computer hardware sales of £54,380 for the month.

Pronto Supplies Limited
Nominal Activity

| Date From: | 01/02/2011 | | N/C From: | 4000 |
| Date To: | 28/02/2011 | | N/C To: | 4000 |

| Transaction From: | 1 |
| Transaction To: | 99,999,999 |

| N/C: | 4000 | Name: | Computer hardware sales | | | Account Balance: | | 139,380.00 CR |

No	Type	Date	Account	Ref	Details	Dept	T/C	Value	Debit	Credit	V	B
48	SI	05/02/2011	JB001	10023	1 x 17" monitor	1	T1	400.00		400.00	N	-
49	SI	06/02/2011	CH001	10024	1 x printer lead	1	T1	16.00		16.00	N	-
53	SC	06/02/2011	LG001	552	Disks returned (hardware)	1	T1	40.00	40.00		N	-
55	SI	13/02/2011	DB001	10028	1 x EF102 Printer	1	T1	600.00		600.00	N	-
56	SI	16/02/2011	LG001	10029	2 x Zap drive	1	T1	180.00		180.00	N	-
58	SI	16/02/2011	CH001	10031	1 x 15" monitor	1	T1	320.00		320.00	N	-
59	SC	12/02/2011	KD001	553	1 Printer lead	1	T1	16.00	16.00		N	-
60	SC	13/02/2011	CR001	554	Zap disks (hardware)	1	T1	20.00	20.00		N	-
79	BR	09/02/2011	1200	10736	Hardware sales	1	T1	12,500.00		12,500.00	N	N
81	BR	16/02/2011	1200	10738	Hardware sales	1	T1	15,840.00		15,840.00	N	N
83	BR	23/02/2011	1200	10740	Hardware sales	1	T1	17,800.00		17,800.00	N	N
101	CR	26/02/2011	1235	10743	Hardware sales	1	T1	5,000.00		5,000.00	N	N
103	CR	27/02/2011	1235	10744	Hardware sales	1	T1	1,200.00		1,200.00	N	N
105	CR	28/02/2011	1235	10745	Hardware sales	1	T1	600.00		600.00	N	N
							Totals:		76.00	54,456.00		
							History Balance:			54,380.00		

aged debtors analysis

It is important to Tom that he knows that his customers who buy on credit pay up on time. The credit period is indicated to them on the bottom of each invoice. Tom allows his customers 30 days from the date of the invoice in which to pay.

An Aged Debtors Analysis shows the amount owing by each customer and splits it up according to the length of time it has been outstanding. The Aged Debtors Analysis can be printed from the REPORTS icon on the CUSTOMERS menu bar. Alternatively an aged balance list can be produced from the AGED icon on CUSTOMERS.

Tom's Aged Debtors Analysis Report as at 28 February 2011 is shown below:

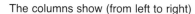

Pronto Supplies Limited
Aged Debtors Analysis (Summary)

Report Date:	28/02/2011	Customer From:	
Include future transactions:	No	Customer To:	ZZZZZZZZ
Exclude later payments:	No		

** NOTE: All report values are shown in Base Currency, unless otherwise indicated **

A/C	Name	Credit Limit	Turnover	Balance	Future	Current	Period 1	Period 2	Period 3	Older
CH001	Charisma Design	£ 5,000.00	2,736.00	376.00	0.00	376.00	0.00	0.00	0.00	0.00
CR001	Crowmatic Ltd	£ 5,000.00	3,314.00	94.00	0.00	94.00	0.00	0.00	0.00	0.00
DB001	David Boossey	£ 5,000.00	3,800.00	705.00	0.00	705.00	0.00	0.00	0.00	0.00
JB001	John Butler & Associates	£ 10,000.00	6,020.00	611.00	0.00	611.00	0.00	0.00	0.00	0.00
KD001	Kay Denz	£ 10,000.00	6,868.00	432.40	0.00	432.40	0.00	0.00	0.00	0.00
LG001	L Garr & Co	£ 15,000.00	8,640.00	164.50	0.00	164.50	0.00	0.00	0.00	0.00
	Totals:		31,378.00	2,382.90	0.00	2,382.90	0.00	0.00	0.00	0.00

The columns show (from left to right)

- the customer account number and name
- the credit limit (the maximum amount of credit Tom will allow on the account)
- the turnover (total net sales for each customer in the current financial year)
- the balance (the total balance on the customer's account)
- any transactions due in future months
- 'current' invoices are February invoices, period 1 is January, and so on

Note that the Report can be dated at any date required. Here it is dated 28 February.

The Report shows the following:

- All the accounts are trading within their credit limits (ie the figure in the 'Balance' column is less than the 'Credit Limit' column) – this is a good sign.

- The total of the Balance column shows that Pronto Supplies Limited is owed a total of £2,382.90 on 28 February. As a further check this figure could be agreed with the balance of Debtors Control Account on the Trial Balance (see page 154).

aged creditors analysis

Tom also needs to check on the amounts that Pronto Supplies Limited owes its Suppliers (creditors) for goods purchased, and to make sure that there are no amounts outstanding for longer than they should be. The Aged Creditors Analysis enables him to do this. It can be printed from REPORTS on the SUPPLIERS menu bar. The layout of the columns works on the same principles as the Aged Debtors Analysis (see previous page). Alternatively the AGED icon on SUPPLIERS can also be used to produce a list of amounts due to suppliers.

Pronto Supplies Limited

Aged Creditors Analysis (Summary)

Report Date:	28/02/2011							Supplier From:		
Include future transactions:	No							Supplier To:		ZZZZZZZ
Exclude Later Payments:	No									

** NOTE: All report values are shown in Base Currency, unless otherwise indicated **

A/C	Name		Credit Limit	Turnover	Balance	Future	Current	Period 1	Period 2	Period 3
DE001	Delco PLC	£	10,000.00	9,270.00	4,700.00	0.00	4,700.00	0.00	0.00	0.00
EL001	Electron Supplies	£	15,000.00	10,860.00	2,773.00	0.00	2,773.00	0.00	0.00	0.00
MA001	MacCity	£	10,000.00	8,142.00	4,324.00	0.00	4,324.00	0.00	0.00	0.00
	Totals:			28,272.00	11,797.00	0.00	11,797.00	0.00	0.00	0.00

This report shows that:

■ Pronto Supplies Limited is up-to-date with payments to suppliers – all amounts due are 'Current', ie there is nothing outstanding for more than 30 days.

■ The total owed by Pronto Supplies Limited is £11,797.00 on 28 February. As a further check this figure should be agreed with the balance of Creditors Control Account on the Trial Balance (see page 154).

customer activity reports

Tom receives a call from John Crow of Crowmatic Limited. John has not yet received his statement of account and wants to find out if there is anything outstanding. Tom needs to bring up this account on screen; he can do this by clicking on the ACTIVITY icon on the CUSTOMERS menu bar with the appropriate account selected. The screen can be printed if required.

Alternatively Tom could select the account on the CUSTOMERS screen and click on the REPORTS icon to select the Customer Activity (Summary) Report. This report shows that there is £94 outstanding on the account; the report shows that this figure is reached by deducting Credit Note 554 for £23.50 from Invoice 10025 for £117.50.

Pronto Supplies Limited

Customer Activity (Summary)

Date From:	01/01/1980							
Date To:	28/02/2011							
Inc b/fwd transaction:	No					Transaction From:	1	
Exc later payment:	No					Transaction To:	99,999,999	

** NOTE: All report values are shown in Base Currency, unless otherwise indicated **

| A/C: | CR001 | | Name: | Crowmatic Ltd | | Contact: | | Tel: | | |

No	Items	Type	Date	Ref	Details	Value	O/S	Debit	Credit
4	1	SI	09/01/2011	10015	Opening Balance	3,234.00	0.00	3,234.00	
50	1	SI	06/02/2011	10025	1 x Macroworx	117.50 *	117.50	117.50	
60	1	SC	13/02/2011	554	Zap disks (hardware)	23.50 *	-23.50		23.50
72	1	SR	28/02/2011	BACS	Sales Receipt	3,234.00	0.00		3,234.00
						94.00	94.00	3,351.50	3,257.50

Amount Outstanding	94.00	
Amount Paid this period	3,234.00	
Credit Limit £	5,000.00	

other useful reports

Tom has also printed a Customer List from his computer; this is an alphabetically sorted account list of customers, together with their contact numbers. A similar report – Customer Address List – produces customer addresses. These reports can be accessed from REPORTS in CUSTOMERS.

Pronto Supplies Limited
Customer List

Customer From:
Customer To: ZZZZZZZZ

A/C	Name	Contact Name	Telephone	Fax
CH001	Charisma Design	Lindsay Foster	01908 345287	01908 345983
CR001	Crowmatic Ltd	John Crow	01908 674237	01908 674345
DB001	David Boossey	David Boossey	01908 333981	01908 333761
JB001	John Butler & Associates	John Butler	01908 824342	01908 824295
KD001	Kay Denz	Kay Denz	01908 624945	01908 624945
LG001	L Garr & Co	Win Norberry	01621 333691	01621 333982

The same exercise can be carried out from the SUPPLIERS menu bar to produce a list of Suppliers with contact numbers.

The computer will also enable Tom to print out name and address labels for Customers and Suppliers. This could be very useful when marketing products to Customers – sending out a catalogue, for example. The labels can be printed by clicking on the LABELS icon on the CUSTOMERS or SUPPLIERS menu bar and selecting an appropriate label format. The labels shown below are extracted from Tom's Customer details printed as Laser Sales Labels (A4).

Lindsay Foster	John Crow	David Boossey
Charisma Design	Crowmatic Ltd	David Boossey
36 Dingle Road	Unit 12 Severnside Estate	17 Harebell Road
Mereford	Mereford	Mereford Green
MR2 8GF	MR3 6FD	MR6 4NB

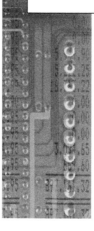

customer statements

At the end of each month Tom will print out statements and send them to his Customers. This can be done in Sage from the STATEMENT icon on the CUSTOMER menu bar. A suitable format can then be chosen from the list shown on the screen. At this point Tom could choose to email statements to his customers using the Email option in the Preview screen. The statements set out the transactions on the Customer account and state the amount owing. Statements are important documents because many customers will pay from the monthly statement rather than the invoice.

An extract from the statement for Crowmatic Limited is shown on the next page.

BANK RECONCILIATION ON THE COMPUTER

the reasons for bank reconciliation

A further routine carried out on a regular basis, with the help of the computer accounting system, is the task of tallying up the entries in the Sage bank account for a set period of time, eg a month, and the entries on the actual bank statement for the same period. This process is known as **bank reconciliation**. It reconciles:

■ the bank statement – what the bank states the balance actually is with . . .

■ the bank account of a business – the balance representing what the accounting records of the business states it has in the bank

It is quite common that **differences** will arise and that the two amounts will not be the same.

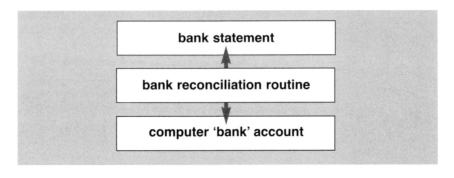

timing differences

These variations can arise from **timing differences**.

For example, a cheque that is issued by the business and sent off to a supplier will be input into the computer accounting records of the business when it is issued, but will not yet have been paid in at the bank by the supplier. Consequently the bank balance on the computer of the business writing the cheque will differ by this amount from the bank balance of the business shown on the bank statement - until, of course, the cheque is paid in and eventually deducted from the bank account. This is a 'timing difference'.

Another timing difference will occur when cheques received from customers of a business have been entered into the bank account on the computer but are still waiting to be paid into the bank on a paying-in slip. The accounting records of the business will show that the money has gone into the bank account, but the actual bank statement will only show the increase after the cheques have been paid into the bank, possibly a day or two later.

Also, there may be items on the bank statement which the business will not immediately know about and will need to enter into the accounting records **after** it has received the bank statement. Examples are bank charges, bank interest paid and bank interest received.

bank reconciliation in Sage

As seen on the previous page, bank reconciliation forms a link between the balances shown in the bank statement and in the accounting records of the business. All the reconciliation is doing in effect is explaining what items make up the difference between the bank statement and the bank account in the accounting records of the business.

The Bank Reconciliation screen, accessed through RECONCILE in BANK, is illustrated in the Case Study which follows. The procedure is as follows:

1. In the statement summary screen enter a statement reference (optional), the closing balance on the bank statement and the bank statement date. Any interest earned or bank charges can be added at this point. Click OK to move to the main bank reconciliation screen.

2. Check that the Matched Balance box at the bottom agrees to the opening balance on the bank statement.

3. Compare the items in the upper window on the screen with the bank statement. Click to select any items that appear on both, then click the Match button to transfer the matched item/s to the lower window. Alternatively double-click the matched items individually to transfer them.

4. Update the computer with any items appearing on the bank statement but not in Sage by inputting them using the Adjust button.

5. When you have transferred all the matched items to the lower screen and made any adjustments, check that the Statement Balance equals the bank statement closing balance and the Difference box shows zero.

6. Click Reconcile.

Now read the Case Study which follows.

PRONTO SUPPLIES LIMITED:
BANK RECONCILIATION ROUTINE

It is 28 February 2011. Tom Cox has just printed out an online bank statement for Pronto Supplies Limited. He has access to this facility from the Albion Bank website.

The bank statement is shown below.

Tom wants to carry out a reconciliation routine and so clicks RECONCILE in BANK. This is shown on the opposite page.

ALBION BANK PLC

Online statement of account as at: 28 02 2011 15.54

Account 90 47 17 11719881 Pronto Supplies Limited

		Paid out	Paid in	Balance
31/01/2011	Balance b/f			14,656.00
01/02/2011	Cheque 122991	100.00		14,556.00
09/02/2011	Credit 10736		14,687.50	29,243.50
09/02/2011	Credit 10737		5,499.00	34,742.50
12/02/2011	Cheque 122992	18,212.50		16,530.00
15/02/2011	DD Xerax	23.27		-1,353.27
15/02/2011	STO F Morton		535.80	-817.47
16/02/2011	Credit 10738		18,612.00	17,794.53
16/02/2011	Credit 10739		4,324.00	22,118.53
16/02/2011	DD Broadwater Properties	5,287.50		16,831.03
19/02/2011	STO Wyvern DC	350.00		16,481.03
19/02/2011	Cheque 122993	11,985.00		4,545.00
19/02/2011	Cheque 122994	5,875.00		-1,330.00
23/02/2011	Credit 10740		20,915.00	37,396.03
23/02/2011	Credit 10741		5,640.00	43,036.03
27/02/2011	Cheque 122995	185.65		42,850.38
28/02/2011	Cheque 122996	364.25		42,486.13
28/02/2011	BACS		3,234.00	45,720.13
28/02/2011	BACS (multiple beneficiary)	18,141.35		27,578.78
28/02/2011	BACS	16,780.00		10,798.78
28/02/2011	122998	4,700.00		6,098.78
28/02/2011	Bank charges	50.00		6,048.78

Note that the BACS supplier payments to Delco, Electron and MacCity (see page 120) on 28 February are shown as one total (£18,141.35)

Tom compares the bank statement with the computer screen.

- He completes the Statement Summary screen with a Statement Reference (he uses the date), the bank statement end balance (£6,048.78) and the statement date (28 February 2011). He clicks OK to move to the main reconciliation screen.

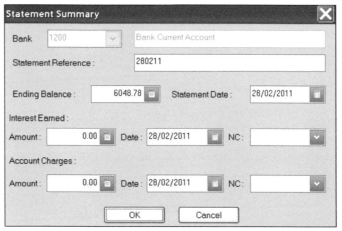

- He checks that the opening balance on the bank statement is the same as the Matched Balance on the screen (it is £14,656.00)

- He selects the items in the upper window that are also on the bank statement. He can use the scroll bar to move up and down or he can change the size of the upper and lower windows by dragging on the horizontal bar between them.

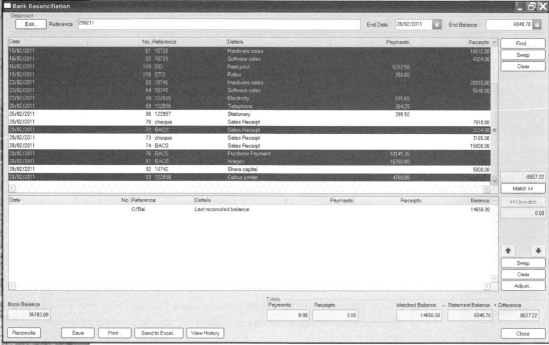

■ Now he clicks the Match button to transfer the matched transactions to the lower window.

■ There is a figure of £50 in the Difference box. This is the Bank charges which have not yet been entered. Tom clicks on the Adjust button to enter this payment. The adjustment screen is shown below. Tom enters the nominal code of 7901, details of 'bank charges', a VAT code of T2 and the Payment of £50. He then clicks Save.

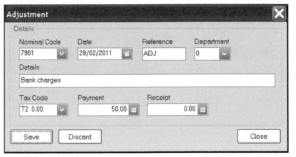

■ Finally Tom is returned to the Bank Reconciliation screen where he checks that the difference box is now showing zero. Now he can click Reconcile to complete the task.

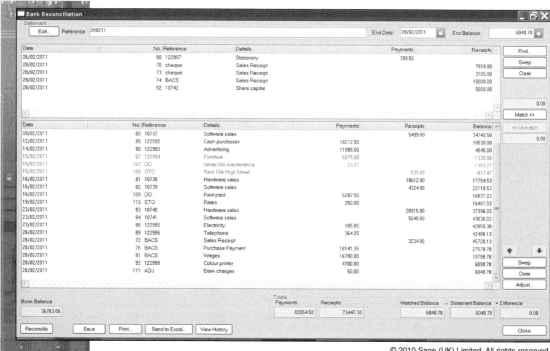

All the unselected (ie 'unreconciled') items on the screen will appear next time the routine is carried out – normally when the next bank statement is received.

By carrying out this routine Tom can make sure that he has entered all his bank transactions correctly, and equally importantly, that the bank has not made any errors.

OTHER MONTH-END ROUTINES

It is important for a business with a computer accounting system to establish an end-of-month routine which will include the production of the reports illustrated in the Case Studies in this chapter. Examples of other month-end routines involving the computer accounting system are explained below.

checking that all transactions have been input

The business must check that all the necessary transactions – sales and purchases transactions, payments made and received – have been input into the computer before extracting the reports.

recurring entries

Recurring entries – standing orders and direct debits – may be processed monthly, and it should become part of the month-end routine to ensure that this is done. Sage helps by displaying a warning message on the screen when you open the program up, letting you know if there are outstanding recurring entries. Recurring entries are dealt with in detail on pages 145 to 147.

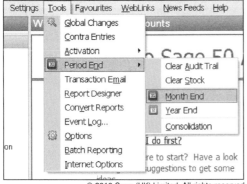

advanced month-end entries

Sage also allows you to process other monthly entries. The month-end procedure is reached from TOOLS on the main menu bar. These include:

■ **clear turnover** – this resets the month-to-date turnover (eg sales and purchases) figures to zero in the customer and supplier records

■ **post prepayments** – payments made in advance of the time period to which they relate; for example, an annual insurance premium can be spread out over twelve months

■ **post accruals** – payments made after the time period to which they relate; for example, a telephone bill for call charges paid at the end of a quarter can be estimated and spread over the previous three months

■ **post depreciation** – regular reductions in the value of assets which can be entered in the accounts each month

EXPORTING REPORT DATA FOR REPORTING PURPOSES

exporting data to Excel

As this chapter has shown, the reporting facilities within Sage are very comprehensive. There may be situations, however, where a business may want to export data for management reporting and 'what if' situations which require the data manipulation facilities of a spreadsheet. Sage allows the user to export data from the Reports Preview window and from certain windows, lists and grids within the program direct to Microsoft Excel. This will then allow the user to edit and format the data to create reports as required.

To export data in the form of a report, preview the report required and then click the Export button. The report can then be saved in a variety of types including Excel files. In the example on the next page an Aged Debtors Analysis has been exported to Excel.

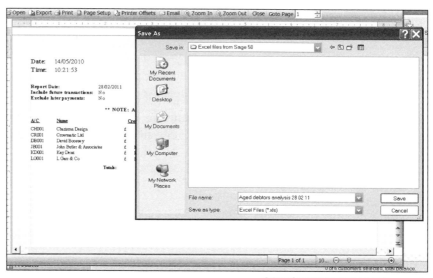

To export data from a screen to Excel, eg customer list, click on the File menu, then Office Integration and Contents to Microsoft Excel (as shown below). Excel will open automatically and show the data transferred. It can then be saved within the Excel program.

exporting reports for email

A report can be emailed directly from a Preview screen using the Email button. The report can be saved as a 'pdf' (Acrobat) file and automatically attached to an email.

Tom in the Pronto Supplies Case Study, for example, could send customer statements by email, or he could send information to his accountant in the form of a Trial Balance or Audit Trail.

screenshots

An image of the screen can be 'exported' to another program using the 'Print Scr' button on the keyboard. The image is held in the computer's memory until it is pasted into another program, eg Word or Paint. It can then be saved and give a suitable filename.

Such images are useful for demonstration purposes (they have been used extensively in this publication) and in a training environment where the student needs to show, or print a copy of, something that appeared on screen.

retention of records

Business records are normally stored for at least **six years** (and a minimum of three years for payroll data). There are a number of legal reasons why financial data should be kept for this period of time:

- accounting records should be kept so that they can be inspected by the Inland Revenue (part of HM Revenue & Customs) if required in the case of a tax inspection
- accounting records should be kept so that they can be inspected by HM Revenue & Customs if there is a VAT inspection

CHAPTER SUMMARY

- A computer accounting system has the advantage that it can provide a wide range of useful printed reports quickly and accurately. These are useful both for the management of the business and also for accounts assistants.

- Reports can be produced to help with checking the accuracy of the records. These are often produced at the end of each month and include:
  - the trial balance – a full list of the Nominal account balances
  - the audit trail – a numbered list of transactions set out in order of input on the computer.

- Reports can be produced to help with day-to-day dealings with customers and suppliers. Month-end reports include:
  - 'aged' analyses – separate lists of customers and suppliers which show when payments are due and if any payments are overdue
  - activity reports – lists of transactions on individual accounts which need to be looked into
  - customer statements of account

  Other day-to-day useful printouts include customer and supplier account lists and label lists – useful for mailing purposes.

KEY
TERMS

■   Another regular routine is the bank reconciliation, which agrees the entries on the actual bank statement with those in the bank account records of the organisation.

■   The end-of-month is the time to process recurring entries and other regular account transfers.

■   Data can be exported to other computer programs and sent by email to other users.`

■   Financial records of a business must be kept for a minimum of 6 years.

trial balance	a list of Nominal account balances set out in debit and credit columns, the totals of which should be the same
audit trail	a numbered list of transactions on the computer produced in order of input
aged debtor analysis	a list of Customer (debtor) balances which are split up according to the length of time they have been outstanding
aged creditor analysis	a list of Supplier (creditor) balances which are split up according to the length of time they have been outstanding
activity report	a list of transactions on individual Nominal, Customer and Supplier accounts
bank reconciliation	the process of checking the bank statement entries against the accounting records of an organisation and identifying the differences that exist between the two documents

STUDENT ACTIVITIES

11.1   What is the purpose of a trial balance in a manual accounting system?

11.2   Why should the debit and credit columns in a trial balance add up to the same total when a computer accounting system is used?

11.3   What else does a trial balance tell the owner of a business?

11.4   An audit trail is a numbered list of transactions input into a computer accounting system. How is it set out – in date order or in order of input?

11.5   What is the main purpose of

(a)   an Aged Debtors Analysis?

(b)   an Aged Creditors Analysis?

11.6   The Aged Debtors Analysis of Pronto Supplies Limited as at 28 February 2011 is shown below. Pronto Supplies allows customers to pay up to 30 days from the date of the invoice.

(a)   What is the total amount owed by the customers of Pronto Supplies Limited?

(b)   Against which figure in the Trial Balance (see next page) should this total in (a) be checked?

(c)   Suppose that in two months time the balance of D Boossey's account still stood at £705 and this figure appeared in the 'Period 2' column. What does this tell Tom about the account? What other document could Tom print out to give him – and the customer – more information?

Pronto Supplies Limited   Page:

Aged Debtors Analysis (Summary)

Report Date: 28/02/2011   Customer From:
Include future transactions: No   Customer To: ZZZZZZZZ
Exclude later payments: No

** NOTE: All report values are shown in Base Currency, unless otherwise indicated **

A/C	Name	Credit Limit	Turnover	Balance	Future	Current	Period 1	Period 2	Period 3	Older
CH001	Charisma Design	£ 5,000.00	2,736.00	376.00	0.00	376.00	0.00	0.00	0.00	0.00
CR001	Crowmatic Ltd	£ 5,000.00	3,314.00	94.00	0.00	94.00	0.00	0.00	0.00	0.00
DB001	David Boossey	£ 5,000.00	3,800.00	705.00	0.00	705.00	0.00	0.00	0.00	0.00
JB001	John Butler & Associates	£ 10,000.00	6,020.00	611.00	0.00	611.00	0.00	0.00	0.00	0.00
KD001	Kay Denz	£ 10,000.00	6,868.00	432.40	0.00	432.40	0.00	0.00	0.00	0.00
LG001	L Garr & Co	£ 15,000.00	8,640.00	164.50	0.00	164.50	0.00	0.00	0.00	0.00
	Totals:		31,378.00	2,382.90	0.00	2,382.90	0.00	0.00	0.00	0.00

11.7 The Trial Balance (extract) of Pronto Supplies Limited at the close of business on 28 February 2011 is shown below. Study the figures and answer the questions that follow.

Date: 14/05/2010	**Pronto Supplies Limited**		Page: 1
Time: 14:47:50	**Period Trial Balance**		

To Period: Month 2, February 2011

N/C	Name	Debit	Credit
0020	Plant and Machinery	35,000.00	
0030	Office Equipment	19,760.00	
0040	Furniture and Fixtures	30,000.00	
1100	Debtors Control Account	2,382.90	
1200	Bank Current Account	36,733.08	
1230	Petty Cash	4.20	
1235	Cash Receipts	9,740.75	
2100	Creditors Control Account		11,797.00
2200	Sales Tax Control Account		30,150.75
2201	Purchase Tax Control Account	35,281.02	
2300	Loans		35,000.00
3000	Ordinary Shares		80,000.00
4000	Computer hardware sales		139,380.00
4001	Computer software sales		29,814.00
4002	Computer consultancy		2,640.00
4904	Rent Income		456.00
5000	Materials Purchased	93,362.00	
5003	Packaging	4.00	
6201	Advertising	22,600.00	
7000	Gross Wages	33,010.00	
7100	Rent	9,000.00	
7103	General Rates	800.00	
7200	Electricity	308.00	
7501	Postage and Carriage	30.00	
7502	Telephone	585.00	
7504	Office Stationery	567.00	
7701	Office Machine Maintenance	19.80	
7901	Bank Charges	50.00	
	Totals:	329,237.75	329,237.75

(a) How much money has the company got in the bank?

(b) How much money has the company got stored on the premises?

(c) What is the company's total sales income (excluding rent) for the period up to 28 February?

11.8 The Administration Supervisor of Pronto Supplies asks for a list of customers together with their contact telephone numbers. Print out the report the supervisor needs.

Optional task: Export the data from the Sage system (either by e-mail or by saving in an appropriate format) and transfer the data into another program and produce a suitable printed version.

PRONTO SUPPLIES INPUTTING TASK

Set the program date to 28 February 2011.

Following the instructions on pages 162 to 165, carry out a bank reconciliation from RECONCILE in BANK.

Check that the opening balance is the same on both the bank statement and the 'reconcile' screen.

Remember to click on the screen only the items which appear in the bank statement.

Carry out any 'adjustments' that need to be done (ie inputting any items on the bank statement which have not yet been input into the computer accounting system).

Check that the Matched Balance is the same as the Statement Balance, ie that the difference is zero, before proceeding to Reconcile. Now print out a Trial Balance. It should agree with the one above..

12 CORRECTIONS AND ADJUSTMENTS

■ *When you are operating a computer accounting program it is inevitable that errors will be made. These might be your own input errors or they might be errors on the part of a customer or a supplier. Whatever the source of the error might be, it will have to be put right.*

■ *The CORRECTIONS function contained in Sage will enable you to change most details on invoices, credit notes and payments. It is most commonly used for internal corrections – before any documents are sent out of the business.*

■ *The JOURNAL function contained in Sage is used for transferring amounts from one nominal account to another. One of its uses is therefore for correcting mistakes where the wrong nominal account number has been used. A knowledge of the use of debits and credits is needed for the JOURNAL.*

■ *If a significant mistake – for example a wrong amount – is discovered after an invoice has been sent out, the invoice will normally be cancelled by a credit note and a new invoice issued in its place. An invoice or credit note can also be cancelled if it has been input on the computer but has not yet been sent out.*

■ *The computer will warn the user, by means of an on-screen message, if an obvious inputting error is being made – for example, a date in the wrong financial year*

■ *Sage provides a Check Data function that should be run regularly. This will highlight and report on some types of errors.*

■ *If data on the computer has become corrupted or is in such a mess that it needs to be input again, Sage provides a REBUILD function which will set up all or part of the accounts again ready for the re-input of data. This is a very drastic measure.*

■ *The computer also allows you to make adjustments to the records, for example:*

  • *you need to 'write off' a customer account because you consider you will never get the money – the customer may have become a bankrupt, for example*

  • *you need to refund a customer because he or she has paid too much*

  • *you need to cancel a cheque you have written or you have received a cheque which has been returned unpaid for some reason by the customer's bank*

THE CORRECTIONS FUNCTION

You will be able to correct most input errors within Sage using the CORRECTIONS function which is part of MAINTENANCE reached through the FILE on the main menu bar.

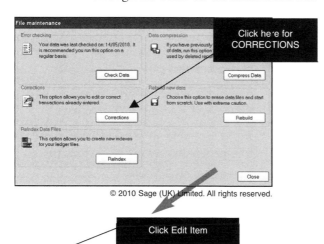

This leads to a screen which lists all the transactions which have passed through the computer accounting system and are available for correction.

You highlight the transaction which needs correcting (see screen below) and click on Edit item to bring up the screen shown at the bottom of the page. The correction has already been made on this screen.

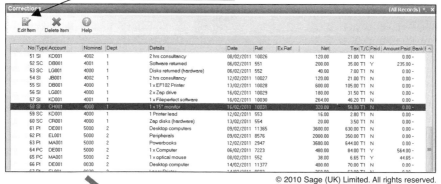

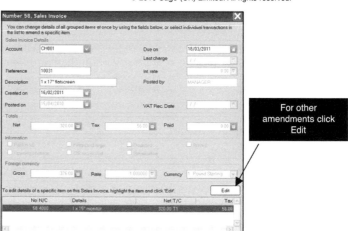

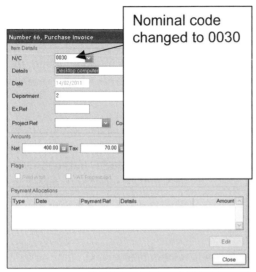

Nominal code changed to 0030

The last screen on the previous page allows correction of:

- the account to which the invoice is posted
- the product description
- the reference and date

Further amendments can be made to an individual item highlighted in the bottom box by clicking Edit. These include:

- the nominal code
- the amounts charged
- the VAT rate and VAT amount

In the example shown (left) the nominal code for transaction number 66, a purchase invoice, has been changed from 5000 to 0030.

JOURNAL ENTRIES

Journal entries enable you to make transfers from one nominal account to another. Journal entries are used, for example, when you are completing a VAT return and need to transfer VAT amounts from one VAT account to another. They are another way of putting things right when you have input the wrong nominal account.

Journals can also be used to enter opening balances and advanced accounting adjustments such as depreciation of fixed assets.

journals and double entry

You need to be confident about **double-entry** book-keeping and using debits and credits when doing journal entries. You will have to decide which accounts have debit entries and which accounts have credit entries. The rule is that for every transaction there are balancing debit and credit entries:

debits	=	money paid into the bank
		purchases and expenses
		an increase in an asset
credits	=	payments out of the bank
		sales and income
		an increase in a liability

If you are still in any doubt about debits and credits, use CORRECTIONS wherever possible to adjust account entries.

example

Suppose you were inputting a batch of Bank Payments which included a number of bills that had to be paid. You have written out a cheque for £94 to RPower for a gas bill, but when inputting it you thought it was for electricity and so posted it to electricity (nominal account 7200) instead of gas (7201).

the solution

You could either use CORRECTIONS, but as you are a double-entry expert you choose to correct your mistake using a journal entry. You bring up the screen by clicking on the JOURNALS icon on the NOMINAL menu bar:

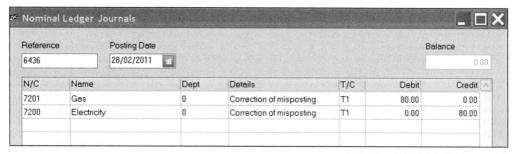

© 2010 Sage (UK) Limited. All rights reserved.

The procedure is:

- enter your reference (this could be the transaction number you can find by opening up the FINANCIALS module and locating the transaction)
- enter the nominal code of the account to which you are going to post the debit; here it is Gas Account because you are recording an expense
- enter the reason for the transaction – here you are adjusting a misposting
- enter the VAT tax code input on the original (wrong) entry
- enter the net amount in the debit column (ie the amount before VAT has been added on) – here the net amount is £80 and VAT (assumed here at standard rate) is £14 and the total is £94; note that neither the VAT nor the total appear on the screen because you are not adjusting the VAT; *only the net amount* has gone to the wrong account

then on the next line . . .

- enter the nominal code of the account to which you are going to post the credit; here it is Electricity Account because you are effectively refunding the amount to the account – it is an income item and so a credit
- enter the remaining data as you did for the debit, but enter the net amount in the right-hand credit column
- make sure the Balance box reads zero – meaning that the debit equals the credit – and SAVE

CORRECTION BY DOCUMENT

Documents such as invoices have to be checked carefully before they are despatched because once they have been sent out by the business they cannot be changed. They must instead be replaced. For example, an invoice sent to a customer with a wrong price used, or a mistake in calculation, a wrong discount, or a wrong VAT code, will need to be refunded in full by the issue of a credit note. A second and correct invoice will then have to be sent to the customer.

The net effect of all this on the accounting system and the input into a computer accounting system is that the final amount owing by the customer will be correct.

If, on the other hand, a problem is discovered with an invoice or credit note *before* it has been sent out, it can be deleted in CORRECTIONS and a replacement document issued and input.

ERROR WARNINGS

Sage will warn the user by an on-screen message if an obvious inputting error is suspected. Some examples are shown below.

CHECK DATA

The File Maintenance option offers a Check Data routine which should be run on a regular basis. An on-screen report will advise any problems or findings. These include data corruption, missing data and date errors.

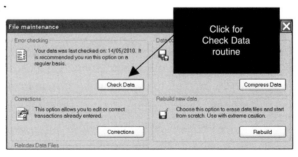

REBUILD

The REBUILD function is exactly what it says it is. Sage provides the facility to reconstruct selections of data files. This could happen for one of two reasons:

- the data is corrupted – something has gone wrong with the computer and the data cannot be used because the program will not work properly

- the data is dummy data – for example in a training situation where new 'companies' are set up each time a new set of exercises is started and the old data has to be deleted

REBUILD can be reached from MAINTENANCE through the FILE menu:

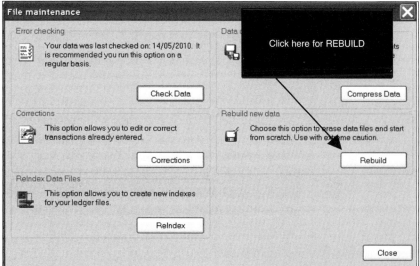

The screen looks like this . . .

You will need to deselect, ie remove the ticks from the data files that you want to reconstruct.

Rebuilding the nominal accounts will also involve reconstructing the chart of accounts (see page 73). You will be asked which chart of accounts you want – including the default layout.

As you can see, REBUILD is a drastic remedy to be used only when all else fails.

Rebuild Data Files	
Files to keep	
Keep my Customer records	☑
Keep my Supplier records	☑
Keep my Nominal Account records	☑
Keep my Transactions	☑
Keep my Chart Of Accounts	☑
Keep my Invoices	☑
Keep my Stock records	☑
Keep my Stock Transactions	☑
Keep my Sales Orders	☑
Keep my Purchase Orders	☑
Keep my Project Records	☑
Keep my Project Transactions	☑
Keep my Assets	☑
Keep my Diary Events	☑
Keep my Deletion Log	☑

ADJUSTMENTS TO THE ACCOUNTS

A business may from time-to-time need to make adjustments to the data which has already been input into the computer accounting system. Situations where this happens include:

- A credit customer is going or has gone 'bust' (bankrupt) and cannot pay invoices – the account will need to be 'written off' as a bad debt
- A credit customer has paid too much and a refund payment has to be made (by cheque or BACS)
- a cheque paid to the business by a credit customer has 'bounced' – it has been returned by the bank after it has been paid in and the money is taken off the account of the business by the bank
- a cheque issued by the business needs to be cancelled – it may have been lost in the post or it may have been stopped

We will look at each of the procedures in turn.

write offs

All businesses from time-to-time will encounter bad debts. A **bad debt** is a credit customer who does not pay. It may be that the customer has gone 'bust' or that the cost of continuing to send statements, reminders and demands is too high in relation to the amount owing. A business will decide in these circumstances to **write off** the debt in the accounts. This involves:

- debiting 'Bad Debts Account' set up in NOMINAL
- crediting the customer with the amount due – wiping it off the account

In Sage this transfer is carried out through the **Write Off/Refund** option on the vertical toolbar when the Customers module is open. This brings up the **Write Off, Refund and Returns** wizard which gives a choice of accounting adjustments …

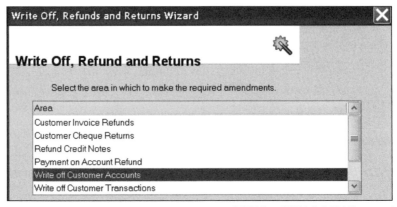

Then a choice of Sales ledger customers . . .

Screens then follow which allow the business to select the outstanding invoices to write off (all of them as the whole account is being written off) and then to date and confirm the details.

After this procedure the customer account will show as a nil balance and a corresponding Bad Debts account in NOMINAL will show the write off amount as an expense to the business. The Debtors Control Account value will also be decreased by the amount of the write off. Eventually a write off – like any expense – will reduce the business profits.

customer refunds

A business may sometimes be asked by a credit customer to send a refund cheque. This could happen when a customer, who has been sold goods on credit and has paid for them, has then decided (with the agreement of the business) to return them. The business will have to refund this amount.

The computer accounting entries in Sage will again be made through the WRITE OFF, REFUNDS AND RETURNS Wizard. If payment has already been made, as in the above example, the 'Refund Credit Notes' option will be chosen as the refund amount will appear with this description on the account. The accounting entries here are:

- adjusting the customer's account with the cheque amount (a debit)
- deducting the cheque amount from the Bank Current Account (a credit)

adjusting for returned cheques

A **returned cheque** is a cheque which has been received by a business and paid in but returned by the cheque issuer's bank for a variety of reasons: there may be a lack of funds, or the cheque may have been stopped, or it may be technically incorrect (eg unsigned by the customer).

The appropriate computer accounting entries in Sage will be made through the WRITE OFF, REFUNDS AND RETURNS Wizard under 'Customer Cheque Returns'. The cheque screen is shown below.

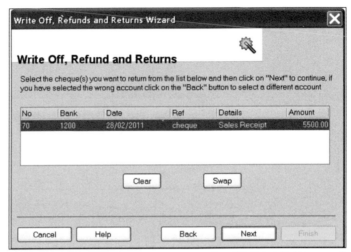

Here a cheque for £5,500 received from John Butler and Associates has been returned from their bank, marked 'Refer to Drawer'. This means that there is not sufficient money in their account and so the money will unfortunately be deducted from Pronto Limited's bank account.

cancelling a cheque

A business may wish to delete from the accounting records a cheque that it has issued. For example, the cheque may have been lost in the post or it may be cancelled before it leaves the business. In these circumstances a new cheque will be issued and input into the computer accounting system.

The appropriate computer accounting entries in Sage will be made using the WRITE OFF, REFUNDS AND RETURNS Wizard (Purchase Ledger) under 'Supplier Cheque Returns'. The screens appear as follows:

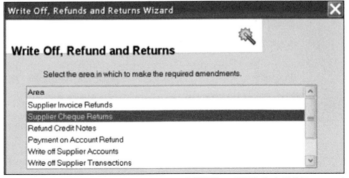

Then the supplier is selected, and then the cheque:

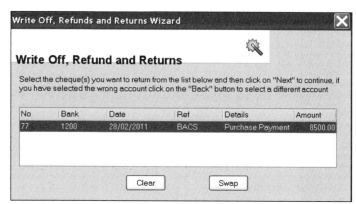

The accounting entries created by this process for this are:

- adding the amount back to the Bank Current Account because the cheque is cancelled (a debit)
- increasing the balance of the supplier's account and the Creditors Control Account with the amount of the cheque (a credit)

CASE STUDY

PRONTO SUPPLIES LIMITED: CORRECTIONS AND ADJUSTMENTS

It is 28 February 2011. Tom is still finalising his accounts. He encounters a number of situations which require him to carry out corrections and adjustments straightaway.

incorrect invoice description

Tom has an email from Charisma Design. The text reads:

> We have just noticed that Sales Invoice 10031 for £376.00 has the product description '1 x 15" monitor'. What we ordered and what was supplied was a 1 x 17" flatscreen. The amount was correct and so no action needs to be taken. You may wish to amend your records.
> Regards. Accounts, Charisma Design.

Tom identifies the invoice from the audit trail he has printed out. It is transaction 58. Tom goes into CORRECTIONS from FILE MAINTENANCE and selects transaction 58. He amends the product description on the Details tab reached via EDIT ITEM.

Number 58, Sales Invoice   ✕

You can change details of all grouped items at once by using the fields below, or select individual transactions in the list to amend a specific item.

Sales Invoice Details

Account	CH001 ▾		Due on	18/03/2011
			Last charge	/ /
Reference	10031		Int. rate	0.00
Description	1 x 17" flatscreen		Posted by	MANAGER
Created on	16/02/2011			
Posted on	15/04/2010		VAT Rec. Date	/ /

Totals

Net	320.00	Tax	56.00	Paid	0.00

Information

☐ Paid in full   ☐ Finance charge   ☐ Disputed   ☐ Printed
☐ Opening balance   ☐ GB reconciled   ☐ Revaluation

Foreign currency

Gross	376.00	Rate	1.000000	Currency	1 Pound Sterling ▾

To edit details of a specific item on this Sales Invoice, highlight the item and click 'Edit'.   [Edit]

No N/C	Details	Net T/C	Tax
58 4000	1 x 15" monitor	320.00 T1	56.00

[How will this affect my data?]   [Save]   [Close]

Clicking on the EDIT button then brings up another screen (see below). Tom has to make the same amendment and then CLOSE and SAVE.

The reason for making this amendment twice is that the second amendment also changes the details in the Audit Trail.

Number 58, Sales Invoice   ✕

Item Details

N/C	4000 ▾
Details	1 x 17" flatscreen
Date	16/02/2011
Department	1 ▾
Ex.Ref	
Project Ref	▾

journal entries

On checking the paperwork relating to the accounts for the month Tom spots that a bill from RPower has been paid but the expense has been posted by mistake to Electricity Account instead of Gas account.

The bill was for £158 plus VAT.

Tom decides to carry out journal entries to switch the expense from one account to the other. In double-entry book-keeping terms this means:

debit   Gas Account (code 7201) £158 – recording an expense

credit   Electricity Account (code 7200) £158 – recording a refund

Tom accesses the Journal through the JOURNALS icon on the NOMINAL menu bar. The journal screen after input appears as follows:

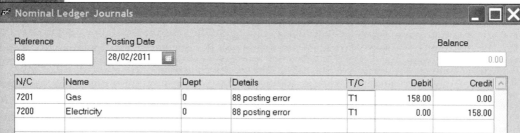

Note that:

- no VAT is involved here because it is only the net amount (amount before VAT is added on) that has gone to the wrong account

- the reference used is the audit trail number of the original transaction

- the Balance box shows as zero because the debit entry equals the credit entry – as you would expect (the Balance is the difference between the entries)

Tom can keep a printed record of his journals by going to Reports in the Nominal module and printing Day Books: Nominal Ledger.

Date:	20/05/2010				**Pronto Supplies Limited**						
					Day Books: Nominal Ledger				D---- 1		
Date To:		/2011 28/02/2011						N/C ғ:ᴏᴍ. N/C To:	99999999		
Transaction From: Transaction To:	1 99,999,999							Dept From: Dept To:	0 999		
No	Type	N/C	Date	Ref	Details	Dept	T/C	Debit	Credit	V	B
112	JD	7201	28/02/2011	88	88 posting error	0	T1	158.00		N	-
113	JC	7200	28/02/2011	88	88 posting error	0	T1		158.00	N	-
							Totals:	158.00	158.00		

cancelling a customer payment

John Butler has phoned to ask Tom to hold the cheque for £5,500.00 which he recently sent because he has a query on the goods charged.

Tom cancels the payment on his computer through WRITE OFF/REFUND on the vertical toolbar of the Customers module. He chooses Customer Cheque Returns in the WRITE OFF, REFUND AND RETURNS Wizard, selects John Butler's account and completes the wizard to delete the payment

checking corrections and adjustments

Sage does not automatically generate a report as a result of corrections to transaction data, so to confirm that the adjustments have been made, the audit trail should be checked.

The way in which a correction is reported depends on how important the change is in accounting terms. Some changes result in a simple substitution, such as a change to Details or Reference (eg the 'monitor' to 'flatscreen' change in the Case Study). Some result in the original transaction being amended and an additional entry being inserted on the audit trail showing what has been deleted, eg where a major alteration like a change to the nominal code has been made. There is an example of this on the Audit Trail on page 252 where transactions 68 and 69 record changes. These will be done in CORRECTIONS.

Changes to amounts of Journals transactions require a different treatment as they cannot be changed in CORRECTIONS. The way to do this is to choose the Reversals option from the Nominal toolbar. This will enable you to reverse (cancel out) the original transaction and to then enter the correct journal debit and credit entries.

CHAPTER SUMMARY

■ Errors inevitably occur when processing accounts on the computer. Errors can involve incorrect descriptions, incorrect prices, wrong VAT codes and wrong accounts used.

■ Most errors within Sage can be corrected using the CORRECTIONS routine within MAINTENANCE. This will enable corrections to be made to invoices, credit notes and payments.

■ Adjustments to Nominal accounts can also be carried out by transfers through the JOURNALS function within Sage. This process requires a knowledge of double-entry book-keeping.

■ After financial documents such as invoices and credit notes have been sent out they can normally only be corrected by document – for example an invoice overcharge adjusted by a credit note.

■ On-screen warnings may appear in the case of some inputting errors

■ Certain data errors can be detected by running the Check Data option

■ If computer files become corrupted beyond repair the Sage REBUILD function can be used to reconstruct the ledgers. This may result in data being lost in the process. REBUILD is also used in a training context.

■ The computer accounting records may also be adjusted for situations such as account write-offs, refunds to customers, returned customer cheques and cheques to suppliers that need to be cancelled.

KEY TERMS

journal	the part of the accounting system which enables you to make transfers from one nominal account to another, and to enter new balances
double-entry	the system of book-keeping which involves each transaction having two entries made – a debit and a credit; computer accounting programs (which are largely single entry systems) deal with the double entry automatically
write off	the removal of a Customer (or Supplier) account balance from the accounting records
bad debt	a debt that is never likely to be paid and so will need to be written off
returned cheque	a cheque that has been paid into a bank account but has been returned unpaid by the bank either because of lack of funds, or because of some technical irregularity on the cheque

STUDENT ACTIVITIES

12.1 What method of adjustment in a computer accounting program would you use if . . .

(a) A customer's cheque which you have paid in is returned to you marked 'cheque stopped by order of drawer'

(b) You discover that a payment for advertising has been input in error to the stationery account.

(c) You need to make a refund to a customer because they have purchased goods on credit, paid for all of them and then returned some of them.

(d) You find you have input an invoice with the wrong amount and Saved it, but you have not yet sent out the invoice to the customer.

(e) You have input an invoice with the wrong products and wrong amount and have Saved it. You have sent out the invoice to the customer who rings you up to say that the wrong goods have arrived.

PRONTO SUPPLIES INPUTTING TASKS

Ensure the program date is set at 28 February 2011.

Task 1

Correct invoice 10031 (transaction 58) in the Case Study on page 182 using CORRECTIONS.

Task 2

Carry out the Journal entries for the misposting in the Case Study on page 182. Use Ref 88.

Task 3

Cancel the cheque for £5,500.00 from John Butler & Associates using the WRITE OFF, REFUNDS AND RETURNS Wizard.

Task 4

When you have completed your corrections, print out a Trial Balance. Check the figures on the Trial Balance with the figures on page 255. Then explain the changes in the Trial Balance to:

(a) Bank Current Account

(b) Electricity Account

These changes can be seen by comparing the two trial balances on pages 254 and 255.

Reminder! Have you made a back-up?

13 SALES INVOICING – FURTHER ASPECTS

chapter introduction

- *In Chapter 6 – 'Selling to customers on credit' – we looked at the way in which Customers are invoiced for goods and services sold. The method of invoicing used was the 'batch' method in which the invoices are produced independently (eg typed out) and the details then entered onto the computer screen. This is the method to be used when first setting up a computer accounting system when you have existing invoices which need to be input onto the system.*

- *In this chapter we illustrate the way in which invoices are printed out by the business using the computer invoicing function and the way in which the details are then updated on the Customer's account.*

- *If the business is selling goods rather than services, producing invoices in this way usually involves setting up stock codes, known in Sage as 'product codes', which are entered on the invoice screen to produce the appropriate price and product description automatically.*

- *If the business is selling services rather than goods, Sage provides a facility known as a 'service invoice' which does not require the setting up of product codes, and so is simpler to operate.*

- *Processing invoices may also involve the use of discounts. There are two main types of discount:*
  - *trade discount, a percentage reduction in the price of goods and services for example for bulk purchases*
  - *cash discount (also known as settlement discount), a percentage reduction in the price of goods and services allowed to customers who pay the invoice early (for example within seven days, rather than the usual thirty days)*

- *We will again look at the business in the Case Study – Pronto Supplies Limited – and see how it deals with printing service invoices and with applying Customer discounts.*

METHODS OF INVOICING IN SAGE

There are two main methods of producing sales invoices in Sage:

■ **batch invoice production** – the business produces invoices independently of the computer and then inputs the details of each invoice on the computer screen to enter the transaction into the computer

■ **computer-produced invoices** – the business uses an invoicing function available in Sage programs to input the details into the computer and to record and print out each invoice

So far in this book we have concentrated on the method of batched invoice entry because of its simplicity and because not all training centres are geared up to print computer-produced invoices. In this chapter, however, we cater for those who are able to print out invoices, and those who may have to do so for certain examination courses.

THE INVOICING FUNCTION IN SAGE

The invoicing function in Sage is reached by opening Modules on the menu bar and choosing Invoicing:

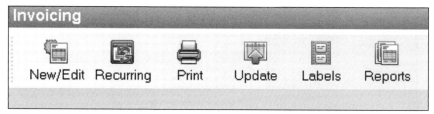

The most important icons here are:

New/Edit	create invoices and credit notes for products and services that you supply to customers
Recurring	if you bill your customers for regular product sales or services (eg rent payable), you can use this feature to create these invoices automatically
Print	print invoices and credit notes
Update	update the ledgers, ie post the entries to the computer accounting records after the input has been checked

PRODUCT INVOICES

Product invoicing in Sage requires the use of the PRODUCTS module to set up product codes. A product code is a reference made up of numbers and/or letters for each item sold. Details of the product such as pricing and re-order levels are included in the Product Record.

Once in operation the PRODUCTS function can record details of all stock held and automatically adjust the recorded stock level each time a product invoice is issued. Setting up the PRODUCTS function is a time-consuming operation which requires much planning and forethought. It is therefore beyond the scope of this book (and most computer accounting examinations).

The product invoice screen (shown at the bottom of the page) is reached by clicking on NEW/EDIT on the INVOICING menu bar.

invoicing without product codes – a short cut

Sage has a short cut to overcome the problem of setting up product codes. If you select a Customer, and click on the Product Code box on the invoice screen you can access a drop down menu which allows you to choose option S1 (goods with VAT) or S2 (goods without VAT). This then produces an 'Edit Item Line' screen (see below) on which you can set out products that you sell.

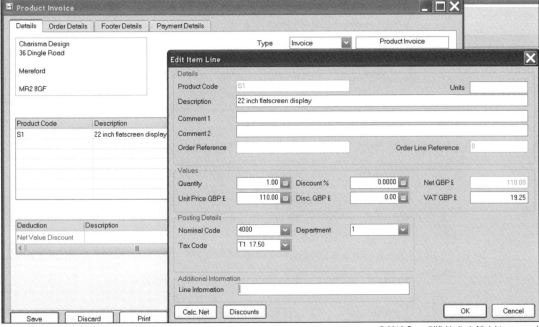

processing the product invoice

There are a number of distinct stages in processing and printing product invoices:

1   Enter the details of the invoice on screen

On the first tab – 'Details' – the invoice number and date are normally set automatically, although they can be over-ridden. The order number and account reference need to be input. The product code also needs to be entered; if S1 or S2 are used, the details and price will also need to be input through the separate screen. If a PRODUCTS function has been set up the product code will automatically generate the details and price.

The details of the order and payment terms also need to be checked on the other tabs and amended as required.

2   Save the invoice when you have checked the details on screen

The invoice should be Saved once it has been correctly entered. It is now ready for printing.

3   Print the invoice

Invoices are normally better printed in batches rather than one by one, which would be very time consuming. Invoices for printing should be selected on the opening INVOICING screen. When the PRINT icon has been clicked you should choose the format in which you want the invoice printed and then set the print run going. Invoices in SAGE are normally preprinted with all the headings and boxes in place; the printer just puts in the figures and details.

4   Updating the ledgers

When the invoices have been printed they should be carefully checked against the appropriate sales order documentation to make sure that the details are correct and that no orders have been missed

When you are satisfied that the invoices are correct they should be selected on the INVOICING screen and updated to the Sales Ledger. This means that the amount of the invoice will be added to the account of the Customer and appropriate entries made to Sales and Sales VAT Account.

5   Printing a report

The final stage in invoice processing is the printing of a report, either the ledger update report which is automatically generated when the update takes place, or a Day Book Customer Invoices (Detailed) report for the appropriate transactions from REPORTS on the CUSTOMERS menu bar.

SERVICE INVOICES

Service invoices are issued for services provided by a business and not for goods sold. The advantage of service invoices is that they do not require product codes. They may be accessed by clicking on New/Edit on the INVOICING menu bar. In the Format box, click on the drop-down arrow and choose 'Service'. A completed input screen looks like this:

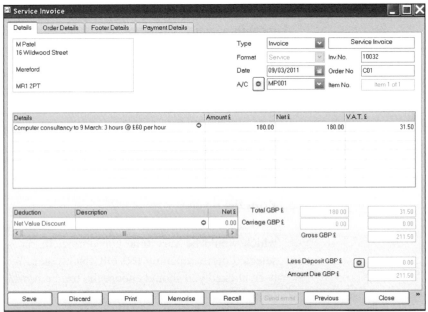

The procedure is much the same as with the Product Invoice (see previous page for the steps to be taken) except that the details and price have to be entered manually, because no product code is entered. Note the following:

Details   You can enter as much text as you like in this box.

Amount   You enter the net amount here, ie the amount before VAT is added on and before discounts are calculated (see later in this chapter for an explanation of discounts).

VAT   This is automatically calculated, based on the tax code entered. The tax code can be checked if you click on the arrow in the Details line (see next page).

Nominal code The Nominal account code to which the invoice is posted (eg Computer Consultancy Account) can also be checked and amended by clicking on the arrow in the Details line (see next page).

The Edit Item Line screen appears as follows:

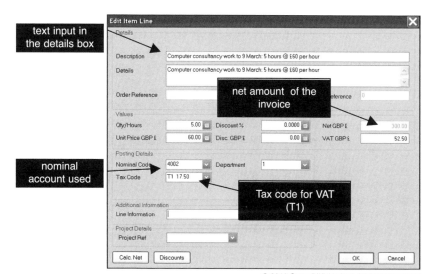

'memorising' invoices

If you repeatedly invoice the same service or product at the same price you can save the details as a 'skeleton' invoice by clicking on the Memorise button at the bottom of the invoice screen and providing a file name and description. If you need to bring up these same details again for another invoice, click the Recall button and select the file you need.

printing and updating – service invoices

The procedure for printing service invoices and **updating** the ledgers is exactly the same as for a product invoice, as explained on page 191. It is advisable also to print out a report for all invoices produced, either when updating the ledgers in INVOICING or as a Day Book Customer Invoices (Detailed) in CUSTOMERS.

CREDIT NOTE PRODUCTION

Exactly the same procedure is followed for processing and printing Product and Service credit notes. These are accessed by amending the options in the Type and Format boxes of the New/Edit screen reached from the INVOICING menu bar.

The Case Study which follows shows how Pronto Supplies Limited decides to process and print its invoices on the computer, starting with service invoices for computer consultancy work carried out by Tom Cox.

CASE STUDY

PRONTO SUPPLIES LIMITED: SERVICE INVOICE PRINTING

During February Tom Cox had placed an advert in the local paper for 'Pronto' computer consultancy services. This was a sideline for Tom's business. Tom had seen that small businesses – particularly start-ups – needed help in setting up computer systems for wordprocessing, databases, spreadsheets and Computer accounting. Tom decided to charge £60 per hour for this service, in view of his qualifications and experience.

It is now 9 March 2011. Tom has already done work for three clients and has decided to invoice them using the Service Invoice function in Sage. He has worked out how to print out the invoices on the office printer and has designed his own stationery to take one of the Sage standard A4 layouts.

setting up the Customer Accounts

The details of the three new customers (with designated account codes) are as follows:

MP001	**M Patel**
	16 Wildwood Street
	Mereford
	MR1 2PT

Contact name: M Patel
Telephone 01908 356745, Fax 01908 356777
Email MPatel@goblin.com
Credit limit £2,000
Computer consultancy work to 9 March; 3 hours @ £60 per hour
Order ref C01

PD001	**Petal Design Company**
	17 Marcus Close
	Mereford
	MR3 1TF

Contact name: Fallon McVeigh
Telephone 01908 640317, Fax 01908 640466
Email mail@petaldesign.co.uk
www.petaldesign.co.uk
Credit limit £2,000
Computer consultancy work to 9 March; 5 hours @ £60 per hour
Order ref C02

EA001   **121 Escort Agency**
2B Verey Close
Stourminster
ST1 9TF

Contact name: Astrid Bergman
Telephone 01603 625150, Fax 01603 625625,
Email mail@121escortagency.co.uk
www.121escortagency.co.uk
Credit limit £2,000
Computer consultancy work to 9 March; 7 hours @ £60 per hour
Order ref C03

Tom first sets up these customers in CUSTOMERS using the RECORD button and the Customer defaults already established. These defaults include:

Payment due days   30 days

Terms of payment   Payment 30 days of invoice

VAT rate   Standard rate of 17.5% (this is Tax Code T1)

Tom realises he will have to be careful about the Nominal Code (normally default 4000, ie computer hardware sales) when processing service invoices for Computer Consultancy (account 4002). He decides to set 4002 as a default account for these three customers.

Tom does not allow discounts on Computer Consultancy at this stage. He ticks the Terms Agreed box on the Credit Control tab for each customer.

The initial input screen for the third customer is shown below.

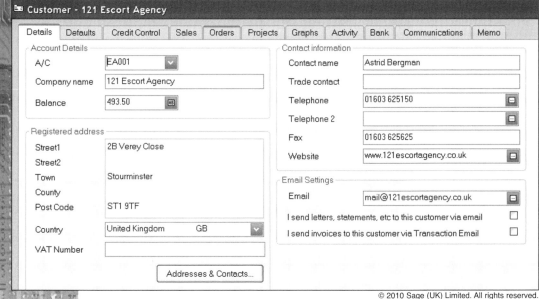

entering the service invoices

Tom has three service invoices to input on 9 March 2011. He selects the INVOICING menu and clicks on New/Edit and selects the Service Invoice format.

He has to set up the invoice number on the first invoice screen. The last invoice he issued was 10031, so he edits the number to 10032. (He can adjust the autonumber settings if necessary by going to Settings/Invoice & Order Defaults and removing the tick from the Lock Autonumber option on the General tab.)

He then inputs the order reference and account reference and types in the text of the service provided in the Details box.

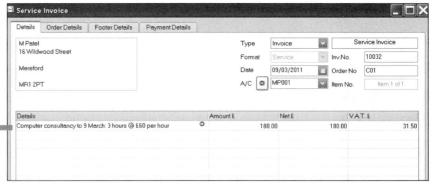

The amount he is charging (before VAT) can be entered in the Amount box and the computer then calculates the VAT amount and invoice total.

Tom should now check that the invoice is posted correctly to Computer Consultancy Account (4002 - the default account for these customers) and so clicks on the Details drop-down arrow to bring up the necessary screen.

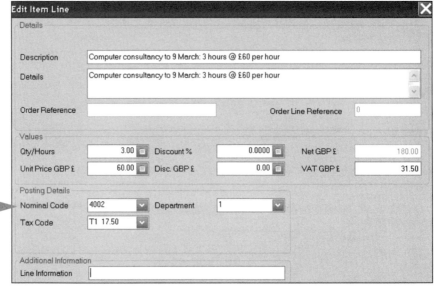

saving and updating

After processing each of the three invoices and Saving them, Tom then selects them on the INVOICING opening screen and clicks on the PRINT icon and selects the invoice layout on screen he has set up for his stationery.

Tom then prints the invoices and checks them. When he is happy that they are all correct he selects the three invoices on the INVOICING opening screen and clicks the Update icon on the menu bar:

This then posts the invoices in the accounting records (Ledgers) as follows

- £900 to Nominal Account 4002 Computer consultancy – the net Sales
- £157.50 to Nominal Account 2200 Sales Tax Control Account – the VAT
- The three invoices (totalling £1,057.50) to the three Customer Accounts and at the same time to Debtors Control Account

printing a report

Tom should check the computer input against his input details by printing a report. This could be the Update Ledgers Report which is generated when the Ledgers are updated, but can only be printed at this time. This shows all the details of the transactions, including the Nominal account to which each invoice is posted.

Tom could alternatively print out a Day Books: Customer Invoices (Detailed) from REPORTS on the CUSTOMERS menu bar. This will also enable him to check his input.

This report is shown below.

Pronto Supplies Limited
Day Books: Customer Invoices (Detailed)

| Date From: | 09/03/2011 | | | | | | | Customer From: | | |
| Date To: | 09/03/2011 | | | | | | | Customer To: | ZZZZZZZZ | |

| Transaction From: | 1 | | | | | | | N/C From: | | |
| Transaction To: | 99,999,999 | | | | | | | N/C To: | 99999999 | |

| Dept From: | 0 | | | | | | | | | |
| Dept To: | 999 | | | | | | | | | |

Tran No.	Type	Date	A/C Ref	N/C	Inv Ref	Dept.	Details	Net Amount	Tax Amount	T/C	Gross Amount	V	B
115	SI	09/03/2011	MP001	4002	10032	1	Computer consultancy work to 9	180.00	31.50	T1	211.50	N	-
116	SI	09/03/2011	PD001	4002	10033	1	Computer consultancy work to 9	300.00	52.50	T1	352.50	N	-
117	SI	09/03/2011	EA001	4002	10034	1	Computer consultancy work to 9	420.00	73.50	T1	493.50	N	-
							Totals:	900.00	157.50		1,057.50		

End of Report

DISCOUNTS ON INVOICES - FURTHER NOTES

As we have seen in Chapter 8 (page 106), a **discount** is a reduction in the selling price of goods or services. The discount will always be shown on the invoice. There are two main types of discount given by sellers:

■ **Trade discount** is a percentage reduction in the price of goods and services, for example in return for large orders.

For example, a supplier may give Customers an overall 20% discount. A sale of goods with a list price of £100 would therefore cost

£100 less £20 (20% trade discount) = £80

■ **Cash discount** (also known as **settlement discount**) is a percentage reduction in the price of goods and services allowed to Customers who pay the invoice early, for example within seven days, rather than the usual thirty days. (Remember that 'cash' means immediate payment).

For example, a supplier may allow a 2.5% cash discount if a Customer pays up within seven days rather than the usual agreed credit period of 30 days. If the original invoice was for £100, the Customer could pay within seven days

£100 less £2.50 (2.5% cash discount) = £97.50

Remember, however, that VAT will normally have to be added on to these amounts.

VAT and discount

The normal practice on an invoice is for VAT to be calculated on the sales amount *after* the discount has been deducted.

In the examples given the total amount charged will be (assuming 17.5% standard rate VAT):

■ **Trade discount**

£80 (ie £100 minus £20) + VAT of £14 = total of £94

■ **Cash discount**

£97.50 (ie £100 minus £2.50) + VAT of £17.06 = total of £114.56

The important thing to remember here is that **the VAT is always calculated on the amount after the discount has been deducted, even if the cash discount is not taken**. It may seem odd and illogical but the printed invoice will always show the *pre-discount total* (in this case £100) as the net total (ie the higher amount) but will then add on the VAT calculated on the amount *after the discount has been deducted!*

discounts and computer accounting

One of the advantages of using a computer accounting package such as Sage is that the program calculates discount automatically and accurately. There are a number of ways in which to input the discount details: using Customer Defaults, amending the Customer Record and editing the invoice itself.

customer defaults

It is possible to set up discount rates on the computer which will apply to all Customer accounts unless the user specifies otherwise.

Trade discounts can be set up in CUSTOMER DEFAULTS under SETTINGS. This would be useful if the business sold goods in a trade where there was a common trade discount rate.

Cash (settlement) discounts can be set up on the Terms tab in the CONFIGURATION EDITOR. In the example shown below a cash (settlement) discount of 2.5% is given if payment is received within 14 days rather than the normal 30 days.

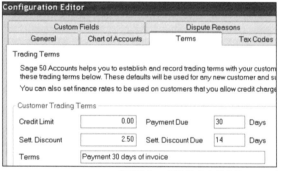

customer record – special terms agreed

The default rates could, if required be over-ridden by amending the RECORD in CUSTOMERS.

The Defaults tab in the Customer Record will enable the user to set up a special trade discount for an individual customer. The screen below shows the application of a 40% trade discount – obviously for a good customer.

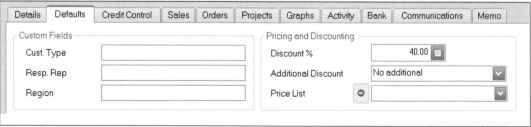

The Credit Control tab in the Customer Record will enable the user to set up a revised cash (settlement) discount; in the case shown below the discount is 5% instead of the normal 2.5%.

customer invoice

Further changes can be made at the invoicing stage, if required. The cash discount can be amended on the invoice footer tab and the trade discount can be amended on the Edit Item screen. A one-off percentage or value discount on the whole invoice value can be given using the net value discount box on the invoice screen

PRONTO SUPPLIES LIMITED: APPLYING DISCOUNTS

It is 9 March 2011. Tom Cox has now been trading for over two months and has been approached by some of his customers asking for **trade discount**.

After some negotiation he has agreed to give 30% trade discount to three customers:

JB001	John Butler & Associates
CR001	Crowmatic Ltd
LG001	L Garr & Co

Tom carries out this procedure by amending the Customer Record in each case, as shown below.

A week later Tom receives an email about **cash discounts** from 121 Escort Agency. The text reads as follows:

Hello Tom

Thanks for your recent invoice for computer work done for us. We will settle it by the end of the month.

As we have a good bank balance these days, is there any possibility of you giving us a cash discount on future invoices of say 5% for settlement within seven days?

Thanks

Astrid

Tom replies:

Hello Astrid

We will be happy to give you a cash discount on future invoices. The highest we can go to at the moment is 3% for settlement within 7 days. Is this OK?

Tom

Astrid replies:

Hello Tom

3% cash settlement discount would be fine. Many thanks.

Regards

Astrid

Tom then amends the RECORD of 121 Escort Agency in CUSTOMERS as follows:

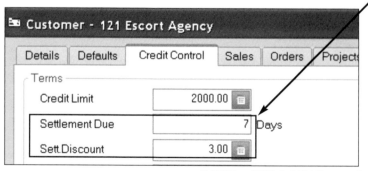

■   Sage provides two ways of processing sales invoices. The first method is batch entry, where the invoice is produced independently of the computer and the details are input afterwards. The second method is the invoicing function in Sage which enables the details to be input and an invoice to be printed from the computer.

■   There are two main types of invoice which can be produced in Sage:
  • a product invoice which is used for invoicing actual goods
  • a service invoice which is used for invoicing services provided
  Invoicing using product invoices normally involves the setting up of the products facility within Sage which provides the product codes needed by the computer. Service invoices do not need product codes.

■   Processing an invoice involves a number of stages:
  • the input of the invoice details
  • saving and printing the invoice
  • updating the ledgers
  • printing a report in order to check the accuracy of the input

■   The issue of credit notes follows the same principles as the issue of invoices.

■   Processing invoices may also involve the use of discounts. There are two main types of discount: trade discount and cash discount.

product code	a reference code made up of letters and/or numbers which is specific to each stock item sold
product invoice	an invoice used for invoicing actual goods
service invoice	an invoice used for invoicing a service provided
ledger update	posting the details of invoices issued to the computer accounting records
trade discount	a percentage reduction in the price of goods and services, eg in return for large orders
cash discount	a percentage reduction in the price of goods and services allowed to customers who pay an invoice early (also known as settlement discount)

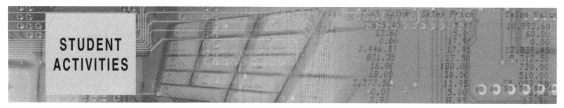

STUDENT ACTIVITIES

13.1   Describe the circumstances in which a business might use the Sage batch invoice input method of invoice production.

13.2   Explain what is meant, with an example, by 'updating the ledger' after processing and printing an invoice on the computer.

13.3   Describe the full range of checking procedures (including the update) that should be carried out when processing and printing an invoice on the computer.

13.4   In what way does a service invoice differ from a product invoice in Sage?

13.5   Explain the difference between trade discount and cash (settlement) discount.

13.6   A stationery wholesaler issues invoices for the goods it sells and gives a 25% trade discount to established customers. Assuming it charges VAT at the standard rate, what would the final invoice total be for goods where the net total (ie total before discount and VAT) is (a) £400 (b) £640.50?

13.7   An advertising agency issues invoices for the services it provides and gives 2.5% cash discount to customers for settlement within seven days. Assuming it charges VAT at 17.5%, what would the final invoice total be for goods where the net total (ie total before discount and VAT) is (a) £4,000.00 (b) £840.00. What would the customer pay in both cases if the discount were taken?

PRONTO SUPPLIES INPUTTING TASKS

Before attempting these tasks, ensure the program date is set at 9 March 2011.

Task 1

Input the three new Customer accounts from the Case Study details (pages 194 to 195) in CUSTOMERS, remembering to use default N/C 4002, and ticking the Terms Agreed box on the Credit Control tab.

Task 2

Process the service invoices for the work done for the three new clients (see Case Study). Remember to check that Nominal code 4002 is set as a default and to check the input before Saving. Print and check the invoices, update the ledgers and print out an Update Ledgers Report or Day Book: Customer Invoices (Detailed) to confirm the batch totals (see page 197).

Task 3

Apply the discounts to the appropriate Customer Records, as in the Case Study (see pages 200 to 201). Take and print out a screenshot of the amendment to Crowmatic Limited's account. Check that it matches the example at the bottom of page 201 (yours will probably show more of the screen than this).

Task 4

Fallon from Petal Design Company telephones on 14 March to say that Tom has only done (order ref. CO2) 4 hours consultancy and not 5 as invoiced. Change the program date to 14 March and process and print a service Credit Note 555 to make the adjustment. Remember to post the credit to Nominal Account 4002 and print out an Update Ledger Report for your records (see page 256).

As a final check of your accuracy, print out a Trial Balance and an Audit Trail as at 14 March and check with the Trial Balance and Audit Trail shown on pages 256-258.

DOUBLE-ENTRY BOOK-KEEPING AND MANUAL SYSTEMS

chapter introduction

- *Earlier chapters in this book have shown how computer accounting involves the use of 'accounts' and 'ledgers' maintained on computer files. It is easy to accept these terms at face value when you are sitting in front of a computer – but they make much more sense once you know how they work in a manual accounting system.*

- *The basis of many manual accounting systems is a set of double-entry accounts grouped into separate ledgers – eg sales ledger, purchases ledger. Each time a transaction is recorded, it is entered twice in the accounts, once as a debit and once as a credit.*

- *The basis of computer accounting is the input of a financial transaction as a single entry on the screen. The computer then processes that entry to two separate accounts (or three accounts if VAT is involved). In other words, the computer does the double-entry for you.*

- *The problem with manual double-entry book-keeping is knowing which entry is the debit and which is the credit. This is best understood when it is seen as part of the 'dual aspect' of double-entry book-keeping, which sets down the principles of which entry is which. These principles are sometimes needed in computer accounting, for example when you are processing a journal entry or a nominal opening balance. You then have to decide whether an amount should be entered as a debit or as a credit. If you understand the principles of manual double-entry book-keeping you are at a great advantage.*

- *Remember that double-entry book-keeping is only one part of the accounting process, whether a manual or a computerised accounting system is used. The first step is the financial transaction and the document it generates, the second is the listing and summarising of financial transactions and the third is the entry of this data in the accounts. The final stage is the summary of the accounts in the Trial Balance and the production of reports such as the Profit & Loss Statement and the Balance Sheet from the double-entry records. We will start off in this chapter by looking at this overall accounting system.*

THE ACCOUNTING SYSTEM

The overall accounting system as it relates to both manual and computer accounting is a simple series of stages which starts off with financial transactions such as sales and purchases and concludes with information used by management such as aged debtor summaries and profit and loss statements. The stages can be summarised as follows:

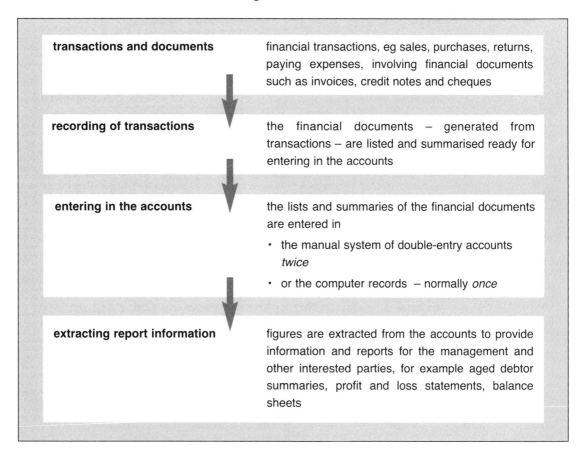

transactions and documents — financial transactions, eg sales, purchases, returns, paying expenses, involving financial documents such as invoices, credit notes and cheques

recording of transactions — the financial documents – generated from transactions – are listed and summarised ready for entering in the accounts

entering in the accounts — the lists and summaries of the financial documents are entered in

- the manual system of double-entry accounts *twice*
- or the computer records – normally *once*

extracting report information — figures are extracted from the accounts to provide information and reports for the management and other interested parties, for example aged debtor summaries, profit and loss statements, balance sheets

stage 1 – transactions and documents

Financial transactions involve financial documents. You will already be familiar with many of these.

sale and purchase of goods and services – the invoice

When a business buys or sells goods or a service the seller prepares an invoice which sets out the amount owing, the date on which it should be paid and the details of the goods sold or the service provided.

refunds – the credit note

If the buyer returns goods which are bought on credit or has a problem with a service supplied on credit, the seller will issue a credit note which is sent to the buyer, reducing the amount of money owed.

small cash payments – the petty cash voucher

If the business operates a petty cash system for making small cash payments, the payments will be recorded and authorised using petty cash vouchers.

paying-in slips, cheques and remittance advices

Businesses need to pay money into the bank current account, and draw out cash and make payments. Money can be paid in on paying-in slips or electronically. Payments made using cheques and BACS transfers are normally issued in conjunction with a remittance advice, a document sent to the person receiving the money, explaining what the payment represents.

stage 2 – recording transactions

Businesses need to list and summarise these documents ready for entry into the accounting records. Manual systems often use cash books for bank and cash transactions and 'day books' for listing sales, purchases and returns. Each day book will usually be totalled on a regular basis. Computer systems often use the **batch** system which is a listing of the items with an overall total to check against the computer input. It is common to find batches for sales, purchases, returns, cheques received, cheques issued.

stage 3 – entering transactions in the accounts

When the financial documents have been suitably listed in a day book or batch they are then entered in the accounts of the business. The format of a manual double-entry account with a debit entry might look like this:

Debit				Computer Account			Credit
Date	**Details**	**Folio**	**£ p**	**Date**	**Details**	**Folio**	**£ p**
01 02 07	**Bank**	**CB007**	**450.00**				
↑	↑	↑	↑	↑	↑	↑	↑
date of the trans-action	name of the account in which the other entry is made	page or reference number of the other account	amount of the trans-action	date of the trans-action	name of the account in which the other entry is made	page or reference number of the other account	amount of the trans-action

The double-entry system used by many manual systems involves two entries for each amount or total (or three entries if VAT is involved). This form of account and the way it works is explained in more detail on page 209.

A computer system, as you know, needs only one entry to be made for each transaction, but will require the account code of the other entry when that single entry is made.

Most accounting systems use the **ledger** system to organise the accounts. The word 'ledger' means 'book' but is used freely by both manual and computer systems to represent a section of the accounts kept on paper or on the computer. The ledgers can be summarised as follows:

■ sales ledger	the accounts of customers who have bought on credit (also known as debtors), referred to in computer accounting as CUSTOMERS
■ purchases ledger	the accounts of suppliers (creditors) who have sold to the business on credit, referred to in computer accounting as SUPPLIERS
■ cash book ledger	the cash and bank accounts of the business – referred to in computer accounting as BANK
■ main 'general' ledger	all the other accounts – expenses, income, assets (items owned) and liabilities (items owed), also referred to in computer accounting as NOMINAL

stage 4 – extracting report information

Financial data in the accounts is only useful when it can be extracted and used by the management of the business or presented to outsiders such as shareholders. The advantage of computer accounting systems is that reports can be generated automatically from a menu. You may encounter a number of different reports in your studies:

■ **trial balance**	a list of account balances in two columns, which will show whether or not the book-keeping (in a manual system) has been accurate
■ **account activity**	a list of the transactions on a particular account which may need investigation, eg an expense account or the account of a customer
■ **aged debtors analysis**	a listing of the balances of credit customers, setting out what they owe, when they need to pay and if any payments are overdue
■ **aged creditors analysis**	a listing of the balances of suppliers, setting out when payments need to be made
■ **financial statements**	these include the **profit and loss statement**, which states what profit/loss has been made and the **balance sheet** which sets out what a business owns and owes and how it is financed

Now study the diagram below which summarises the various stages in a manual and a computerised accounting system. The workings of double-entry used in a manual system are explained on the next page.

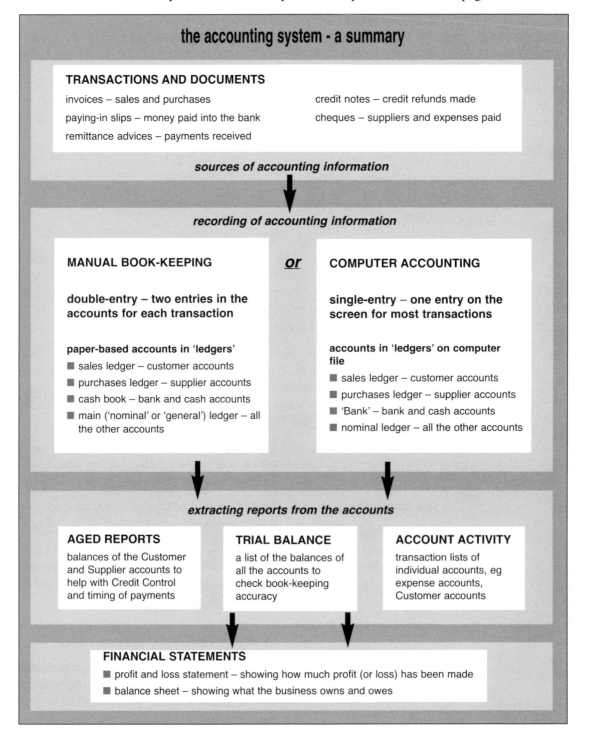

the accounting system - a summary

TRANSACTIONS AND DOCUMENTS

invoices – sales and purchases

paying-in slips – money paid into the bank

remittance advices – payments received

credit notes – credit refunds made

cheques – suppliers and expenses paid

sources of accounting information

recording of accounting information

MANUAL BOOK-KEEPING

double-entry – two entries in the accounts for each transaction

paper-based accounts in 'ledgers'
- sales ledger – customer accounts
- purchases ledger – supplier accounts
- cash book – bank and cash accounts
- main ('nominal' or 'general') ledger – all the other accounts

or

COMPUTER ACCOUNTING

single-entry – one entry on the screen for most transactions

accounts in 'ledgers' on computer file
- sales ledger – customer accounts
- purchases ledger – supplier accounts
- 'Bank' – bank and cash accounts
- nominal ledger – all the other accounts

extracting reports from the accounts

AGED REPORTS
balances of the Customer and Supplier accounts to help with Credit Control and timing of payments

TRIAL BALANCE
a list of the balances of all the accounts to check book-keeping accuracy

ACCOUNT ACTIVITY
transaction lists of individual accounts, eg expense accounts, Customer accounts

FINANCIAL STATEMENTS
- profit and loss statement – showing how much profit (or loss) has been made
- balance sheet – showing what the business owns and owes

DOUBLE-ENTRY ACCOUNTS

Double-entry book-keeping in a manual accounting system involves entries being made in accounts for each transaction – debit entries (on the left-hand side of the account) and credit entries (on the right-hand side of the account). If a transaction does not involve VAT there will be two entries: an equal debit and credit. If VAT is involved there will be three entries, but the debit(s) must always equal the credit(s).

The questions faced by anyone operating the system are:

- deciding which two (or three) accounts should be used for each transaction, and more critically …
- deciding which entry is the debit and which is the credit

There are simple rules which guide you here, but, as with learning to drive a car, the early stages require both thought and concentration!

We will first look at the layout of a typical double-entry account. The illustration here shows an account for computer equipment purchased.

Debit				Computer Account				Credit
Date	**Details**	**Folio**	**£ p**	**Date**	**Details**	**Folio**	**£ p**
01 02 07	Bank	CB007	450.00				
date of the trans-action	*name of the account in which the other entry is made*	*page or reference number of the other account*	*amount of the trans-action*				

Note the following:

- the name of the account – Computer Account – is written at the top
- the account is divided into two identical halves, separated by a central double vertical line: the left-hand side is called the 'debit' side ('debit' is abbreviated to 'Dr'), the right-hand side is called the 'credit' (or 'Cr') side

  A note for UK drivers! –   **Dr**ive on the left   **Cr**ash on the right
- the date, details and amount of the transaction are entered in the columns:

  - in the 'details' column is entered the name of the other account involved in the book-keeping transaction – here it is the Bank Account

  - the 'folio' column is used as a cross-referencing system to the other entry of the double-entry book-keeping transaction – here CB007 stands for page 7 in the Cash Book where the Bank Account entry is made

In a manual book-keeping system each account would occupy a whole page or more, but in textbooks to save space it is usual to simplify the format and put several accounts on a page. The Computer Account set out in this way is shown at the bottom of this page.

You will see that the Folio column has gone and the column divisions have also disappeared. It is all much simpler, with just a single vertical line dividing the debit and credit sides.

The problem remains: if you are given a transaction to enter, how do you decide which is the debit entry and which is the credit entry?

dual aspect theory of double-entry

The principle of double-entry book-keeping is that every business transaction has a dual aspect: one account gains value (the debit), the other gives value (the credit). The Computer Account shows a gain in value for the business (the debit), ie the new computer, while the Bank Account will give value as the purchase price is paid (the credit).

practical aspects of double-entry

If this sounds too theoretical, look at the *practical* aspects of the system. For each double-entry transaction (ignoring any VAT for the sake of simplicity):

■ one account is debited (entry on the left of the account)

■ another account is credited (entry on the right of the account)

The *practical* rules for debits and credits are:

debit entry	**credit entry**
■ money paid into the bank	■ money paid out of the bank
■ purchases made, expenses paid	■ an income item
■ an asset (item owned) is acquired or increased	■ a liability (item owed) is incurred or increased

Look at the example below and read the text in the grey boxes:

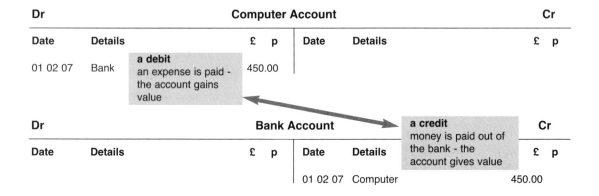

CASE STUDY

HARRY PORTER LIMITED: DOUBLE-ENTRY TRANSACTIONS

Harry Porter runs a magic and jokes shop. During the first week of July 2007 he has five transactions to enter in his double-entry accounts:

2 Jul 2007   Sale of goods for £12,000 cheque received.

3 Jul 2007   Payment of wages of £1,200 by cheque.

4 Jul 2007   Purchase of goods for £3,000, paid for by cheque.

5 Jul 2007   Received loan of £5,000 from D B Dore, and paid cheque into bank.

6 Jul 2007   Purchase of computer costing £4,000, paid for by cheque.

Again, for the sake of simplicity we have ignored any Sales or Purchases VAT.

If you look at these five transactions for Harry Porter Limited, you will see that they all involve the bank account. One invariable rule for the bank account is that money received is recorded on the left-hand (debit) side, and money paid out is recorded on the right-hand (credit) side. By applying this rule, you can say that for a bank account:

Money in is a debit (on the left); money out is a credit (on the right)

Using this rule, the bank account for Harry Porter Limited, after entering the five transactions, appears as follows:

Dr					Bank Account			Cr	
Date	Details			£	p	Date	Details		£	p
2007		**money in**				2007		**money out**		
02 Jul	Sales			12,000.00		03 Jul	Wages		1,200.00	
05 Jul	D B Dore Loan			5,000.00		04 Jul	Purchases		3,000.00	
						06 Jul	Computer		4,000.00	

It is now a simple step to work out onto which side, debit or credit, the entries are recorded in the other accounts involved. If you bear in mind that money received is a debit (left hand side) and money paid out is a credit (right hand side), by looking at any double-entry transaction which involves the bank account you should:

• identify on which side of the bank account, debit (money in) or credit (money out), the item is recorded

• record the other double-entry item on the other side of the appropriate account

We are now in a position to set out the other accounts involved in the five transactions entered in the bank account. Note that in each case the description in the account is 'Bank'.

transaction

2 July 2007: sale of goods for £12,000, cheque received

double-entry

Debit Bank Account (money in); Credit Sales Account (an income item)

Dr				Sales Account			Cr
Date	**Details**		**£ p**	**Date**	**Details**		**£ p**
2007				2007			
				02 Jul	Bank		12,000.00

transaction

3 July 2007: payment of wages £1,200 by cheque

double-entry

Debit Wages Account (an expense); Credit Bank Account (money paid out)

Dr				Wages Account			Cr
Date	**Details**		**£ p**	**Date**	**Details**		**£ p**
2007				2007			
03 Jul	Bank		1,200.00				

transaction

4 July 2007: purchase of goods for £3,000, paid for by cheque

double-entry

Debit Purchases Account (an expense); Credit Bank Account (money paid out)

Dr				Purchases Account			Cr
Date	**Details**		**£ p**	**Date**	**Details**		**£ p**
2007				2007			
04 Jul	Bank		3,000.00				

transaction

5 July 2007: received loan from D B Dore, £5,000, and paid cheque into bank

double-entry

Debit Bank Account (money in); Credit D B Dore Loan Account (a liability)

Dr				D B Dore Loan Account			Cr
Date	**Details**		**£ p**	**Date**	**Details**		**£ p**
2007				2007			
				05 Jul	Bank		5,000.00

transaction

6 July 2007: purchase of computer costing £4,000, paid for by cheque

double-entry

Debit Computer Account (asset acquired); Credit Bank Account (money paid out)

Dr			Computer Account			Cr
Date	**Details**	**£ p**	**Date**	**Details**		**£ p**
2007			2007			
06 Jul	Bank	4,000.00				

Note that the acquisition of a computer is the purchase of an item which will be retained in the business. It is therefore a fixed asset and will be recorded in a separate account, and not in Purchases Account, which is used solely for recording the purchase of goods which the business is going to sell – ie magic and joke products.

DOUBLE-ENTRY FOR CREDIT SALES AND CREDIT PURCHASES

So far in this chapter we have examined the treatment of double-entry transactions involving the bank account, and have used the bank account as a guide to working out which entry is a debit and which is a credit. In business many entries will involve the bank account, because cash, cheques and BACS are common methods of payment.

There will, however, be some transactions which do not involve the bank account. Purchases and sales on credit (ie where payment is made later) are the most common, and the double-entry rules for these follow the same logic: the book-keeper, on entering a credit purchase or credit sale, records the item in the sales account or purchases account as normal, but then records the second entry in the relevant account in the name of either the customer or the supplier, instead of in the bank account, because no money has yet changed hands. The entries (again ignoring any VAT) are therefore:

- credit sale   Debit   Customer's Account
                        Credit   Sales Account

- credit purchase   Credit   Supplier's Account
                        Debit   Purchases Account

Let us now take an example of a credit sale made by Harry Porter Limited, and payment received after thirty days. On 10 July 2007 Harry Porter Limited sells goods invoiced at £5,000 on credit to Owl Promotions. The ledger entries are: debit Owl Promotions' Account; credit Sales Account.

Dr   **Sales Account**   **Cr**

Date	Details	£	p	Date	Details	£	p
2007				2007			
				10 Jul	Owl Promotions	5,000.00	

Dr   **Owl Promotions**   **Cr**

Date	Details	£	p	Date	Details	£	p
2007				2007			
10 Jul	Sales	5,000.00					

On 10 October, thirty days after this sale has been made, Harry Porter Limited receives a cheque for £5,000 from Owl Promotions in settlement of the amount due; the cheque is paid into the bank. Harry Porter Limited's book-keeper will:

- debit Bank Account £5,000 (money received)

- credit the account of Owl Promotions £5,000

The accounts will appear as set out below. Note the existing entry from 10 July on the account of Owl Promotions.

Dr   **Bank Account**   **Cr**

Date	Details	£	p	Date	Details	£	p
2007				2007			
10 Oct	Owl Promotions	5,000.00					

Dr   **Owl Promotions**   **Cr**

Date	Details	£	p	Date	Details	£	p
2007				2007			
10 Jul	Sales	5,000.00		10 Oct	Bank	5,000.00	

double-entry and credit purchases

Credit purchases made by a business are recorded in a similar way. If Harry Porter Limited purchases £2,500 of goods from H A Gridd Supplies on 12 July, and is given 30 days in which to pay, the entries in the books will be:

- debit Purchases Account £2,500

- credit H A Gridd Supplies' Account £2,500

Dr				Purchases Account			Cr
Date	**Details**	**£**	**p**	**Date**	**Details**	**£**	**p**
2007				2007			
12 Jul	H A Gridd Supplies	2,500.00					

Dr				H A Gridd Supplies			Cr
Date	**Details**	**£**	**p**	**Date**	**Details**	**£**	**p**
2007				2007			
				12 Jul	Purchases	2,500.00	

Settlement of the invoice by Harry Porter Limited in thirty days' time will be recorded by the book-keeper with the following entries:

■ debit H A Gridd Supplies Account £2,500

■ credit Bank Account £2,500 (money paid out)

Dr				H A Gridd Supplies			Cr
Date	**Details**	**£**	**p**	**Date**	**Details**	**£**	**p**
2007				2007			
12 Oct	Bank	2,500.00		12 Jul	Purchases	2,500.00	

Dr				Bank Account			Cr
Date	**Details**	**£**	**p**	**Date**	**Details**	**£**	**p**
2007				2007			
				12 Oct	H A Gridd Supplies	2,500.00	

balancing off accounts

You will probably have noticed that in the above examples, the accounts of the customer (Owl Promotions) and the supplier (H A Gridd Supplies) have finished up with the same amounts on each side. In these cases, nothing is owing to Harry Porter Limited, or is owed by Harry Porter Limited.

In practice, as the business trades, there will be many entries on both sides of customer and supplier accounts. It is a useful exercise to balance off each account periodically, to see how much in total each customer owes, and how much is owed to each supplier of the business. This balancing off procedure is also applied to other accounts in the books of the business. A computer accounting system will, of course, do this balancing automatically.

- The accounting system of a business involves a number of stages:
  - financial transactions and the documents they generate
  - recording and listing of transactions ready for entering in the accounts
  - entering the data into the accounts of the business – either manual accounts or a computer accounting system
  - extracting report information from the accounts

- Double-entry book-keeping transactions involve two entries, a credit and a debit. Debits are recorded on the left-hand side of an account, credits on the right-hand side.

- The dual aspect theory of double-entry accounting states that one account gains value (the debit entry) while the other gives value (the credit entry).

- In practical terms, debit entries include:
  - money paid into the bank
  - an expense incurred or a purchase made
  - an acquisition of an asset or an increase in that asset
  - money owing by customers (debtors)

- In practical terms, credit entries include:
  - money paid out of the bank
  - income item
  - a liability incurred or increased
  - money owed to suppliers (creditors)

batch	a group of items totalled together for input into an accounting system
ledger	a section of the accounts of a business
trial balance	a list of the balances of accounts compiled to check the accuracy of the book-keeping
account activity	a list of the transactions on a particular account
aged debtors analysis	a list of credit customers showing what they owe and if payment is overdue
aged creditors analysis	a list of suppliers showing what they are owed and when payment is due
profit and loss statement	a financial statement showing the amount of profit or loss made by a business
balance sheet	a financial statement showing what a business owns and owes and how it is financed

STUDENT
ACTIVITIES

You are a trainee accountant in the firm of Arthur Andrews & Co. Your job is to assist with the accounts of start-up businesses, a number of which have no double-entry records. You are to carry out the following tasks.

14.1 Will Abbott has kept his bank account up-to-date, but has not got around to the other double-entry items. Rule out the other accounts for him, and make the appropriate entries.

Dr			Bank Account			Cr
20-7		£	20-7			£
1 Feb	Sales	5,000	1 Feb	Purchases		3,500
2 Feb	Sales	7,500	2 Feb	Wages		2,510
3 Feb	Bank Loan	12,500	3 Feb	Van purchase		12,500
5 Feb	Sales	9,300	3 Feb	Purchases		5,000
			4 Feb	Rent paid		780

14.2 Sarah Banks has opened up a health food shop 'Just Nuts', but has not yet started to write up the books. As she is inexperienced she asks you to set up an accounting system for her.

She provides you with the following list of transactions for the first week's trading, starting on Monday 8 June 20-7. You are to enter up the double-entry accounts for her.

Monday

Paid £ 5,000 cheque as capital into the bank; purchases of £4,000, paid by cheque.

Paid £750 sales into the bank; paid week's rent £75 by cheque.

Tuesday

Paid £500 sales into the bank; made purchases of £425 by cheque.

Wednesday

Paid £420 sales into the bank; bought computer £890 by cheque.

Thursday

Paid £550 sales into the bank; made purchases £510 by cheque.

Friday

Paid £925 sales into the bank; paid assistant's wages £75 by cheque.

14.3 Anu Sharma has made a mess of recording entries in the bank account. You are to set out the bank account as it should appear, rule up the other double-entry accounts and make the appropriate entries.

Dr			Bank Account			Cr
20-7		£	20-7			£
1 Jan	Purchases	1,000	2 Jan	Sales		5,000
5 Jan	Wages	2,700	3 Jan	Sales		7,000
5 Jan	Rent paid	150	4 Jan	Bank Loan		5,500
8 Jan	Rates paid	6,210	9 Jan	Machine purchased		4,000
9 Jan	Sales	5,205	10 Jan	Sales		9,520
10 Jan	Purchases	6,750	12 Jan	Wages		2,850
11 Jan	Car purchase	5,500	12 Jan	Rent paid		150

14.4 Sam McRae is a lazy individual and has not entered up his double-entry accounts. He has listed all his transactions, and mentions that all cheques are paid into the bank account on the day of receipt. You are to draw up the accounts for Sam McRae and make the necessary entries.

20-7	
1 March	Received £5,000 cheque as loan from brother
2 March	Bought goods £200; paid by cheque
3 March	Bought goods £1,200 on credit from H Lomax
4 March	Sold goods £800; cheque received
5 March	Sold goods £1,200 on credit to V Firth
6 March	Paid rent £955 by cheque
9 March	Bought cash register £1,200 on credit from Broadheath Business Supplies
10 March	Paid wages £780 by cheque
11 March	Bought goods on credit £5,920 from W Gould
12 March	V Firth pays for goods £1,200 by cheque
15 March	Bought goods £1,650 on credit from H Lomax
16 March	Made payment £750 by cheque to H Lomax

extended exercise

Interlingo Translation Services

exercise introduction

This is a 'standalone' extended exercise which puts into practice all the computer accounting skills you will have developed while working through this book.

It features a small company run by Jo Lane who has set up a translation bureau 'Interlingo' which sells language books and CDs as a sideline. Jo has been operating for a month using a manual book-keeping system and has then decided to set up the accounting records in a Sage system in the second month.

The activities to be covered are:

1   *Setting up the business in Sage.*

2   *Setting up customers and supplier records and inputting opening balances.*

3   *Setting up the Nominal Ledger in Sage and inputting opening balances from the Trial Balance produced at the end of the first month of trading.*

4   *Processing and printing service sales invoices and credit notes.*

5   *Processing purchase invoices and credit notes.*

6   *Processing payments received – including payments from credit customers, contra entry and cash payments from small translation jobs, and books and CDs over the counter.*

7   *Processing payments made to suppliers and for running expenses.*

8   *Setting up a Petty Cash Account and processing Petty Cash Payments.*

9   *Setting up recurring payments through the bank current account.*

10 *Printing month-end reports and extracting information from the computer accounting records for use in the business.*

11 *Dealing with security aspects – formulating a back up policy, setting up passwords and access rights.*

ACTIVITY 1 – SETTING UP THE BUSINESS IN SAGE

introduction

Interlingo Translation Services Limited is a small company business run by Jo Lane, a linguist who has worked as a translator with the European Commission in Brussels and has now settled back in her home town of Mereford. The business is very much a 'one person' business. Jo rents a small office in the town and does everything herself.

Interlingo Translation Services provides translation services and also sells books and CDs.

translation services

Larger clients, for example importers and exporters who need documents translated into English and sales literature translated into foreign languages are supplied by Jo on credit terms (ie they are invoiced and pay later).

Small local 'private' translating jobs which come about from local adverts are normally paid for on a cash basis (ie cash or cheque) and are not invoiced.

language books and CDs

Jo has found that selling language books and CDs is a useful sideline. They are all sold for cash, but are bought on credit from the publishers.

the accounting system

Interlingo Translation Services was set up on 2 July 2011. The business is registered for VAT and after a month of using a manual accounting system Jo has decided to transfer her accounts to Sage 50 software and sign up for a year's telephone technical support. Her main problem, common to so many small businesses, is that of time – finding time to process her accounts and to see how she is getting on in financial terms.

Jo has chosen Sage 50 because it will enable her to:

• process the invoices issued to business customers who are supplied on credit

• record the cash sales of books and CDs and small translation jobs

• pay the publishers of the books and CDs on the due date

• keep a record of money received and paid out

• print out reports which will tell her who has not paid on time

• print out reports which will tell her what she is spending

In short Jo hopes that Sage will help her save time (and money) in running her accounting system.

backups

Remember to backup your data after each inputting Task, just as Jo would.

task 1

Ensure that the computer is set up correctly. A Sage Rebuild may be necessary.

The financial year should be set to start in July 2011. This can be done in SETTINGS or as part of the Rebuild process.

As part of this process you should adopt the 'General Business: Standard Accounts' as the chart of accounts to be used.

task 2

Set up the details of the business in Sage. Company Preferences in SETTINGS can be used if you are not using the ActiveSetup Wizard.

■ Enter the address details: Interlingo Translation Services
14 Privet Road
Mereford
MR5 1HP

Tel: 01908 335876

Fax: 01908 335899

Email: mail@interlingo.co.uk

www.interlingo.co.uk

VAT Reg: 416 1385 51

■ Ensure that the non-VAT code in Parameters in Company Preferences (SETTINGS) is set at T9. Also check that the VAT Cash Accounting box is blank.

■ Set the program date to 31 July 2011 (SETTINGS).

ACTIVITY 2 – SETTING UP THE CUSTOMER AND SUPPLIER RECORDS

introduction

Interlingo Translation sells on credit to five businesses that use its translation services on a regular basis. Jo will have to set up the details of these customers on the computer.

The business also buys its books and CDs from two wholesale suppliers. These will also have to be input onto the computer.

task 1

The defaults for the customers, reached through SETTINGS, should be set up as follows:

Configuration Editor (Terms):

Payment due days	30 days
Terms	Payment 30 days of invoice

Customer Defaults:

VAT rate	17.5% standard rate (code T1)
Default nominal code	4000

task 2

Input the details and opening balance for each of the five customers through RECORD in CUSTOMERS. The opening balance in each case is the total of the invoice already issued and is a gross amount. You do not need to deal with VAT at this stage. Do not post these invoices as a separate batch.

The credit limits and 'Terms Agreed' will also need to be entered (in the Credit Control tab).

Account name	**RS Export Agency**
Account reference	RS001
Address	46 Chancery Street Mereford MR1 9FD
Contact name	Raspal Singh

Telephone 01908 564187, Fax 01908 564911
Email rsingh@zipnet.co.uk

Credit limit £1,000

Invoice reference 10010 for £850.00 issued on 06 07 11.

Account name	**Playgames PLC**
Account reference	PL001
Address	Consul House
	Viney Street
	Mereford
	MR2 6PL
Contact name	Jacquie Mills

Telephone 01908 749724, Fax 01908 749355
Email mail@playgames.com
www.playgames.com

Credit limit £1,000

Invoice reference 10011 for £795.00 issued on 12 07 11

Account name	**Rotherway Limited**
Account reference	RT001
Address	78 Sparkhouse Street
	Millway
	MY5 8HG
Contact name	Darsha Patel

Telephone 01987 875241, Fax 01987 875267
Email mail@rotherway.co.uk
www.rotherway.co.uk

Credit limit £2,000

Invoice reference 10012 for £1,210.00 issued on 17 07 11

Account name	**Hill & Dale & Co, Solicitors**
Account reference	HD001
Address	17 Berkeley Chambers
	Penrose Street
	Mereford
	MR2 6GF
Contact name	Helen Lexington

Telephone 01908 875432, Fax 01908 875444
Email hlex@hilldale.co.uk

Credit limit £1,000

Invoice reference 10013 for £345.00 issued on 19 07 11

Account name	**Schafeld Ltd**
Account reference	SC001
Address	86 Tanners Lane
	Millway
	MY7 5VB
Contact name	Hans Rautmann

Telephone 01987 619086, Fax 01987 619097
Email hrautmann@schafeld.com
www.schafeld.com
Credit limit £1,000

Invoice reference 10014 for £800.00 issued on 20 07 11

task 3

Print out a Day Books: Customer Invoices (Detailed) Report and check your printout against the printout on page 259. The batch total should be £4,000.

task 4

The SUPPLIER defaults (reached through SETTINGS) should be set up as follows:

VAT rate	17.5% standard rate (code T1)
Default nominal code	5000

task 5

Input the details and opening balance for the two suppliers of books and CDs through RECORD in SUPPLIERS. The credit limits and payment terms agreed will also need to be entered on the Credit Control screen. The 'Terms Agreed' box will also need to be ticked.

Account name	**TDI Wholesalers**
Account reference	TD001
Address	Markway Estate
	Nottingham
	NG1 7GH
Contact name	Ron Beasley

Telephone 0115 295992, Fax 0115 295976, Email sales@tdi.co.uk
www.tdi.co.uk

Credit limit granted £5,000, payment terms 30 days of invoice date

Invoice reference 2347 for £780.00 issued on 05 07 11.

TDI Wholesalers supply Jo with language CDs, which are standard-rated for VAT.

Account name	**Bardners Books**
Account reference	BB001
Address	Purbeck House
	College Street
	Cambridge
	CB3 8HP
Contact name	Sarah Rooney

Telephone 01223 400652, Fax 01223 400648
Email sales@bardners.co.uk
www.bardners.co.uk

Credit limit granted £2,000, payment terms 30 days of invoice date

Invoice reference 9422 for £420.00 issued on 06 07 11.

Bardners Books supply Jo with language books, which are zero-rated for VAT. This supplier account may therefore be set up with a default tax code of T0.

task 6

Print out a Day Books: Supplier Invoices (Detailed) Report and check your printout against the printout on page 259. The batch total should be £1,200.

task 7

Print out a Trial Balance Report from FINANCIALS to check the total of the Debtors Control Account (the total of the Customer invoices) and the Creditors Control Account (the total of the Supplier invoices). The report should appear as follows:

	Interlingo Translation Services		**Page:** 1
	Period Trial Balance		

To Period: Month 1, July 2011

N/C	Name	Debit	Credit
1100	Debtors Control Account	4,000.00	
2100	Creditors Control Account		1,200.00
9998	Suspense Account		2,800.00
	Totals:	4,000.00	4,000.00

End of Report

ACTIVITY 3 – SETTING UP THE NOMINAL LEDGER

introduction

Interlingo Translation Services has been set up in Sage with a default Chart of Accounts (nominal accounts list) which can be used as a structure for the nominal account balances which were outstanding at the end of July.

Jo has already set up a Trial Balance on a spreadsheet. The figures are shown below. The right-hand column shows the Nominal Account number which Jo has allocated to each account from the list of Nominal Accounts. The grey backgrounds show where the default account name needs changing.

	Dr	Cr	Account
	£	£	
Office computers	5000		0020
Office equipment	2500		0030
Furniture and fixtures	3000		0040
Debtors control account	4000		1100
Bank current account	7085		1200
Creditors control account		1200	2100
Sales tax control account		814	2200
Purchase tax control account	623		2201
Loans		5000	2300
Ordinary Shares		15000	3000
Translation services income		3660	4000
Sales of language books		456	4100
Sales of language CDs		950	4101
Purchases of books	300		5000
Purchases of CDs	750		5001
Advertising	550		6201
Gross wages	2000		7000
Rent	250		7100
General rates	129		7103
Electricity	61		7200
Postage & Carriage	86		7501
Telephone	275		7502
Office Stationery	471		7504
	27,080	27,080	

task 1

Ensure the program date is set at 31 July 2011.

Select the accounts that you wish to enter in the records from the NOMINAL opening screen. Use the account numbers in the right-hand column. Do not worry if the account names are different - they will be amended in Task 3. But do not select the Debtors Control Account or the Creditors Control Account as they should already show their balances.

Select RECORD from NOMINAL and enter the balance of each account from the Trial Balance, using the 31 July date. You may need to click on the Balance field or the O/B button to bring up the balance entry screen. Ensure that the amount is recorded in the correct debit or credit box.

task 2

Print out a Trial Balance as at 1 August 2011 from FINANCIALS.

task 3

Now change the account names that need changing (see the accounts with grey backgrounds on page 227) in RECORD in NOMINAL. Print out a further Trial Balance to check your corrections. The print out should appear as shown below. Check your input against this Report.

Interlingo Translation Services
Period Trial Balance

To Period: Month 2, August 2011

N/C	Name	Debit	Credit
0020	Office computers	5,000.00	
0030	Office Equipment	2,500.00	
0040	Furniture and Fixtures	3,000.00	
1100	Debtors Control Account	4,000.00	
1200	Bank Current Account	7,085.00	
2100	Creditors Control Account		1,200.00
2200	Sales Tax Control Account		814.00
2201	Purchase Tax Control Account	623.00	
2300	Loans		5,000.00
3000	Ordinary Shares		15,000.00
4000	Translation services income		3,660.00
4100	Sales of language books		456.00
4101	Sales of language CDs		950.00
5000	Purchases of books	300.00	
5001	Purchases of CDs	750.00	
6201	Advertising	550.00	
7000	Gross Wages	2,000.00	
7100	Rent	250.00	
7103	General Rates	129.00	
7200	Electricity	61.00	
7501	Postage and Carriage	86.00	
7502	Telephone	275.00	
7504	Office Stationery	471.00	
	Totals:	27,080.00	27,080.00

ACTIVITY 4 – ISSUING INVOICES AND CREDIT NOTES FOR TRANSLATIONS

introduction

It is 31 August and Jo has to process customer invoices and a credit note for work done during the month. She uses batch entry to enter the details into Sage 50.

task 1

Set the program date to 31 August 2011. Input the following invoices using the batch entry system.

invoice	account	date	net(£)	VAT(£)	description
10015	HD001	10 08 2011	520.00	91.00	Translation of sales contracts
10016	PL001	16 08 2011	120.00	21.00	Translation of sales literature
10017	RS001	20 08 2011	100.00	17.50	Translation of shipping docs
10018	RT001	20 08 2011	320.00	56.00	Translation of sales contracts
10019	SC001	22 08 2011	160.00	28.00	Translation of sales contracts

task 2

Hill & Dale & Co, who have passed substantial work to Interlingo, have written formally to ask for a 10% discount backdated to the beginning of the month..

Enter the following credit note to Hill & Dale & Co:

ref	account	date	net(£)	VAT(£)	description
501	HD001	31 08 2011	52.00	9.10	Refund of 10% discount, invoice 10015

task 3

Jo agreed that Rotherway Limited should be allowed 2.5% settlement discount for payment within 7 days, with effect from 22 August. She also agreed an increase in their credit limit to £3,000.

Amend the customer record then take and print a screenshot showing the new terms. Check it against the detail on page 261.

Now input the following invoice for Rotherway Limited.

invoice	account	date	net(£)	VAT(£)	description
10020	RT001	22 08 2011	1200.00	204.75	Translation of contract tender

Note: The VAT value is reduced because of the settlement discount offered. You will need to amend the VAT figure in Sage.

task 4

Print out detailed Day Books reports for the customer invoices and credit note entered. Check them against the those on page 262.

ACTIVITY 5 – PROCESSING PURCHASE INVOICES AND CREDIT NOTES

introduction

Jo's purchases on credit are her supplies of language CDs and books. During August she received two invoices in total. They are shown below and on the next page.

task 1

Set the program date to 31 August 2011.

Input the two invoices below and on the next page as a batch into Invoices in SUPPLIERS.

Note that the Nominal code for CDs is 5001 and for books is 5000.

task 2

Interlingo's customer RS Export Agency supplies delivery services for Interlingo and is therefore both a customer and a supplier. A supplier account should be set up (see page 223 for address details) using an appropriate account number and then the following supplier invoice details entered. The nominal code is 5100 (Carriage).

invoice	date	net(£)	VAT(£)	description
72/554	15 08 2011	100.00	17.50	Same day delivery to London

task 3

Print out a Day Books: Supplier Invoices (Detailed) and check your printout against the printout on page 263. The transaction dates are 15 August to 20 August. The total should be £1,622.75.

INVOICE

TDI Wholesalers

Markway Estate, Nottingham, NG1 7GH
Tel 0115 295992 Fax 0115 295976 www.TDI.co.uk

invoice to

Interlingo Translation Services
14 Privet Road
Mereford
MR5 1HP

invoice no	2561
account	3023
your reference	984
date/tax point	15 08 11

product code	description	quantity	price	unit	total	VAT	total
2421	Beginners French CDs	100	5.00	set	500.00	87.50	587.50
2634	Advanced Italian CDs	50	6.00	set	300.00	52.50	352.50

goods total	800.00
VAT	140.00
TOTAL	940.00

INVOICE

BARDNERS BOOKS

Purbeck House, College Street, Cambridge CB3 8HP
Tel 01223 400652 Fax 01223 400648 www.Bardners.co.uk

invoice to

Interlingo Translation Services	invoice no — 11231
14 Privet Road	account — IL9987
Mereford	your reference — 985
MR5 1HP	date/tax point — 20 08 11

product code	description	quantity	price	unit	total	VAT zero-rate	total
G778	German First Course	60	4.95	each	297.00	00.00	297.00
2634	French Second Course	45	5.95	each	267.75	00.00	267.75
					goods total		564.75
					VAT		00.00
					TOTAL		564.75

task 4

Jo discovers that ten of the sets of Beginners French CDs are faulty. She sends them back and asks for a credit note. This arrives on 31 August. Input the document (see below) into Credit in SUPPLIERS (Nominal Code 5001) and print out a Day Books: Suppliers Credits (Detailed) report. Check your printout against the printout on page 263.

credit note from TDI Wholesalers (extract)

Interlingo Translation Services	credit note no — 1919
14 Privet Road	account — 3023
Mereford	your reference — 984
MR5 1HP	date/tax point — 28 08 11

product code	description	quantity	price	unit	total	VAT	total
2421	Beginners French CDs	10	5.00	set	50.00	8.75	58.75
					goods total		50.00
					VAT		8.75
					TOTAL		58.75

REASON FOR CREDIT
Faulty CDs returned

ACTIVITY 6 – PROCESSING PAYMENTS RECEIVED

introduction

Jo has received payments from a number of different sources during August:

• payments from customers who have bought on credit during July

• cash payments for small translation jobs

• cash payments for books and CDs

They all have to be input into the computer accounting system.

task 1

Ensure the program date is set at 31 August 2011.

Input in BANK (Customer) the following payments received during August and paid into the bank current account on the dates indicated. The reference number is the paying-in slip number.

account	date	customer	amount (£)	reference
HD001	10 08 2011	Hill & Dale & Co	345.00	100110
PL001	17 08 2011	Playgames PLC	795.00	100112
RS001	24 08 2011	RS Export Agency	850.00	100114
RT001	24 08 2011	Rotherway Limited	1,210.00	100114
SC001	31 08 2011	Schafeld Ltd	800.00	100116
RT001	31 08 2011	Rotherway Limited	1,374.75*	100116
		Total	5,374.75	

*This pays invoice 10020 less settlement discount of £30.00.

task 2

Print out a Day Books: Customer Receipts (Summary) report for the month from BANK and check your printout against the printout on page 264.

task 3

Jo has also paid the takings from cash sales (ie from small translation jobs, books and CDs) into the bank current account each week. She has totalled up each week's takings from these three sources and paid them in on one paying-in slip each Friday (the reference is shown in the right-hand column). The manual records she has kept show the cash receipts as follows:

date paid in	description	net (£)	VAT (£)	gross (£)	reference
10 08 2011	Translations	96.00	16.80	112.80	100111
	CDs	240.00	42.00	282.00	
	Books	160.00	T0 code	160.00	
	Paying-in slip total			554.80	

date paid in	description	net (£)	VAT (£)	gross (£)	reference
17 08 2011	Translations	116.00	20.30	136.30	100113
	CDs	180.00	31.50	211.50	
	Books	107.00	T0 code	107.00	
	Paying-in slip total			454.80	
24 08 2011	Translations	104.00	18.20	122.20	100115
	CDs	220.00	38.50	258.50	
	Books	84.00	T0 code	84.00	
	Paying-in slip total			464.70	
31 08 2011	Translations	82.00	14.35	96.35	100117
	CDs	190.00	33.25	223.25	
	Books	113.00	T0 code	113.00	
	Paying-in slip total			432.60	
BATCH TOTALS		1,692.00	214.90	1,906.90	

Input each of these cash receipts in BANK as BANK RECEIPTS. Remember to use the correct Nominal Codes for each type of sale: 4000 for translations, 4100 for books, 4101 for CDs. The reference in the right-hand column is the paying-in slip reference and should be used for each line of input.

task 4

Print out a Day Books: Bank Receipts (Detailed) report for the month from BANK and check your printout against the printout on page 264.

task 5

Process a set off (contra entry) for the amount owed by RS Export Agency against the amount owed to RS Export Agency. Use the Contra Entries option in the Tools menu.

ACTIVITY 7 – PAYING SUPPLIERS AND EXPENSES

introduction

During August Jo has had to pay her suppliers (of books and CDs) who have invoiced her in July on 30 days terms. She has also had to pay a number of expenses.

task 1

Ensure the program date is set at 31 August 2011.

Input in BANK (Supplier) these two outstanding items which were paid on 6 August:

TDI Wholesalers	Invoice 2347	£780.00	Due 05 08 2011	Cheque 120006
Bardners Books	Invoice 9422	£420.00	Due 06 08 2011	Cheque 120007

If possible, print out remittance advices from the computer to accompany the cheques.

task 2

Print out a Day Books: Supplier Payments (Summary) report for 6 August from BANK and check your printout against the printout on page 265.

task 3

Input the following expense payments through Payment in BANK.

In most cases you will need to work out the nominal codes from the Trial Balance on page 228.

The cheque number should be used as the reference.

The tax code is T1 unless indicated otherwise.

date	cheque	details	net(£)	VAT(£)
07 08 2011	120009	Office furniture	140.00	24.50
08 08 2011	120010	Advertising	600.00	105.00
15 08 2011	120011	Rent	250.00	43.75
17 08 2011	120012	Stationery	126.00	22.05
20 08 2011	120013	Rates	129.00	T2
22 08 2011	120014	Telephone	186.00	32.55
24 08 2011	120015	Electricity	84.00	14.70
30 08 2011	120016	Postages	45.60	T2
31 08 2011	BACS	Salaries	2,240.00	T9
		Totals	3,800.60	242.55
				4,043.15

task 4

Print out a Day Books: Bank Payments (Detailed) report for 7 - 31 August from BANK and check your printout against the printout on page 265.

ACTIVITY 8 – SETTING UP A PETTY CASH SYSTEM

introduction

Jo finds that her temporary office assistant, Ella, often needs to make small payments in cash for items such as postage stamps and stationery for the office. She therefore decides to set up a petty cash system and cashes a cheque for £80 on 6 August to provide the funds.

task 1

Set the program date to 31 August 2011.

Process a Transfer in BANK for the £80 cheque (No. 120008) cashed on 6 August 2011. The accounts involved are Bank Current Account 1200 and Petty Cash Account 1230.

task 2

Input into BANK (Payments) Petty Cash Account the transactions represented by the four petty cash vouchers shown below and opposite.

Note that on one of them you will have to calculate the VAT on screen.

Postage stamps are VAT exempt (Tax code T2)

task 3

Print out a Day Books: Cash Payments (Detailed) report from BANK and check your printout against the printout on page 266. Remember to select Petty Cash Account on the Bank opening screen first.

The net total should be £72.00 and the VAT total £6.30.

petty cash voucher			Number *0001*
		date	*7 Aug 2011*
description			amount
		£	p
Copy paper		*16*	*00*
		16	*00*
	VAT	*2*	*80*
VAT receipt obtained		*18*	*80*
signature *Ella Smith*			
authorised *Jo Lane*			

petty cash voucher

Number *0002*

date *7 Aug 2011*

description		amount	
		£	p
Postage stamps		*24*	*00*
	VAT		
		24	*00*

signature *Ella Smith*

authorised *Jo Lane*

---

petty cash voucher

Number *0003*

date *15 Aug 2011*

description		amount	
		£	p
Box files		*23*	*50*
	VAT		
Receipt obtained (VAT not shown)		*23*	*50*

signature *Ella Smith*

authorised *Jo Lane*

note that the receipt in this case does not show the VAT that has been charged – it will have to be worked out on input

---

petty cash voucher

Number *0004*

date *22 Aug 2011*

description		amount	
		£	p
Postage stamps		*12*	*00*
	VAT		
		12	*00*

signature *Ella Smith*

authorised *Jo Lane*

ACTIVITY 9 – SETTING UP RECURRING PAYMENTS IN BANK

introduction

Jo has set up monthly standing order and direct debit payments through the bank current account. She can process these in Sage by setting up Recurring Payments in RECURRING in BANK. Click on the ADD button at the bottom of the screen to bring up the necessary window.

task 1

Set up a Recurring Payment for the following:

Bank Account	1200
Payment type	Direct Debit (Transaction ref: DD)
Payee	Suresafe Insurance (premises insurance)
Nominal code	7104
Tax code	T2
Amount	£98.50 per month
Frequency	12 monthly payments, starting 10 August 2011

task 2

Set up a Recurring Payment for the following:

Bank Account	1200
Payment type	Standing order (Transaction ref: STO)
Payee	Albion Bank (standing charge)
Nominal code	7901
Tax code	T2
Amount	£15.00 per month
Frequency	Monthly, until further notice, starting 25 August 2011

task 3

Set the program date to 31 August 2011 and process the Recurring Payments for August in BANK.

task 4

Print out a trial balance of the business as at 31 August 2011. It should agree with the Trial balance shown on the next page.

<h3 style="text-align:center">Interlingo Translation Services
Period Trial Balance</h3>

To Period: Month 2, August 2011

N/C	Name	Debit	Credit
0020	Office Computers	5,000.00	
0030	Office Equipment	2,500.00	
0040	Furniture and Fixtures	3,140.00	
1100	Debtors Control Account	1,254.90	
1200	Bank Current Account	8,930.00	
1230	Petty Cash	1.70	
2100	Creditors Control Account		1,446.00
2200	Sales Tax Control Account		1,438.05
2201	Purchase Tax Control Account	1,020.60	
2300	Loans		5,000.00
3000	Ordinary Shares		15,000.00
4000	Translation services income		6,426.00
4009	Discounts Allowed	30.00	
4100	Sales of language books		920.00
4101	Sales of language CDs		1,780.00
5000	Purchases of books	864.75	
5001	Purchases of CDs	1,500.00	
5100	Carriage	100.00	
6201	Advertising	1,150.00	
7000	Gross Wages	2,000.00	
7003	Staff Salaries	2,240.00	
7100	Rent	500.00	
7103	General Rates	258.00	
7104	Premises Insurance	98.50	
7200	Electricity	145.00	
7501	Postage and Carriage	167.60	
7502	Telephone	461.00	
7504	Office Stationery	633.00	
7901	Bank Charges	15.00	
	Totals:	32,010.05	32,010.05

Trial balance of Interlingo Translation Services as at 31 August 2011

ACTIVITY 10 – END-OF-MONTH PROCEDURES

introduction

At the end of August Jo is ready to print out her end-of-month reports.

task 1

Print out the following reports and write a brief explanation of their function and how they can help Jo in running the business:

■ the month-end Trial Balance (note that this is the Trial Balance printed in Activity 9, Task 4).

■ customer statements of account from Reports in CUSTOMERS

■ an Aged Debtors Analysis from Reports in CUSTOMERS (see page 267)

■ a Summary Audit Trail from Reports in FINANCIALS (see pages 268-269)

task 2

Jo remembers that she had negotiations over discounts with her account customer Rotherway Limited earlier in the month. Obtain a Customer Activity (Detailed) report (see page 270) and examine the Customer Record. Describe what has happened on the account and explain to Jo what the discount position is on this account.

task 3

Print out a Supplier Activity (Detailed) report for TDI Wholesalers (see page 270) and examine the Supplier Record. Describe what has happened on the account during the month and advise Jo what the amount of her next payment should be.

task 4

Jim Draxman, a friend of Jo, who is helping her with her marketing, asks her for a list of the names and addresses of her customers as soon as possible and send the data electronically by email (see page 271).

Produce a suitable list, either from Labels or from a Customer Address List Report (both accessible in CUSTOMERS) and send the data electronically by email.

ACTIVITY 11 – DEALING WITH SECURITY

introduction

At the end of August Jo is concerned that the security of her computer and the data kept on it is not as good as it could be. She takes measures to improve the safety of her machines and data.

task 1

Jo finds that her temporary assistant, Ella, has been looking at the computer accounting files which relate to business expenditure and to Wages in particular. Ella normally only deals with Customer files.

How can Jo prevent this happening in the future?

task 2

Jo sometimes gets in a muddle over her data backup disks for her computer accounting program and has on one occasion had to reinput data.

Recommend to Jo a back up system using disks which will prevent this happening in the future.

task 3

Jo has been talking to her solicitor customers Hill & Dale & Co. They have said in passing that they "presume she is complying with the terms of the Data Protection Act". She says that she is.

Describe the main purposes of this Act.

SAGE PRINTOUT CHECKLIST

The Sage printouts that follow are provided so that tutors and students carrying out the processing exercises and extended activities can periodically check their progress.

The page numbers for the relevant printouts can be found by referring to the index below.

book chapters

Chapter 4	243
Chapter 5	244
Chapter 6	244
Chapter 7	246
Chapter 8	247
Chapter 9	248
Chapter 10	250
Chapter 11	254
Chapter 12	255
Chapter 13	256

extended activity

Interlingo Translation Services

Activity 2	259
Activity 3	260
Activity 4	262
Activity 5	263
Activity 6	264
Activity 7	265
Activities 8,9,10	266

Chapter 4

Task 3

Pronto Supplies Limited

Day Books: Customer Invoices (Summary)

| Date From: | 01/01/1980 | | | | | Customer From: | | |
| Date To: | 31/12/2019 | | | | | Customer To: | ZZZZZZZZ | |

| Transaction From: | 1 |
| Transaction To: | 99,999,999 |

Tran No.	Items	Tp	Date	A/C Ref	Inv Ref	Details	Net Amount	Tax Amount	Gross Amount
1	1	SI	05/01/2011	JB001	10013	Opening Balance	5,500.00	0.00	5,500.00
3	1	SI	05/01/2011	CH001	10014	Opening Balance	2,400.00	0.00	2,400.00
4	1	SI	09/01/2011	CR001	10015	Opening Balance	3,234.00	0.00	3,234.00
5	1	SI	10/01/2011	DB001	10016	Opening Balance	3,400.00	0.00	3,400.00
6	1	SI	10/01/2011	KD001	10017	Opening Balance	6,500.00	0.00	6,500.00
7	1	SI	17/01/2011	LG001	10019	Opening Balance	8,500.00	0.00	8,500.00
						Totals:	29,534.00	0.00	29,534.00

Task 4

Pronto Supplies Limited

Day Books: Supplier Invoices (Summary)

| Date From: | 04/01/2011 | | | | | Supplier From: | | |
| Date To: | 09/01/2011 | | | | | Supplier To: | ZZZZZZZZ | |

| Transaction From: | 1 |
| Transaction To: | 99,999,999 |

Tran No.	Item	Type	Date	A/C Ref	Inv Ref	Details	Net Amount	Tax Amount	Gross Amount
2	1	PI	04/01/2011	DE001	4563	Opening Balance	5,750.00	0.00	5,750.00
8	1	PI	05/01/2011	EL001	8122	Opening Balance	8,500.00	0.00	8,500.00
9	1	PI	09/01/2011	MA001	9252	Opening Balance	4,500.00	0.00	4,500.00
						Totals	18,750.00	0.00	18,750.00

Task 5

Pronto Supplies Limited

Period Trial Balance

To Period: Month 1, January 2011

N/C	Name	Debit	Credit
1100	Debtors Control Account	29,534.00	
2100	Creditors Control Account		18,750.00
9998	Suspense Account		10,784.00
	Totals:	29,534.00	29,534.00

Chapter 5

Task 3

Pronto Supplies Limited
Period Trial Balance

To Period: Month 1, January 2011

N/C	Name	Debit	Credit
0020	Plant and Machinery	35,000.00	
0030	Office Equipment	15,000.00	
0040	Furniture and Fixtures	25,000.00	
1100	Debtors Control Account	29,534.00	
1200	Bank Current Account	14,656.00	
2100	Creditors Control Account		18,750.00
2200	Sales Tax Control Account		17,920.00
2201	Purchase Tax Control Account	26,600.00	
2300	Loans		35,000.00
3000	Ordinary Shares		75,000.00
4000	Sales Type A		85,000.00
4001	Sales Type B		15,000.00
4002	Sales Type C		2,400.00
5000	Materials Purchased	69,100.00	
6201	Advertising	12,400.00	
7000	Gross Wages	16,230.00	
7100	Rent	4,500.00	
7103	General Rates	450.00	
7200	Electricity	150.00	
7502	Telephone	275.00	
7504	Office Stationery	175.00	
	Totals:	249,070.00	249,070.00

Chapter 6

Task 3

Pronto Supplies Limited
Day Books: Customer Invoices (Detailed)

Time: 15:51:56

Date From:	12/02/2011		Customer From:	
Date To:	16/02/2011		Customer To:	ZZZZZZZZ
Transaction From:	1		N/C From:	
Transaction To:	99,999,999		N/C To:	99999999
Dept From:	0			
Dept To:	999			

Tran No.	Type	Date	A/C Ref	N/C	Inv Ref	Dept.	Details	Net Amount	Tax Amount	T/C	Gross Amount	V	B
54	SI	12/02/2011	JB001	4002	10027	1	2 hrs consultancy	120.00	21.00	T1	141.00	N	-
55	SI	13/02/2011	DB001	4000	10028	1	1 x EF102 Printer	600.00	105.00	T1	705.00	N	-
56	SI	16/02/2011	LG001	4000	10029	1	2 x Zap drive	180.00	31.50	T1	211.50	N	-
57	SI	16/02/2011	KD001	4001	10030	1	1 x Fileperfect software	264.00	46.20	T1	310.20	N	-
58	SI	16/02/2011	CH001	4000	10031	1	1 x 15" monitor	320.00	56.00	T1	376.00	N	-
							Totals:	1,484.00	259.70		1,743.70		

Task 4

Pronto Supplies Limited

Day Books: Customer Credits (Detailed)

Date From: 12/02/2011
Date To: 13/02/2011
Transaction From: 1
Transaction To: 99,999,999
Dept From: 0
Dept To: 999

Customer From:
Customer To: ZZZZZZZZ
N/C From:
N/C To: 99999999

Tran No.	Type	Date	A/C Ref	N/C	Inv Ref	Dept.	Details	Net Amount	Tax Amount	T/C	Gross Amount	V	B
59	SC	12/02/2011	KD001	4000	553	1	1 Printer lead	16.00	2.80	T1	18.80	N	-
60	SC	13/02/2011	CR001	4000	554	1	Zap disks (hardware)	20.00	3.50	T1	23.50	N	-
							Totals:	36.00	6.30		42.30		

Task 4

Pronto Supplies Limited

Period Trial Balance

To Period: Month 2, February 2011

N/C	Name	Debit	Credit
0020	Plant and Machinery	35,000.00	
0030	Office Equipment	15,000.00	
0040	Furniture and Fixtures	25,000.00	
1100	Debtors Control Account	31,700.70	
1200	Bank Current Account	14,656.00	
2100	Creditors Control Account		18,750.00
2200	Sales Tax Control Account		18,242.70
2201	Purchase Tax Control Account	26,600.00	
2300	Loans		35,000.00
3000	Ordinary Shares		75,000.00
4000	Computer hardware sales		86,440.00
4001	Computer software sales		15,164.00
4002	Computer consultancy		2,640.00
5000	Materials Purchased	69,100.00	
6201	Advertising	12,400.00	
7000	Gross Wages	16,230.00	
7100	Rent	4,500.00	
7103	General Rates	450.00	
7200	Electricity	150.00	
7502	Telephone	275.00	
7504	Office Stationery	175.00	
	Totals:	251,236.70	251,236.70

Chapter 7

Task 3

Pronto Supplies Limited

Day Books: Supplier Invoices (Detailed)

Date From:	14/02/2011				Supplier From:		
Date To:	14/02/2011				Supplier To:	ZZZZZZZZ	
Transaction From:	1				N/C From:		
Transaction To:	99,999,999				N/C To:	99999999	
Dept From:	0						
Dept To:	999						

Tran No.	Type	Date	A/C Ref	N/C	Inv Ref	Dept	Details	Net Amount	Tax Amount	T/C	Gross Amount	V	B
66	PI	14/02/2011	DE001	0030	11377	2	Desktop computer	400.00	70.00	T1	470.00	N	-
67	PI	14/02/2011	EL001	0030	8603	2	Laser Printer	360.00	63.00	T1	423.00	N	-
							Totals	760.00	133.00		893.00		

Pronto Supplies Limited

Period Trial Balance

To Period: Month 2, February 2011

N/C	Name	Debit	Credit
0020	Plant and Machinery	35,000.00	
0030	Office Equipment	15,760.00	
0040	Furniture and Fixtures	25,000.00	
1100	Debtors Control Account	31,700.70	
1200	Bank Current Account	14,656.00	
2100	Creditors Control Account		29,938.35
2200	Sales Tax Control Account		18,242.70
2201	Purchase Tax Control Account	28,266.35	
2300	Loans		35,000.00
3000	Ordinary Shares		75,000.00
4000	Computer hardware sales		86,440.00
4001	Computer software sales		15,164.00
4002	Computer consultancy		2,640.00
5000	Materials Purchased	77,862.00	
6201	Advertising	12,400.00	
7000	Gross Wages	16,230.00	
7100	Rent	4,500.00	
7103	General Rates	450.00	
7200	Electricity	150.00	
7502	Telephone	275.00	
7504	Office Stationery	175.00	
	Totals:	262,425.05	262,425.05

Chapter 8

Task 1

Pronto Supplies Limited

Day Books: Customer Receipts (Summary)

Date From:	28/02/2011								**Bank From:**	1200
DateTo:	28/02/2011								**Bank To:**	1200

Transaction From:	1					Customer From :	
Transaction To:	99,999,999					Customer To:	ZZZZZZZZ

Bank	1200			**Currency**	Pound Sterling							
No	**Type**	**Date**	**Account**	**Ref**	**Details**	**Net £**		**Tax £**		**Gross £ B**		**Bank Rec. Date**
70	SR	28/02/2011	JB001	cheque	Sales Receipt	5,500.00		0.00		5,500.00 N		
71	SR	28/02/2011	CH001	cheque	Sales Receipt	2,418.80		0.00		2,418.80 N		
72	SR	28/02/2011	CR001	BACS	Sales Receipt	3,234.00		0.00		3,234.00 N		
73	SR	28/02/2011	DB001	cheque	Sales Receipt	3,165.00		0.00		3,165.00 N		
74	SR	28/02/2011	KD001	BACS	Sales Receipt	6,500.00		0.00		6,500.00 N		
75	SR	28/02/2011	LG001	BACS	Sales Receipt	8,500.00		0.00		8,500.00 N		
					Totals £	29,317.80		0.00		29,317.80		

Task 2

Pronto Supplies Limited

Day Books: Supplier Payments (Summary)

Date From:	28/02/2011								**Bank From:**	1200
DateTo:	28/02/2011								**Bank To:**	1200

Transaction From:	1					Supplier From:	
Transaction To:	99,999,999					Supplier To:	ZZZZZZZZ

Bank	1200			**Currency**	Pound Sterling							
No	**Type**	**Date**	**Supplier**	**Ref**	**Details**	**Net £**		**Tax £**		**Gross £ B**		**Bank Rec. Date**
76	PP	28/02/2011	DE001	BACS	Purchase Payment	5,186.00		0.00		5,186.00 N		
77	PP	28/02/2011	EL001	BACS	Purchase Payment	8,500.00		0.00		8,500.00 N		
78	PP	28/02/2011	MA001	BACS	Purchase Payment	4,455.35		0.00		4,455.35 N		
					Totals £	18,141.35		0.00		18,141.35		

Task 3

Pronto Supplies Limited

Period Trial Balance

To Period: Month 2, February 2011

N/C	Name	Debit	Credit
0020	Plant and Machinery	35,000.00	
0030	Office Equipment	15,760.00	
0040	Furniture and Fixtures	25,000.00	
1100	Debtors Control Account	2,382.90	
1200	Bank Current Account	25,832.45	
2100	Creditors Control Account		11,797.00
2200	Sales Tax Control Account		18,242.70
2201	Purchase Tax Control Account	28,266.35	
2300	Loans		35,000.00
3000	Ordinary Shares		75,000.00
4000	Computer hardware sales		86,440.00
4001	Computer software sales		15,164.00
4002	Computer consultancy		2,640.00
5000	Materials Purchased	77,862.00	
6201	Advertising	12,400.00	
7000	Gross Wages	16,230.00	
7100	Rent	4,500.00	
7103	General Rates	450.00	
7200	Electricity	150.00	
7502	Telephone	275.00	
7504	Office Stationery	175.00	
	Totals:	244,283.70	244,283.70

Chapter 9

Task 1

Pronto Supplies Limited   Page: 1

Day Books: Bank Receipts (Detailed)

| Date From: | 09/02/2011 | | | | Bank From: | 1200 |
| DateTo: | 23/02/2011 | | | | Bank To: | 1200 |

| Transaction From: | 1 | | | N/C From: | |
| Transaction To: | 99,999,999 | | | N/C To: | 99999999 |

| Dept From: | 0 |
| Dept To: | 999 |

Bank: 1200   **Currency:** Pound Sterling

No	Type	N/C	Date	Ref	Details	Dept	Net £	Tax £ T/C	Gross £ V B	Bank Rec. Date
79	BR	4000	09/02/2011	10736	Hardware sales	1	12,500.00	2,187.50 T1	14,687.50 N N	
80	BR	4001	09/02/2011	10737	Software sales	1	4,680.00	819.00 T1	5,499.00 N N	
81	BR	4000	16/02/2011	10738	Hardware sales	1	15,840.00	2,772.00 T1	18,612.00 N N	
82	BR	4001	16/02/2011	10739	Software sales	1	3,680.00	644.00 T1	4,324.00 N N	
83	BR	4000	23/02/2011	10740	Hardware sales	1	17,800.00	3,115.00 T1	20,915.00 N N	
84	BR	4001	23/02/2011	10741	Software sales	1	4,800.00	840.00 T1	5,640.00 N N	
						Totals £	59,300.00	10,377.50	69,677.50	

Task 2

Pronto Supplies Limited

Day Books: Bank Payments (Detailed)

Date From:		12/02/2011								Bank From:	1200	
DateTo:		28/02/2011								Bank To:	1200	
Transaction From:		1								N/C From:		
Transaction To:		99,999,999								N/C To:	99999999	
Dept From:		0										
Dept To:		999										

Bank: 1200   **Currency:** Pound Sterling

No	Type	N/C	Date	Ref	Details	Dept	Net £	Tax £ T/C	Gross £ V B	Bank Re Date
85	BP	5000	12/02/2011	122992	Cash purchases	2	15,500.00	2,712.50 T1	18,212.50 N N	
86	BP	6201	14/02/2011	122993	Advertising	2	10,200.00	1,785.00 T1	11,985.00 N N	
87	BP	0040	15/02/2011	122994	Furniture	2	5,000.00	875.00 T1	5,875.00 N N	
88	BP	7200	23/02/2011	122995	Electricity	2	158.00	27.65 T1	185.65 N N	
89	BP	7502	26/02/2011	122996	Telephone	2	310.00	54.25 T1	364.25 N N	
90	BP	7504	26/02/2011	122997	Stationery	2	340.00	59.50 T1	399.50 N N	
91	BP	7000	28/02/2011	BACS	Wages	2	16,780.00	0.00 T9	16,780.00 - N	
						Totals £	48,288.00	5,513.90	53,801.90	

Task 4

Date:	29/04/2010	**Pronto Supplies Limited**	**Page:**	1
Time:	17:29:08	**Period Trial Balance**		

To Period: Month 2, February 2011

N/C	Name	Debit	Credit
0020	Plant and Machinery	35,000.00	
0030	Office Equipment	19,760.00	
0040	Furniture and Fixtures	30,000.00	
1100	Debtors Control Account	2,382.90	
1200	Bank Current Account	42,008.05	
2100	Creditors Control Account		11,797.00
2200	Sales Tax Control Account		28,620.20
2201	Purchase Tax Control Account	34,480.25	
2300	Loans		35,000.00
3000	Ordinary Shares		80,000.00
4000	Computer hardware sales		132,580.00
4001	Computer software sales		28,324.00
4002	Computer consultancy		2,640.00
5000	Materials Purchased	93,362.00	
6201	Advertising	22,600.00	
7000	Gross Wages	33,010.00	
7100	Rent	4,500.00	
7103	General Rates	450.00	
7200	Electricity	308.00	
7502	Telephone	585.00	
7504	Office Stationery	515.00	
	Totals:	318,961.20	318,961.20

Chapter 10

Task 2

Pronto Supplies Limited

Day Books: Cash Payments (Detailed)

| Date From: | 01/02/2011 | | | | | | Bank From: | 1230 |
| Date To: | 28/02/2011 | | | | | | Bank To: | 1230 |

| Transaction From: | 1 | | | N/C From: | |
| Transaction To: | 99,999,999 | | | N/C To: | 99999999 |

| Dept From: | 0 |
| Dept To: | 999 |

Bank: 1230   **Currency:** Pound Sterling

No	Type	N/C	Date	Ref	Details	Dept	Net £	Tax £	T/C	Gross £	V	B
96	CP	7504	07/02/2011	PC101	Copy paper	2	36.00	6.30	T1	42.30	N	N
97	CP	7501	14/02/2011	PC102	Postage stamps	2	25.00	0.00	T2	25.00	N	N
98	CP	7504	20/02/2011	PC103	Envelopes	2	16.00	2.80	T1	18.80	N	N
99	CP	7501	28/02/2011	PC104	Postage stamps	2	5.00	0.00	T2	5.00	N	N
100	CP	5003	28/02/2011	PC105	Packing tape	2	4.00	0.70	T1	4.70	N	N
						Totals £	86.00	9.80		95.80		

Task 3

Pronto Supplies Limited

Day Books: Cash Receipts (Detailed)

| Date From: | 26/02/2011 | | | | | | Bank From: | 1235 |
| Date To: | 28/02/2011 | | | | | | Bank To: | 1235 |

| Transaction From: | 1 | | | N/C From: | |
| Transaction To: | 99,999,999 | | | N/C To: | 99999999 |

| Dept From: | 0 |
| Dept To: | 999 |

Bank: 1235   **Currency:** Pound Sterling

No	Type	N/C	Date	Ref	Details	Dept	Net £	Tax £	T/C	Gross £	V	B
101	CR	4000	26/02/2011	10743	Hardware sales	1	5,000.00	875.00	T1	5,875.00	N	N
102	CR	4001	26/02/2011	10743	Software sales	1	480.00	84.00	T1	564.00	N	N
103	CR	4000	27/02/2011	10744	Hardware sales	1	1,200.00	210.00	T1	1,410.00	N	N
104	CR	4001	27/02/2011	10744	Software sales	1	890.00	155.75	T1	1,045.75	N	N
105	CR	4000	28/02/2011	10745	Hardware sales	1	600.00	105.00	T1	705.00	N	N
106	CR	4001	28/02/2011	10745	Software sales	1	120.00	21.00	T1	141.00	N	N
						Totals £	8,290.00	1,450.75		9,740.75		

Task 5 (a)

| Date: | 06/05/2010 | | **Pronto Supplies Limited** | | Page: | 1 |
| Time: | 11:17:37 | | **Audit Trail (Summary)** | | | |

| Date From: | 01/01/1980 | Customer From: | |
| Date To: | 31/12/2019 | Customer To: | ZZZZZZZZ |

| Transaction From: | 1 | Supplier From: | |
| Transaction To: | 99,999,999 | Supplier To: | ZZZZZZZZ |

| Dept From: | 0 | N/C From: | |
| Dept To: | 999 | N/C To: | 99999999 |

Exclude Deleted Tran: No

No	Type	Date	A/C	N/C	Dept	Ref	Details	Net	Tax	T/C	Pd	Paid	V	B	Bank Rec. Date
1	SI	05/01/2011	JB001	9998	0	10013	Opening Balance	5,500.00	0.00	T9	Y	5,500.00	-	-	
2	PI	04/01/2011	DE001	9998	0	4563	Opening Balance	5,750.00	0.00	T9	Y	5,750.00	-	-	
3	SI	05/01/2011	CH001	9998	0	10014	Opening Balance	2,400.00	0.00	T9	Y	2,400.00	-	-	
4	SI	09/01/2011	CR001	9998	0	10015	Opening Balance	3,234.00	0.00	T9	Y	3,234.00	-	-	
5	SI	10/01/2011	DB001	9998	0	10016	Opening Balance	3,400.00	0.00	T9	Y	3,400.00	-	-	
6	SI	10/01/2011	KD001	9998	0	10017	Opening Balance	6,500.00	0.00	T9	Y	6,500.00	-	-	
7	SI	17/01/2011	LG001	9998	0	10019	Opening Balance	8,500.00	0.00	T9	Y	8,500.00	-	-	
8	PI	05/01/2011	EL001	9998	0	8122	Opening Balance	8,500.00	0.00	T9	Y	8,500.00	-	-	
9	PI	09/01/2011	MA001	9998	0	9252	Opening Balance	4,500.00	0.00	T9	Y	4,500.00	-	-	
10	JD	31/01/2011	0020	0020	0	O/Bal	Opening Balance	35,000.00	0.00	T9	Y	35,000.00	-	-	
11	JC	31/01/2011	9998	9998	0	O/Bal	Opening Balance	35,000.00	0.00	T9	Y	35,000.00	-	-	
12	JD	31/01/2011	0030	0030	0	O/Bal	Opening Balance	15,000.00	0.00	T9	Y	15,000.00	-	-	
13	JC	31/01/2011	9998	9998	0	O/Bal	Opening Balance	15,000.00	0.00	T9	Y	15,000.00	-	-	
14	JD	31/01/2011	0040	0040	0	O/Bal	Opening Balance	25,000.00	0.00	T9	Y	25,000.00	-	-	
15	JC	31/01/2011	9998	9998	0	O/Bal	Opening Balance	25,000.00	0.00	T9	Y	25,000.00	-	-	
16	JD	31/01/2011	1200	1200	0	O/Bal	Opening Balance	14,656.00	0.00	T9	Y	14,656.00	-	-	15/04/2010
17	JC	31/01/2011	9998	9998	0	O/Bal	Opening Balance	14,656.00	0.00	T9	Y	14,656.00	-	-	
18	JC	31/01/2011	2200	2200	0	O/Bal	Opening Balance	17,920.00	0.00	T9	Y	17,920.00	-	-	
19	JD	31/01/2011	9998	9998	0	O/Bal	Opening Balance	17,920.00	0.00	T9	Y	17,920.00	-	-	
20	JD	31/01/2011	2201	2201	0	O/Bal	Opening Balance	26,600.00	0.00	T9	Y	26,600.00	-	-	
21	JC	31/01/2011	9998	9998	0	O/Bal	Opening Balance	26,600.00	0.00	T9	Y	26,600.00	-	-	
22	JC	31/01/2011	2300	2300	0	O/Bal	Opening Balance	35,000.00	0.00	T9	Y	35,000.00	-	-	
23	JD	31/01/2011	9998	9998	0	O/Bal	Opening Balance	35,000.00	0.00	T9	Y	35,000.00	-	-	
24	JC	31/01/2011	3000	3000	0	O/Bal	Opening Balance	75,000.00	0.00	T9	Y	75,000.00	-	-	
25	JD	31/01/2011	9998	9998	0	O/Bal	Opening Balance	75,000.00	0.00	T9	Y	75,000.00	-	-	
26	JC	31/01/2011	4000	4000	0	O/Bal	Opening Balance	85,000.00	0.00	T9	Y	85,000.00	-	-	
27	JD	31/01/2011	9998	9998	0	O/Bal	Opening Balance	85,000.00	0.00	T9	Y	85,000.00	-	-	
28	JC	31/01/2011	4001	4001	0	O/Bal	Opening Balance	15,000.00	0.00	T9	Y	15,000.00	-	-	
29	JD	31/01/2011	9998	9998	0	O/Bal	Opening Balance	15,000.00	0.00	T9	Y	15,000.00	-	-	
30	JC	31/01/2011	4002	4002	0	O/Bal	Opening Balance	2,400.00	0.00	T9	Y	2,400.00	-	-	
31	JD	31/01/2011	9998	9998	0	O/Bal	Opening Balance	2,400.00	0.00	T9	Y	2,400.00	-	-	
32	JD	31/01/2011	5000	5000	0	O/Bal	Opening Balance	69,100.00	0.00	T9	Y	69,100.00	-	-	
33	JC	31/01/2011	9998	9998	0	O/Bal	Opening Balance	69,100.00	0.00	T9	Y	69,100.00	-	-	
34	JD	31/01/2011	6201	6201	0	O/Bal	Opening Balance	12,400.00	0.00	T9	Y	12,400.00	-	-	
35	JC	31/01/2011	9998	9998	0	O/Bal	Opening Balance	12,400.00	0.00	T9	Y	12,400.00	-	-	
36	JD	31/01/2011	7000	7000	0	O/Bal	Opening Balance	16,230.00	0.00	T9	Y	16,230.00	-	-	
37	JC	31/01/2011	9998	9998	0	O/Bal	Opening Balance	16,230.00	0.00	T9	Y	16,230.00	-	-	
38	JD	31/01/2011	7100	7100	0	O/Bal	Opening Balance	4,500.00	0.00	T9	Y	4,500.00	-	-	
39	JC	31/01/2011	9998	9998	0	O/Bal	Opening Balance	4,500.00	0.00	T9	Y	4,500.00	-	-	
40	JD	31/01/2011	7103	7103	0	O/Bal	Opening Balance	450.00	0.00	T9	Y	450.00	-	-	
41	JC	31/01/2011	9998	9998	0	O/Bal	Opening Balance	450.00	0.00	T9	Y	450.00	-	-	
42	JD	31/01/2011	7200	7200	0	O/Bal	Opening Balance	150.00	0.00	T9	Y	150.00	-	-	
43	JC	31/01/2011	9998	9998	0	O/Bal	Opening Balance	150.00	0.00	T9	Y	150.00	-	-	
44	JD	31/01/2011	7502	7502	0	O/Bal	Opening Balance	275.00	0.00	T9	Y	275.00	-	-	
45	JC	31/01/2011	9998	9998	0	O/Bal	Opening Balance	275.00	0.00	T9	Y	275.00	-	-	
46	JD	31/01/2011	7504	7504	0	O/Bal	Opening Balance	175.00	0.00	T9	Y	175.00	-	-	
47	JC	31/01/2011	9998	9998	0	O/Bal	Opening Balance	175.00	0.00	T9	Y	175.00	-	-	
48	SI	05/02/2011	JB001	4000	1	10023	1 x 17" monitor	400.00	70.00	T1	N	0.00	N	-	
49	SI	06/02/2011	CH001	4000	1	10024	1 x printer lead	16.00	2.80	T1	N	18.80	N	-	
50	SI	06/02/2011	CR001	4001	1	10025	1 x Macroworx	100.00	17.50	T1	N	0.00	N	-	
51	SI	08/02/2011	KD001	4002	1	10026	2 hrs consultancy	120.00	21.00	T1	N	0.00	N	-	
52	SC	06/02/2011	DB001	4001	1	551	Software returned	200.00	35.00	T1	Y	235.00	N	-	
53	SC	06/02/2011	LG001	4000	1	552	Disks returned (hardware)	40.00	7.00	T1	N	0.00	N	-	
54	SI	12/02/2011	JB001	4002	1	10027	2 hrs consultancy	120.00	21.00	T1	N	0.00	N	-	
55	SI	13/02/2011	DB001	4000	1	10028	1 x EF102 Printer	600.00	105.00	T1	N	0.00	N	-	
56	SI	16/02/2011	LG001	4000	1	10029	2 x Zap drive	180.00	31.50	T1	N	0.00	N	-	
57	SI	16/02/2011	KD001	4001	1	10030	1 x Fileperfect software	264.00	46.20	T1	N	0.00	N	-	
58	SI	16/02/2011	CH001	4000	1	10031	1 x 15" monitor	320.00	56.00	T1	N	0.00	N	-	
59	SC	12/02/2011	KD001	4000	1	553	1 Printer lead	16.00	2.80	T1	N	0.00	N	-	
60	SC	13/02/2011	CR001	4000	1	554	Zap disks (hardware)	20.00	3.50	T1	N	0.00	N	-	
61	PI	09/02/2011	DE001	5000	2	11365	Desktop computers	3,600.00	630.00	T1	N	0.00	N	-	
62	PI	09/02/2011	EL001	5000	2	8576	Peripherals	2,000.00	350.00	T1	N	0.00	N	-	

Task 5 (a) continued

Date: 06/05/2010
Time: 11:17:37

Pronto Supplies Limited
Audit Trail (Summary)

No	Type	Date	A/C	N/C	Dept	Ref	Details	Net	Tax	T/C	Pd	Paid	V	B	Bank Rec. Date
63	PI	12/02/2011	MA001	5000	2	2947	Powerbooks	3,680.00	644.00	T1	N	0.00	N	-	
64	PC	06/02/2011	DE001	5000	2	7223	1 x Computer	480.00	84.00	T1	Y	564.00	N	-	
65	PC	08/02/2011	MA001	5000	2	552	1 x optical mouse	38.00	6.65	T1	Y	44.65	N	-	
66	PI	14/02/2011	DE001	0030	2	11377	Desktop computer	400.00	70.00	T1	N	0.00	N	-	
67	PI	14/02/2011	EL001	0030	2	8603	Laser Printer	360.00	63.00	T1	N	0.00	N	-	
68	PI	14/02/2011	DE001	5000	2	11377	Deleted - see tran 66	400.00	70.00	T1	N	0.00	-	-	
69	PI	14/02/2011	EL001	5000	2	8603	Deleted - see tran 67	360.00	63.00	T1	N	0.00	-	-	
70	SR	28/02/2011	JB001	1200	0	cheque	Sales Receipt	5,500.00	0.00	T9	Y	5,500.00	-	N	
71	SR	28/02/2011	CH001	1200	0	cheque	Sales Receipt	2,418.80	0.00	T9	Y	2,418.80	-	N	
72	SR	28/02/2011	CR001	1200	0	BACS	Sales Receipt	3,234.00	0.00	T9	Y	3,234.00	-	N	
73	SR	28/02/2011	DB001	1200	0	cheque	Sales Receipt	3,165.00	0.00	T9	Y	3,165.00	-	N	
74	SR	28/02/2011	KD001	1200	0	BACS	Sales Receipt	6,500.00	0.00	T9	Y	6,500.00	-	N	
75	SR	28/02/2011	LG001	1200	0	BACS	Sales Receipt	8,500.00	0.00	T9	Y	8,500.00	-	N	
76	PP	28/02/2011	DE001	1200	0	BACS	Purchase Payment	5,186.00	0.00	T9	Y	5,186.00	-	N	
77	PP	28/02/2011	EL001	1200	0	BACS	Purchase Payment	8,500.00	0.00	T9	Y	8,500.00	-	N	
78	PP	28/02/2011	MA001	1200	0	BACS	Purchase Payment	4,455.35	0.00	T9	Y	4,455.35	-	N	
79	BR	09/02/2011	1200	4000	1	10736	Hardware sales	12,500.00	2,187.50	T1	Y	14,687.50	N	N	
80	BR	09/02/2011	1200	4001	1	10737	Software sales	4,680.00	819.00	T1	Y	5,499.00	N	N	
81	BR	16/02/2011	1200	4000	1	10738	Hardware sales	15,840.00	2,772.00	T1	Y	18,612.00	N	N	
82	BR	16/02/2011	1200	4001	1	10739	Software sales	3,680.00	644.00	T1	Y	4,324.00	N	N	
83	BR	23/02/2011	1200	4000	1	10740	Hardware sales	17,800.00	3,115.00	T1	Y	20,915.00	N	N	
84	BR	23/02/2011	1200	4001	1	10741	Software sales	4,800.00	840.00	T1	Y	5,640.00	N	N	
85	BP	12/02/2011	1200	5000	2	122992	Cash purchases	15,500.00	2,712.50	T1	Y	18,212.50	N	N	
86	BP	14/02/2011	1200	6201	2	122993	Advertising	10,200.00	1,785.00	T1	Y	11,985.00	N	N	
87	BP	15/02/2011	1200	0040	2	122994	Furniture	5,000.00	875.00	T1	Y	5,875.00	N	N	
88	BP	23/02/2011	1200	7200	2	122995	Electricity	158.00	27.65	T1	Y	185.65	N	N	
89	BP	26/02/2011	1200	7502	2	122996	Telephone	310.00	54.25	T1	Y	364.25	N	N	
90	BP	26/02/2011	1200	7504	2	122997	Stationery	340.00	59.50	T1	Y	399.50	N	N	
91	BP	28/02/2011	1200	7000	2	BACS	Wages	16,780.00	0.00	T9	Y	16,780.00	-	N	
92	BR	28/02/2011	1200	3000	1	10742	Share capital	5,000.00	0.00	T9	Y	5,000.00	-	N	
93	BP	28/02/2011	1200	0030	2	122998	Colour printer	4,000.00	700.00	T1	Y	4,700.00	N	N	
94	JC	01/02/2011	1200	1200	0	122991	From bank to petty cash	100.00	0.00	T9	Y	100.00	-	N	
95	JD	01/02/2011	1230	1230	0	122991	From bank to petty cash	100.00	0.00	T9	Y	100.00	-	N	
96	CP	07/02/2011	1230	7504	2	PC101	Copy paper	36.00	6.30	T1	Y	42.30	N	N	
97	CP	14/02/2011	1230	7501	2	PC102	Postage stamps	25.00	0.00	T2	Y	25.00	N	N	
98	CP	20/02/2011	1230	7504	2	PC103	Envelopes	16.00	2.80	T1	Y	18.80	N	N	
99	CP	28/02/2011	1230	7501	2	PC104	Postage stamps	5.00	0.00	T2	Y	5.00	N	N	
100	CP	28/02/2011	1230	5003	2	PC105	Packing tape	4.00	0.70	T1	Y	4.70	N	N	
101	CR	26/02/2011	1235	4000	1	10743	Hardware sales	5,000.00	875.00	T1	Y	5,875.00	N	N	
102	CR	26/02/2011	1235	4001	1	10743	Software sales	480.00	84.00	T1	Y	564.00	N	N	
103	CR	27/02/2011	1235	4000	1	10744	Hardware sales	1,200.00	210.00	T1	Y	1,410.00	N	N	
104	CR	27/02/2011	1235	4001	1	10744	Software sales	890.00	155.75	T1	Y	1,045.75	N	N	
105	CR	28/02/2011	1235	4000	1	10745	Hardware sales	600.00	105.00	T1	Y	705.00	N	N	
106	CR	28/02/2011	1235	4001	1	10745	Software sales	120.00	21.00	T1	Y	141.00	N	N	
107	BP	15/02/2011	1200	7701	0	DD	Xerax 566 maintenance	19.80	3.47	T1	Y	23.27	N	N	
108	BR	15/02/2011	1200	4904	0	STO	Rent 10A High Street	456.00	79.80	T1	Y	535.80	N	N	
109	BP	16/02/2011	1200	7100	0	DD	Rent paid	4,500.00	787.50	T1	Y	5,287.50	N	N	
110	BP	19/02/2011	1200	7103	0	STO	Rates	350.00	0.00	T2	Y	350.00	N	N	

End of Report

Note: in this audit trail the nominal codes for transactions 66 and 67 have been corrected. Transactions 68 and 69 show the deleted entries. Corrections are dealt with in Chapter 12.

Task 5 (b)

Date: 06/05/2010		**Pronto Supplies Limited**	
Time: 11:15:35		**Period Trial Balance**	

To Period: Month 2, February 2011

N/C	Name	Debit	Credit
0020	Plant and Machinery	35,000.00	
0030	Office Equipment	19,760.00	
0040	Furniture and Fixtures	30,000.00	
1100	Debtors Control Account	2,382.90	
1200	Bank Current Account	36,783.08	
1230	Petty Cash	4.20	
1235	Cash Receipts	9,740.75	
2100	Creditors Control Account		11,797.00
2200	Sales Tax Control Account		30,150.75
2201	Purchase Tax Control Account	35,281.02	
2300	Loans		35,000.00
3000	Ordinary Shares		80,000.00
4000	Computer hardware sales		139,380.00
4001	Computer software sales		29,814.00
4002	Computer consultancy		2,640.00
4904	Rent Income		456.00
5000	Materials Purchased	93,362.00	
5003	Packaging	4.00	
6201	Advertising	22,600.00	
7000	Gross Wages	33,010.00	
7100	Rent	9,000.00	
7103	General Rates	800.00	
7200	Electricity	308.00	
7501	Postage and Carriage	30.00	
7502	Telephone	585.00	
7504	Office Stationery	567.00	
7701	Office Machine Maintenance	19.80	
	Totals:	329,237.75	329,237.75

Pronto Supplies Limited
Period Trial Balance

To Period: Month 2, February 2011

N/C	Name	Debit	Credit
0020	Plant and Machinery	35,000.00	
0030	Office Equipment	19,760.00	
0040	Furniture and Fixtures	30,000.00	
1100	Debtors Control Account	2,382.90	
1200	Bank Current Account	36,733.08	
1230	Petty Cash	4.20	
1235	Cash Receipts	9,740.75	
2100	Creditors Control Account		11,797.00
2200	Sales Tax Control Account		30,150.75
2201	Purchase Tax Control Account	35,281.02	
2300	Loans		35,000.00
3000	Ordinary Shares		80,000.00
4000	Computer hardware sales		139,380.00
4001	Computer software sales		29,814.00
4002	Computer consultancy		2,640.00
4904	Rent Income		456.00
5000	Materials Purchased	93,362.00	
5003	Packaging	4.00	
6201	Advertising	22,600.00	
7000	Gross Wages	33,010.00	
7100	Rent	9,000.00	
7103	General Rates	800.00	
7200	Electricity	308.00	
7501	Postage and Carriage	30.00	
7502	Telephone	585.00	
7504	Office Stationery	567.00	
7701	Office Machine Maintenance	19.80	
7901	Bank Charges	50.00	
	Totals:	329,237.75	329,237.75

Chapter 12

Task 4

Pronto Supplies Limited

Period Trial Balance

To Period: Month 2, February 2011

N/C	Name	Debit	Credit
0020	Plant and Machinery	35,000.00	
0030	Office Equipment	19,760.00	
0040	Furniture and Fixtures	30,000.00	
1100	Debtors Control Account	7,882.90	
1200	Bank Current Account	31,233.08	
1230	Petty Cash	4.20	
1235	Cash Receipts	9,740.75	
2100	Creditors Control Account		11,797.00
2200	Sales Tax Control Account		30,150.75
2201	Purchase Tax Control Account	35,281.02	
2300	Loans		35,000.00
3000	Ordinary Shares		80,000.00
4000	Computer hardware sales		139,380.00
4001	Computer software sales		29,814.00
4002	Computer consultancy		2,640.00
4904	Rent Income		456.00
5000	Materials Purchased	93,362.00	
5003	Packaging	4.00	
6201	Advertising	22,600.00	
7000	Gross Wages	33,010.00	
7100	Rent	9,000.00	
7103	General Rates	800.00	
7200	Electricity	150.00	
7201	Gas	158.00	
7501	Postage and Carriage	30.00	
7502	Telephone	585.00	
7504	Office Stationery	567.00	
7701	Office Machine Maintenance	19.80	
7901	Bank Charges	50.00	
	Totals:	329,237.75	329,237.75

Chapter 13

Task 4

Pronto Supplies Limited

Update Ledgers

Inv	Type	Tran	Date	A/C	N/C	Stock Code	Details	Quantity	Net	Tax	Gross
555	SC	118	14/03/2011	PD001	4002		Refund 1 hour consultancy work @ £60 per hour		-60.00	-10.50	-70.50
							Credit Total:		-60.00	-10.50	-70.50
							Grand Total for Invoices:		0.00	0.00	0.00
							Grand Total for All:		-60.00	-10.50	-70.50

Pronto Supplies Limited

Period Trial Balance

To Period: Month 3, March 2011

N/C	Name	Debit	Credit
0020	Plant and Machinery	35,000.00	
0030	Office Equipment	19,760.00	
0040	Furniture and Fixtures	30,000.00	
1100	Debtors Control Account	8,869.90	
1200	Bank Current Account	31,233.08	
1230	Petty Cash	4.20	
1235	Cash Receipts	9,740.75	
2100	Creditors Control Account		11,797.00
2200	Sales Tax Control Account		30,297.75
2201	Purchase Tax Control Account	35,281.02	
2300	Loans		35,000.00
3000	Ordinary Shares		80,000.00
4000	Computer hardware sales		139,380.00
4001	Computer software sales		29,814.00
4002	Computer consultancy		3,480.00
4904	Rent Income		456.00
5000	Materials Purchased	93,362.00	
5003	Packaging	4.00	
6201	Advertising	22,600.00	
7000	Gross Wages	33,010.00	
7100	Rent	9,000.00	
7103	General Rates	800.00	
7200	Electricity	150.00	
7201	Gas	158.00	
7501	Postage and Carriage	30.00	
7502	Telephone	585.00	
7504	Office Stationery	567.00	
7701	Office Machine Maintenance	19.80	
7901	Bank Charges	50.00	
	Totals:	330,224.75	330,224.75

Pronto Supplies Limited
Audit Trail (Summary)

Date From:	01/01/1980			**Customer From:**		
Date To:	31/12/2019			**Customer To:**		ZZZZZZZZ
Transaction From:	1			**Supplier From:**		
Transaction To:	99,999,999			**Supplier To:**		ZZZZZZZZ
Dept From:	0			**N/C From:**		
Dept To:	999			**N/C To:**		99999999
Exclude Deleted Tran:	No					

No	Type	Date	A/C	N/C	Dept	Ref	Details	Net	Tax	T/C	Pd	Paid	V	B	Bank Rec. Date
1	SI	05/01/2011	JB001	9998	0	10013	Opening Balance	5,500.00	0.00	T9	Y	5,500.00	-	-	
2	PI	04/01/2011	DE001	9998	0	4563	Opening Balance	5,750.00	0.00	T9	Y	5,750.00	-	-	
3	SI	05/01/2011	CH001	9998	0	10014	Opening Balance	2,400.00	0.00	T9	Y	2,400.00	-	-	
4	SI	09/01/2011	CR001	9998	0	10015	Opening Balance	3,234.00	0.00	T9	Y	3,234.00	-	-	
5	SI	10/01/2011	DB001	9998	0	10016	Opening Balance	3,400.00	0.00	T9	Y	3,400.00	-	-	
6	SI	10/01/2011	KD001	9998	0	10017	Opening Balance	6,500.00	0.00	T9	Y	6,500.00	-	-	
7	SI	17/01/2011	LG001	9998	0	10019	Opening Balance	8,500.00	0.00	T9	Y	8,500.00	-	-	
8	PI	05/01/2011	EL001	9998	0	8122	Opening Balance	8,500.00	0.00	T9	Y	8,500.00	-	-	
9	PI	09/01/2011	MA001	9998	0	9252	Opening Balance	4,500.00	0.00	T9	Y	4,500.00	-	-	
10	JD	31/01/2011	0020	0020	0	O/Bal	Opening Balance	35,000.00	0.00	T9	Y	35,000.00	-	-	
11	JC	31/01/2011	9998	9998	0	O/Bal	Opening Balance	35,000.00	0.00	T9	Y	35,000.00	-	-	
12	JD	31/01/2011	0030	0030	0	O/Bal	Opening Balance	15,000.00	0.00	T9	Y	15,000.00	-	-	
13	JC	31/01/2011	9998	9998	0	O/Bal	Opening Balance	15,000.00	0.00	T9	Y	15,000.00	-	-	
14	JD	31/01/2011	0040	0040	0	O/Bal	Opening Balance	25,000.00	0.00	T9	Y	25,000.00	-	-	
15	JC	31/01/2011	9998	9998	0	O/Bal	Opening Balance	25,000.00	0.00	T9	Y	25,000.00	-	-	
16	JD	31/01/2011	1200	1200	0	O/Bal	Opening Balance	14,656.00	0.00	T9	Y	14,656.00	-	-	15/04/2010
17	JC	31/01/2011	9998	9998	0	O/Bal	Opening Balance	14,656.00	0.00	T9	Y	14,656.00	-	-	
18	JC	31/01/2011	2200	2200	0	O/Bal	Opening Balance	17,920.00	0.00	T9	Y	17,920.00	-	-	
19	JD	31/01/2011	9998	9998	0	O/Bal	Opening Balance	17,920.00	0.00	T9	Y	17,920.00	-	-	
20	JD	31/01/2011	2201	2201	0	O/Bal	Opening Balance	26,600.00	0.00	T9	Y	26,600.00	-	-	
21	JC	31/01/2011	9998	9998	0	O/Bal	Opening Balance	26,600.00	0.00	T9	Y	26,600.00	-	-	
22	JC	31/01/2011	2300	2300	0	O/Bal	Opening Balance	35,000.00	0.00	T9	Y	35,000.00	-	-	
23	JD	31/01/2011	9998	9998	0	O/Bal	Opening Balance	35,000.00	0.00	T9	Y	35,000.00	-	-	
24	JC	31/01/2011	3000	3000	0	O/Bal	Opening Balance	75,000.00	0.00	T9	Y	75,000.00	-	-	
25	JD	31/01/2011	9998	9998	0	O/Bal	Opening Balance	75,000.00	0.00	T9	Y	75,000.00	-	-	
26	JC	31/01/2011	4000	4000	0	O/Bal	Opening Balance	85,000.00	0.00	T9	Y	85,000.00	-	-	
27	JD	31/01/2011	9998	9998	0	O/Bal	Opening Balance	85,000.00	0.00	T9	Y	85,000.00	-	-	
28	JC	31/01/2011	4001	4001	0	O/Bal	Opening Balance	15,000.00	0.00	T9	Y	15,000.00	-	-	
29	JD	31/01/2011	9998	9998	0	O/Bal	Opening Balance	15,000.00	0.00	T9	Y	15,000.00	-	-	
30	JC	31/01/2011	4002	4002	0	O/Bal	Opening Balance	2,400.00	0.00	T9	Y	2,400.00	-	-	
31	JD	31/01/2011	9998	9998	0	O/Bal	Opening Balance	2,400.00	0.00	T9	Y	2,400.00	-	-	
32	JD	31/01/2011	5000	5000	0	O/Bal	Opening Balance	69,100.00	0.00	T9	Y	69,100.00	-	-	
33	JC	31/01/2011	9998	9998	0	O/Bal	Opening Balance	69,100.00	0.00	T9	Y	69,100.00	-	-	
34	JD	31/01/2011	6201	6201	0	O/Bal	Opening Balance	12,400.00	0.00	T9	Y	12,400.00	-	-	
35	JC	31/01/2011	9998	9998	0	O/Bal	Opening Balance	12,400.00	0.00	T9	Y	12,400.00	-	-	
36	JD	31/01/2011	7000	7000	0	O/Bal	Opening Balance	16,230.00	0.00	T9	Y	16,230.00	-	-	
37	JC	31/01/2011	9998	9998	0	O/Bal	Opening Balance	16,230.00	0.00	T9	Y	16,230.00	-	-	
38	JD	31/01/2011	7100	7100	0	O/Bal	Opening Balance	4,500.00	0.00	T9	Y	4,500.00	-	-	
39	JC	31/01/2011	9998	9998	0	O/Bal	Opening Balance	4,500.00	0.00	T9	Y	4,500.00	-	-	
40	JD	31/01/2011	7103	7103	0	O/Bal	Opening Balance	450.00	0.00	T9	Y	450.00	-	-	
41	JC	31/01/2011	9998	9998	0	O/Bal	Opening Balance	450.00	0.00	T9	Y	450.00	-	-	
42	JD	31/01/2011	7200	7200	0	O/Bal	Opening Balance	150.00	0.00	T9	Y	150.00	-	-	
43	JC	31/01/2011	9998	9998	0	O/Bal	Opening Balance	150.00	0.00	T9	Y	150.00	-	-	
44	JD	31/01/2011	7502	7502	0	O/Bal	Opening Balance	275.00	0.00	T9	Y	275.00	-	-	
45	JC	31/01/2011	9998	9998	0	O/Bal	Opening Balance	275.00	0.00	T9	Y	275.00	-	-	
46	JD	31/01/2011	7504	7504	0	O/Bal	Opening Balance	175.00	0.00	T9	Y	175.00	-	-	
47	JC	31/01/2011	9998	9998	0	O/Bal	Opening Balance	175.00	0.00	T9	Y	175.00	-	-	
48	SI	05/02/2011	JB001	4000	1	10023	1 x 17" monitor	400.00	70.00	T1	N	0.00	N	-	
49	SI	06/02/2011	CH001	4000	1	10024	1 x printer lead	16.00	2.80	T1	Y	18.80	N	-	
50	SI	06/02/2011	CR001	4001	1	10025	1 x Macroworx	100.00	17.50	T1	N	0.00	N	-	
51	SI	08/02/2011	KD001	4002	1	10026	2 hrs consultancy	120.00	21.00	T1	N	0.00	N	-	
52	SC	06/02/2011	DB001	4001	1	551	Software returned	200.00	35.00	T1	Y	235.00	N	-	
53	SC	06/02/2011	LG001	4000	1	552	Disks returned (hardware)	40.00	7.00	T1	N	0.00	N	-	
54	SI	12/02/2011	JB001	4002	1	10027	2 hrs consultancy	120.00	21.00	T1	N	0.00	N	-	
55	SI	13/02/2011	DB001	4000	1	10028	1 x EF102 Printer	600.00	105.00	T1	N	0.00	N	-	
56	SI	16/02/2011	LG001	4000	1	10029	2 x Zap drive	180.00	31.50	T1	N	0.00	N	-	
57	SI	16/02/2011	KD001	4001	1	10030	1 x Fileperfect software	264.00	46.20	T1	N	0.00	N	-	
58	SI	16/02/2011	CH001	4000	1	10031	1 x 17" flatscreen	320.00	56.00	T1	N	0.00	N	-	
59	SC	12/02/2011	KD001	4000	1	553	1 Printer lead	16.00	2.80	T1	N	0.00	N	-	
60	SC	13/02/2011	CR001	4000	1	554	Zap disks (hardware)	20.00	3.50	T1	N	0.00	N	-	
61	PI	09/02/2011	DE001	5000	2	11365	Desktop computers	3,600.00	630.00	T1	N	0.00	N	-	
62	PI	09/02/2011	EL001	5000	2	8576	Peripherals	2,000.00	350.00	T1	N	0.00	N	-	

Pronto Supplies Limited

Audit Trail (Summary)

No	Type	Date	A/C	N/C	Dept	Ref	Details	Net	Tax	T/C	Pd	Paid	V	B	Bank Rec. Date
63	PI	12/02/2011	MA001	5000	2	2947	Powerbooks	3,680.00	644.00	T1	N	0.00	N	-	
64	PC	06/02/2011	DE001	5000	2	7223	1 x Computer	480.00	84.00	T1	Y	564.00	N	-	
65	PC	08/02/2011	MA001	5000	2	552	1 x optical mouse	38.00	6.65	T1	Y	44.65	N	-	
66	PI	14/02/2011	DE001	0030	2	11377	Desktop computer	400.00	70.00	T1	N	0.00	N	-	
67	PI	14/02/2011	EL001	0030	2	8603	Laser Printer	360.00	63.00	T1	N	0.00	N	-	
68	PI	14/02/2011	DE001	5000	2	11377	Deleted - see tran 66	400.00	70.00	T1	N	0.00	-	-	
69	PI	14/02/2011	EL001	5000	2	8603	Deleted - see tran 67	360.00	63.00	T1	N	0.00	-	-	
70	SR	28/02/2011	JB001	1200	0	CANCEL	Sales Receipt	5,500.00	0.00	T9	Y	5,500.00	-	N	
71	SR	28/02/2011	CH001	1200	0	cheque	Sales Receipt	2,418.80	0.00	T9	Y	2,418.80	-	N	
72	SR	28/02/2011	CR001	1200	0	BACS	Sales Receipt	3,234.00	0.00	T9	Y	3,234.00	-	R	28/02/2011
73	SR	28/02/2011	DB001	1200	0	cheque	Sales Receipt	3,165.00	0.00	T9	Y	3,165.00	-	N	
74	SR	28/02/2011	KD001	1200	0	BACS	Sales Receipt	6,500.00	0.00	T9	Y	6,500.00	-	N	
75	SR	28/02/2011	LG001	1200	0	BACS	Sales Receipt	8,500.00	0.00	T9	Y	8,500.00	-	N	
76	PP	28/02/2011	DE001	1200	0	BACS	Purchase Payment	5,186.00	0.00	T9	Y	5,186.00	-	R	28/02/2011
77	PP	28/02/2011	EL001	1200	0	BACS	Purchase Payment	8,500.00	0.00	T9	Y	8,500.00	-	R	28/02/2011
78	PP	28/02/2011	MA001	1200	0	BACS	Purchase Payment	4,455.35	0.00	T9	Y	4,455.35	-	R	28/02/2011
79	BR	09/02/2011	1200	4000	1	10736	Hardware sales	12,500.00	2,187.50	T1	Y	14,687.50	N	R	28/02/2011
80	BR	09/02/2011	1200	4001	1	10737	Software sales	4,680.00	819.00	T1	Y	5,499.00	N	R	28/02/2011
81	BR	16/02/2011	1200	4000	1	10738	Hardware sales	15,840.00	2,772.00	T1	Y	18,612.00	N	R	28/02/2011
82	BR	16/02/2011	1200	4001	1	10739	Software sales	3,680.00	644.00	T1	Y	4,324.00	N	R	28/02/2011
83	BR	23/02/2011	1200	4000	1	10740	Hardware sales	17,800.00	3,115.00	T1	Y	20,915.00	N	R	28/02/2011
84	BR	23/02/2011	1200	4001	1	10741	Software sales	4,800.00	840.00	T1	Y	5,640.00	N	R	28/02/2011
85	BP	12/02/2011	1200	5000	2	122992	Cash purchases	15,500.00	2,712.50	T1	Y	18,212.50	N	R	28/02/2011
86	BP	14/02/2011	1200	6201	2	122993	Advertising	10,200.00	1,785.00	T1	Y	11,985.00	N	R	28/02/2011
87	BP	15/02/2011	1200	0040	2	122994	Furniture	5,000.00	875.00	T1	Y	5,875.00	N	R	28/02/2011
88	BP	23/02/2011	1200	7200	2	122995	Electricity	158.00	27.65	T1	Y	185.65	N	R	28/02/2011
89	BP	26/02/2011	1200	7502	2	122996	Telephone	310.00	54.25	T1	Y	364.25	N	R	28/02/2011
90	BP	26/02/2011	1200	7504	2	122997	Stationery	340.00	59.50	T1	Y	399.50	N	N	
91	BP	28/02/2011	1200	7000	2	BACS	Wages	16,780.00	0.00	T9	Y	16,780.00	-	R	28/02/2011
92	BR	28/02/2011	1200	3000	1	10742	Share capital	5,000.00	0.00	T9	Y	5,000.00	-	N	
93	BP	28/02/2011	1200	0030	2	122998	Colour printer	4,000.00	700.00	T1	Y	4,700.00	N	R	28/02/2011
94	JC	01/02/2011	1200	1200	0	122991	From bank to petty cash	100.00	0.00	T9	Y	100.00	-	R	28/02/2011
95	JD	01/02/2011	1230	1230	0	122991	From bank to petty cash	100.00	0.00	T9	Y	100.00	-	N	
96	CP	07/02/2011	1230	7504	2	PC101	Copy paper	36.00	6.30	T1	Y	42.30	N	N	
97	CP	14/02/2011	1230	7501	2	PC102	Postage stamps	25.00	0.00	T2	Y	25.00	N	N	
98	CP	20/02/2011	1230	7504	2	PC103	Envelopes	16.00	2.80	T1	Y	18.80	N	N	
99	CP	28/02/2011	1230	7501	2	PC104	Postage stamps	5.00	0.00	T2	Y	5.00	N	N	
100	CP	28/02/2011	1230	5003	2	PC105	Packing tape	4.00	0.70	T1	Y	4.70	N	N	
101	CR	26/02/2011	1235	4000	1	10743	Hardware sales	5,000.00	875.00	T1	Y	5,875.00	N	N	
102	CR	26/02/2011	1235	4001	1	10743	Software sales	480.00	84.00	T1	Y	564.00	N	N	
103	CR	27/02/2011	1235	4000	1	10744	Hardware sales	1,200.00	210.00	T1	Y	1,410.00	N	N	
104	CR	27/02/2011	1235	4001	1	10744	Software sales	890.00	155.75	T1	Y	1,045.75	N	N	
105	CR	28/02/2011	1235	4000	1	10745	Hardware sales	600.00	105.00	T1	Y	705.00	N	N	
106	CR	28/02/2011	1235	4001	1	10745	Software sales	120.00	21.00	T1	Y	141.00	N	N	
107	BP	15/02/2011	1200	7701	0	DD	Xerax 566 maintenance	19.80	3.47	T1	Y	23.27	N	R	28/02/2011
108	BR	15/02/2011	1200	4904	0	STO	Rent 10A High Street	456.00	79.80	T1	Y	535.80	N	R	28/02/2011
109	BP	16/02/2011	1200	7100	0	DD	Rent paid	4,500.00	787.50	T1	Y	5,287.50	N	R	28/02/2011
110	BP	19/02/2011	1200	7103	0	STO	Rates	350.00	0.00	T2	Y	350.00	N	R	28/02/2011
111	BP	28/02/2011	1200	7901	0	ADJ	Bank charges	50.00	0.00	T2	Y	50.00	N	R	28/02/2011
112	JD	28/02/2011	7201	7201	0	88	88 posting error	158.00	0.00	T1	Y	158.00	N	-	
113	JC	28/02/2011	7200	7200	0	88	88 posting error	158.00	0.00	T1	Y	158.00	N	-	
114	SP	28/02/2011	JB001	1200	0	CANCEL	Cancelled Cheque	5,500.00	0.00	T9	Y	0.00	-	N	
115	SI	09/03/2011	MP001	4002	1	10032	Computer consultancy	180.00	31.50	T1	N	0.00	N	-	
116	SI	09/03/2011	PD001	4002	1	10033	Computer consultancy	300.00	52.50	T1	N	0.00	N	-	
117	SI	09/03/2011	EA001	4002	1	10034	Computer consultancy	420.00	73.50	T1	N	0.00	N	-	
118	SC	14/03/2011	PD001	4002	1	555	Refund 1 hour consultancy	60.00	10.50	T1	N	0.00	N	-	

End of Report

Interlingo Limited Extended Exercise: Activity 2

Task 3

Interlingo Translation Services

Day Books: Customer Invoices (Detailed)

Date From:	01/07/2011										Customer From:		
Date To:	31/07/2011										Customer To:	ZZZZZZZZ	
Transaction From:	1										N/C From:		
Transaction To:	99,999,999										N/C To:	99999999	
Dept From:	0												
Dept To:	999												

Tran No.	Type	Date	A/C Ref	N/C	Inv Ref	Dept.	Details	Net Amount	Tax Amount	T/C	Gross Amount	V	B
1	SI	06/07/2011	RS001	9998	10010	0	Opening Balance	850.00	0.00	T9	850.00	-	-
2	SI	12/07/2011	PL001	9998	10011	0	Opening Balance	795.00	0.00	T9	795.00	-	-
3	SI	17/07/2011	RT001	9998	10012	0	Opening Balance	1,210.00	0.00	T9	1,210.00	-	-
4	SI	19/07/2011	HD001	9998	10013	0	Opening Balance	345.00	0.00	T9	345.00	-	-
5	SI	20/07/2011	SC001	9998	10014	0	Opening Balance	800.00	0.00	T9	800.00	-	-
							Totals:	4,000.00	0.00		4,000.00		

End of Report

Task 6

Interlingo Translation Services

Day Books: Supplier Invoices (Detailed)

Date From:	01/07/2011										Supplier From:		
Date To:	31/07/2011										Supplier To:	ZZZZZZZZ	
Transaction From:	1										N/C From:		
Transaction To:	99,999,999										N/C To:	99999999	
Dept From:	0												
Dept To:	999												

Tran No.	Type	Date	A/C Ref	N/C	Inv Ref	Dept	Details	Net Amount	Tax Amount	T/C	Gross Amount	V	B
6	PI	05/07/2011	TD001	9998	2347	0	Opening Balance	780.00	0.00	T9	780.00	-	-
7	PI	06/07/2011	BB001	9998	9422	0	Opening Balance	420.00	0.00	T9	420.00	-	-
							Totals	1,200.00	0.00		1,200.00		

End of Report

Task 7

Interlingo Translation Services

Period Trial Balance

To Period: Month 1, July 2011

N/C	Name	Debit	Credit
1100	Debtors Control Account	4,000.00	
2100	Creditors Control Account		1,200.00
9998	Suspense Account		2,800.00
	Totals:	4,000.00	4,000.00

End of Report

Interlingo Limited Extended Exercise: Activity 3

Task 2

Date:			
Time:			

Interlingo Translation Services

Period Trial Balance

To Period: Month 2, August 2011

N/C	Name	Debit	Credit
0020	Plant and Machinery	5,000.00	
0030	Office Equipment	2,500.00	
0040	Furniture and Fixtures	3,000.00	
1100	Debtors Control Account	4,000.00	
1200	Bank Current Account	7,085.00	
2100	Creditors Control Account		1,200.00
2200	Sales Tax Control Account		814.00
2201	Purchase Tax Control Account	623.00	
2300	Loans		5,000.00
3000	Ordinary Shares		15,000.00
4000	Sales Type A		3,660.00
4100	Sales Type D		456.00
4101	Sales Type E		950.00
5000	Materials Purchased	300.00	
5001	Materials Imported	750.00	
6201	Advertising	550.00	
7000	Gross Wages	2,000.00	
7100	Rent	250.00	
7103	General Rates	129.00	
7200	Electricity	61.00	
7501	Postage and Carriage	86.00	
7502	Telephone	275.00	
7504	Office Stationery	471.00	
	Totals:	27,080.00	27,080.00

End of Report

Task 3

<u>Interlingo Translation Services</u>
<u>Period Trial Balance</u>

To Period: Month 2, August 2011

N/C	Name	Debit	Credit
0020	Office computers	5,000.00	
0030	Office Equipment	2,500.00	
0040	Furniture and Fixtures	3,000.00	
1100	Debtors Control Account	4,000.00	
1200	Bank Current Account	7,085.00	
2100	Creditors Control Account		1,200.00
2200	Sales Tax Control Account		814.00
2201	Purchase Tax Control Account	623.00	
2300	Loans		5,000.00
3000	Ordinary Shares		15,000.00
4000	Translation services income		3,660.00
4100	Sales of language books		456.00
4101	Sales of language CDs		950.00
5000	Purchases of books	300.00	
5001	Purchases of CDs	750.00	
6201	Advertising	550.00	
7000	Gross Wages	2,000.00	
7100	Rent	250.00	
7103	General Rates	129.00	
7200	Electricity	61.00	
7501	Postage and Carriage	86.00	
7502	Telephone	275.00	
7504	Office Stationery	471.00	
	Totals:	27,080.00	27,080.00

End of Report

Task 4

Interlingo Translation Services

Day Books: Customer Invoices (Detailed)

Date From:	01/08/2011		Customer From:	
Date To:	31/08/2011		Customer To:	ZZZZZZZZ
Transaction From:	1		N/C From:	
Transaction To:	99,999,999		N/C To:	99999999
Dept From:	0			
Dept To:	999			

Tran No.	Type	Date	A/C Ref	N/C	Inv Ref	Dept.	Details	Net Amount	Tax Amount	T/C	Gross Amount	V	B
50	SI	10/08/2011	HD001	4000	10015	1	Translation of sales contracts	520.00	91.00	T1	611.00	N	-
51	SI	16/08/2011	PL001	4000	10016	1	Translation of sales literature	120.00	21.00	T1	141.00	N	-
52	SI	20/08/2011	RS001	4000	10017	1	Translation of shipping docs	100.00	17.50	T1	117.50	N	-
53	SI	20/08/2011	RT001	4000	10018	1	Translation of sales contracts	320.00	56.00	T1	376.00	N	-
54	SI	22/08/2011	SC001	4000	10019	1	Translation of sales contracts	160.00	28.00	T1	188.00	N	-
56	SI	22/08/2011	RT001	4000	10020	1	Translation of contract tender	1,200.00	204.75	T1	1,404.75	N	-
							Totals:	2,420.00	418.25		2,838.25		

Interlingo Translation Services

Day Books: Customer Credits (Detailed)

Date From:	01/08/2011		Customer From:	
Date To:	31/08/2011		Customer To:	ZZZZZZZZ
Transaction From:	1		N/C From:	
Transaction To:	99,999,999		N/C To:	99999999
Dept From:	0			
Dept To:	999			

Tran No.	Type	Date	A/C Ref	N/C	Inv Ref	Dept.	Details	Net Amount	Tax Amount	T/C	Gross Amount	V	B
55	SC	31/08/2011	HD001	4000	501	1	Refund of 10% discount , invoice	52.00	9.10	T1	61.10	N	-
							Totals:	52.00	9.10		61.10		

Interlingo Limited Extended Exercise: Activity 5

Task 3

Interlingo Translation Services

Day Books: Supplier Invoices (Detailed)

Date From:	01/08/2011										Supplier From:		
Date To:	31/08/2011										Supplier To:	ZZZZZZZZ	

Transaction From:	1										N/C From:		
Transaction To:	99,999,999										N/C To:	99999999	

Dept From:	0
Dept To:	999

Tran No.	Type	Date	A/C Ref	N/C	Inv Ref	Dept	Details	Net Amount	Tax Amount	T/C	Gross Amount	V	B
57	PI	15/08/2011	TD001	5001	2561	2	Beginners French CDs	500.00	87.50	T1	587.50	N	-
58	PI	15/08/2011	TD001	5001	2561	2	Advanced Italian CDs	300.00	52.50	T1	352.50	N	-
59	PI	20/08/2011	BB001	5000	11231	2	German First Coure	297.00	0.00	T0	297.00	N	-
60	PI	20/08/2011	BB001	5000	11231	2	French Second Course	267.75	0.00	T0	267.75	N	-
61	PI	15/08/2011	RE001	5100	72/554	2	Same day delivery to London	100.00	17.50	T1	117.50	N	-
							Totals	1,464.75	157.50		1,622.25		

End of Report

Task 4

Interlingo Translation Services

Day Books: Supplier Credits (Detailed)

Date From:	01/08/2011										Supplier From:		
Date To:	31/08/2011										Supplier To:	ZZZZZZZZ	

Transaction From:	1										N/C From:		
Transaction To:	99,999,999										N/C To:	99999999	

Dept From:	0
Dept To:	999

Tran No.	Type	Date	A/C Ref	N/C	Inv Ref	Dept	Details	Net Amount	Tax Amount	T/C	Gross Amount	V	B
62	PC	28/08/2011	TD001	5001	1919	2	Beginners French CDs	50.00	8.75	T1	58.75	N	-
							Totals	50.00	8.75		58.75		

End of Report

Interlingo Limited Extended Exercise: Activity 6

Task 2

Interlingo Translation Services
Day Books: Customer Receipts (Summary)

Transaction From:		1						Customer From :			
Transaction To:		99,999,999						Customer To:		ZZZZZZZZ	

Bank   1200   **Currency**   Pound Sterling

No	Type	Date	Account	Ref	Details	Net £	Tax £	Gross £ B	Bank Re
63	SR	10/08/2011	HD001	100110	Sales Receipt	345.00	0.00	345.00 N	
64	SR	17/08/2011	PL001	100112	Sales Receipt	795.00	0.00	795.00 N	
65	SR	24/08/2011	RS001	100114	Sales Receipt	850.00	0.00	850.00 N	
66	SR	24/08/2011	RT001	100114	Sales Receipt	1,210.00	0.00	1,210.00 N	
67	SR	31/08/2011	SC001	100116	Sales Receipt	800.00	0.00	800.00 N	
68	SR	31/08/2011	RT001	100116	Sales Receipt	1,374.75	0.00	1,374.75 N	
					Totals £	5,374.75	0.00	5,374.75	

Task 4

Interlingo Translation Services
Day Books: Bank Receipts (Detailed)

Transaction From:		1									
Transaction To:		99,999,999									
Dept From:		0									
Dept To:		999									

Bank: 1200   **Currency:**   Pound Sterling

No	Type	N/C	Date	Ref	Details	Dept	Net £	Tax £ T/C	Gross £ V	B
70	BR	4000	10/08/2011	100111	Translations	1	96.00	16.80 T1	112.80 N	N
71	BR	4101	10/08/2011	100111	CDs	1	240.00	42.00 T1	282.00 N	N
72	BR	4100	10/08/2011	100111	Books	1	160.00	0.00 T0	160.00 N	N
73	BR	4000	17/08/2011	100113	Translations	1	116.00	20.30 T1	136.30 N	N
74	BR	4101	17/08/2011	100113	CDs	1	180.00	31.50 T1	211.50 N	N
75	BR	4100	17/08/2011	100113	Books	1	107.00	0.00 T0	107.00 N	N
76	BR	4000	24/08/2011	100115	Translations	1	104.00	18.20 T1	122.20 N	N
77	BR	4101	24/08/2011	100115	CDs	1	220.00	38.50 T1	258.50 N	N
78	BR	4100	24/08/2011	100115	Books	1	84.00	0.00 T0	84.00 N	N
79	BR	4000	31/08/2011	100117	Translations	1	82.00	14.35 T1	96.35 N	N
80	BR	4101	31/08/2011	100117	CDs	1	190.00	33.25 T1	223.25 N	N
81	BR	4100	31/08/2011	100117	Books	1	113.00	0.00 T0	113.00 N	N
						Totals £	1,692.00	214.90	1,906.90	

Interlingo Limited Extended Exercise: Activity 7

Task 2

Interlingo Translation Services
Day Books: Supplier Payments (Summary)

Date From:	06/08/2011			Bank From:	1200
DateTo:	06/08/2011			Bank To:	1200
Transaction From:	1			Supplier From:	
Transaction To:	99,999,999			Supplier To:	ZZZZZZZZ

Bank 1200   **Currency** Pound Sterling

No	Type	Date	Supplier	Ref	Details	Net £	Tax £	Gross £	B	Bank Rec
84	PP	06/08/2011	TD001	120006	Purchase Payment	780.00	0.00	780.00	N	
85	PP	06/08/2011	BB001	120007	Purchase Payment	420.00	0.00	420.00	N	
					Totals £	1,200.00	0.00	1,200.00		

Task 4

Interlingo Translation Services
Day Books: Bank Payments (Detailed)

Transaction From:	1			N/C From:	
Transaction To:	99,999,999			N/C To:	99999999
Dept From:	0				
Dept To:	999				

Bank: 1200   **Currency:** Pound Sterling

No	Type	N/C	Date	Ref	Details	Dept	Net £	Tax £	T/C	Gross £	V	B
86	BP	0040	07/08/2011	120009	Office furniture	2	140.00	24.50	T1	164.50	N	N
87	BP	6201	08/08/2011	120010	Advertising	2	600.00	105.00	T1	705.00	N	N
88	BP	7100	15/08/2011	120011	Rent	2	250.00	43.75	T1	293.75	N	N
89	BP	7504	17/08/2011	120012	Stationery	2	126.00	22.05	T1	148.05	N	N
90	BP	7103	20/08/2011	120013	Rates	2	129.00	0.00	T2	129.00	N	N
91	BP	7502	22/08/2011	120014	Telephone	2	186.00	32.55	T1	218.55	N	N
92	BP	7200	24/08/2011	120015	Electricity	2	84.00	14.70	T1	98.70	N	N
93	BP	7501	30/08/2011	120016	Postages	2	45.60	0.00	T2	45.60	N	N
94	BP	7003	31/08/2011	BACS	Salaries	2	2,240.00	0.00	T9	2,240.00	-	N
					Totals £		3,800.60	242.55		4,043.15		

Interlingo Limited Extended Exercise: Activity 8

Task 3

Interlingo Translation Services

Day Books: Cash Payments (Detailed)

| Date From: | 01/08/2011 |
| DateTo: | 31/08/2011 |

| Transaction From: | 1 | | | N/C From: | |
| Transaction To: | 99,999,999 | | | N/C To: | 99999999 |

| Dept From: | 0 |
| Dept To: | 999 |

| Bank: | 1230 | | **Currency:** | Pound Sterling |

No	Type	N/C	Date	Ref	Details	Dept	Net £	Tax £	T/C	Gross £	V	B
97	CP	7504	07/08/2011	0001	Copy paper	2	16.00	2.80	T1	18.80	N	N
98	CP	7501	07/08/2011	0002	Postage stamps	2	24.00	0.00	T2	24.00	N	N
99	CP	7504	15/08/2011	0003	Box files	2	20.00	3.50	T1	23.50	N	N
100	CP	7501	22/08/2011	0004	Postage stamps	2	12.00	0.00	T2	12.00	N	N
						Totals £	72.00	6.30		78.30		

Interlingo Limited Extended Exercise: Activities 9 & 10

Activity 9 Task 4, Activity 10 Task 1 (trial balance extract)

N/C	Name	Debit	Credit
0020	Office Computers	5,000.00	
0030	Office Equipment	2,500.00	
0040	Furniture and Fixtures	3,140.00	
1100	Debtors Control Account	1,254.90	
1200	Bank Current Account	8,930.00	
1230	Petty Cash	1.70	
2100	Creditors Control Account		1,446.00
2200	Sales Tax Control Account		1,438.05
2201	Purchase Tax Control Account	1,020.60	
2300	Loans		5,000.00
3000	Ordinary Shares		15,000.00
4000	Translation services income		6,426.00
4009	Discounts Allowed	30.00	
4100	Sales of language books		920.00
4101	Sales of language CDs		1,780.00
5000	Purchases of books	864.75	
5001	Purchases of CDs	1,500.00	
5100	Carriage	100.00	
6201	Advertising	1,150.00	
7000	Gross Wages	2,000.00	
7003	Staff Salaries	2,240.00	
7100	Rent	500.00	
7103	General Rates	258.00	
7104	Premises Insurance	98.50	
7200	Electricity	145.00	
7501	Postage and Carriage	167.60	
7502	Telephone	461.00	
7504	Office Stationery	633.00	
7901	Bank Charges	15.00	
	Totals:	32,010.05	32,010.05

Interlingo Limited Extended Exercise: Activity 10

Task 1

Interlingo Translation Services
Aged Debtors Analysis (Summary)

Report Date: 31/08/2011   Customer From:
Include future transactions: No   Customer To: ZZZZZZZZ
Exclude later payments: No

** NOTE: All report values are shown in Base Currency, unless otherwise indicated **

A/C	Name	Credit Limit	Turnover	Balance	Future	Current	Period 1	Period 2	Period 3	Older
HD001	Hill & Dale & Co, Solicitors	£ 1,000.00	813.00	549.90	0.00	549.90	0.00	0.00	0.00	0.00
PL001	Playgames PLC	£ 1,000.00	915.00	141.00	0.00	141.00	0.00	0.00	0.00	0.00
RT001	Rotherway Limited	£ 3,000.00	2,730.00	376.00	0.00	376.00	0.00	0.00	0.00	0.00
SC001	Schafeld Ltd	£ 1,000.00	960.00	188.00	0.00	188.00	0.00	0.00	0.00	0.00
	Totals:		5,418.00	1,254.90	0.00	1,254.90	0.00	0.00	0.00	0.00

Task 1 (continued)

Interlingo Translation Services

Audit Trail (Summary)

Page: 1

Customer From:											
Customer To:						ZZZZZZZZ					
Transaction From:	1										
Transaction To:	99,999,999					Supplier From:					
						Supplier To:		ZZZZZZZZ			
Dept From:	0										
Dept To:	999					N/C From:					
						N/C To:		99999999			
Exclude Deleted Tran:	No										

No	Type	Date	A/C	N/C	Dept	Ref	Details	Net	Tax	T/C	Pd	Paid	V	B	Bank Rec. Date
1	SI	06/07/2011	RS001	9998	0	10010	Opening Balance	850.00	0.00	T9	Y	850.00	-	-	
2	SI	12/07/2011	PL001	9998	0	10011	Opening Balance	795.00	0.00	T9	Y	795.00	-	-	
3	SI	17/07/2011	RT001	9998	0	10012	Opening Balance	1,210.00	0.00	T9	Y	1,210.00	-	-	
4	SI	19/07/2011	HD001	9998	0	10013	Opening Balance	345.00	0.00	T9	Y	345.00	-	-	
5	SI	20/07/2011	SC001	9998	0	10014	Opening Balance	800.00	0.00	T9	Y	800.00	-	-	
6	PI	05/07/2011	TD001	9998	0	2347	Opening Balance	780.00	0.00	T9	Y	780.00	-	-	
7	PI	06/07/2011	BB001	9998	0	9422	Opening Balance	420.00	0.00	T9	Y	420.00	-	-	
8	JD	31/07/2011	0020	0020	0	O/Bal	Opening Balance	5,000.00	0.00	T9	Y	5,000.00	-	-	
9	JC	31/07/2011	9998	9998	0	O/Bal	Opening Balance	5,000.00	0.00	T9	Y	5,000.00	-	-	
10	JD	31/07/2011	0030	0030	0	O/Bal	Opening Balance	2,500.00	0.00	T9	Y	2,500.00	-	-	
11	JC	31/07/2011	9998	9998	0	O/Bal	Opening Balance	2,500.00	0.00	T9	Y	2,500.00	-	-	
12	JD	31/07/2011	0040	0040	0	O/Bal	Opening Balance	3,000.00	0.00	T9	Y	3,000.00	-	-	
13	JC	31/07/2011	9998	9998	0	O/Bal	Opening Balance	3,000.00	0.00	T9	Y	3,000.00	-	-	
14	JD	31/07/2011	1200	1200	0	O/Bal	Opening Balance	7,085.00	0.00	T9	Y	7,085.00	-	-	
15	JC	31/07/2011	9998	9998	0	O/Bal	Opening Balance	7,085.00	0.00	T9	Y	7,085.00	-	-	31/07/2011
16	JC	31/07/2011	2200	2200	0	O/Bal	Opening Balance	814.00	0.00	T9	Y	814.00	-	-	
17	JD	31/07/2011	9998	9998	0	O/Bal	Opening Balance	814.00	0.00	T9	Y	814.00	-	-	
18	JD	31/07/2011	2201	2201	0	O/Bal	Opening Balance	623.00	0.00	T9	Y	623.00	-	-	
19	JC	31/07/2011	9998	9998	0	O/Bal	Opening Balance	623.00	0.00	T9	Y	623.00	-	-	
20	JC	31/07/2011	2300	2300	0	O/Bal	Opening Balance	5,000.00	0.00	T9	Y	5,000.00	-	-	
21	JD	31/07/2011	9998	9998	0	O/Bal	Opening Balance	5,000.00	0.00	T9	Y	5,000.00	-	-	
22	JC	31/07/2011	3000	3000	0	O/Bal	Opening Balance	15,000.00	0.00	T9	Y	15,000.00	-	-	
23	JD	31/07/2011	9998	9998	0	O/Bal	Opening Balance	15,000.00	0.00	T9	Y	15,000.00	-	-	
24	JC	31/07/2011	4000	4000	0	O/Bal	Opening Balance	3,660.00	0.00	T9	Y	3,660.00	-	-	
25	JD	31/07/2011	9998	9998	0	O/Bal	Opening Balance	3,660.00	0.00	T9	Y	3,660.00	-	-	
26	JC	31/07/2011	4100	4100	0	O/Bal	Opening Balance	456.00	0.00	T9	Y	456.00	-	-	
27	JD	31/07/2011	9998	9998	0	O/Bal	Opening Balance	456.00	0.00	T9	Y	456.00	-	-	
28	JC	31/07/2011	4101	4101	0	O/Bal	Opening Balance	950.00	0.00	T9	Y	950.00	-	-	
29	JD	31/07/2011	9998	9998	0	O/Bal	Opening Balance	950.00	0.00	T9	Y	950.00	-	-	
30	JD	31/07/2011	5000	5000	0	O/Bal	Opening Balance	300.00	0.00	T9	Y	300.00	-	-	
31	JC	31/07/2011	9998	9998	0	O/Bal	Opening Balance	300.00	0.00	T9	Y	300.00	-	-	
32	JD	31/07/2011	5001	5001	0	O/Bal	Opening Balance	750.00	0.00	T9	Y	750.00	-	-	
33	JC	31/07/2011	9998	9998	0	O/Bal	Opening Balance	750.00	0.00	T9	Y	750.00	-	-	
34	JD	31/07/2011	6201	6201	0	O/Bal	Opening Balance	550.00	0.00	T9	Y	550.00	-	-	
35	JC	31/07/2011	9998	9998	0	O/Bal	Opening Balance	550.00	0.00	T9	Y	550.00	-	-	
36	JD	31/07/2011	7000	7000	0	O/Bal	Opening Balance	2,000.00	0.00	T9	Y	2,000.00	-	-	
37	JC	31/07/2011	9998	9998	0	O/Bal	Opening Balance	2,000.00	0.00	T9	Y	2,000.00	-	-	
38	JD	31/07/2011	7100	7100	0	O/Bal	Opening Balance	250.00	0.00	T9	Y	250.00	-	-	
39	JC	31/07/2011	9998	9998	0	O/Bal	Opening Balance	250.00	0.00	T9	Y	250.00	-	-	
40	JD	31/07/2011	7103	7103	0	O/Bal	Opening Balance	129.00	0.00	T9	Y	129.00	-	-	
41	JC	31/07/2011	9998	9998	0	O/Bal	Opening Balance	129.00	0.00	T9	Y	129.00	-	-	
42	JD	31/07/2011	7200	7200	0	O/Bal	Opening Balance	61.00	0.00	T9	Y	61.00	-	-	
43	JC	31/07/2011	9998	9998	0	O/Bal	Opening Balance	61.00	0.00	T9	Y	61.00	-	-	
44	JD	31/07/2011	7501	7501	0	O/Bal	Opening Balance	86.00	0.00	T9	Y	86.00	-	-	
45	JC	31/07/2011	9998	9998	0	O/Bal	Opening Balance	86.00	0.00	T9	Y	86.00	-	-	
46	JD	31/07/2011	7502	7502	0	O/Bal	Opening Balance	275.00	0.00	T9	Y	275.00	-	-	
47	JC	31/07/2011	9998	9998	0	O/Bal	Opening Balance	275.00	0.00	T9	Y	275.00	-	-	
48	JD	31/07/2011	7504	7504	0	O/Bal	Opening Balance	471.00	0.00	T9	Y	471.00	-	-	
49	JC	31/07/2011	9998	9998	0	O/Bal	Opening Balance	471.00	0.00	T9	Y	471.00	-	-	
50	SI	10/08/2011	HD001	4000	1	10015	Translation of sales	520.00	91.00	T1	N	0.00	N	-	
51	SI	16/08/2011	PL001	4000	1	10016	Translation of sales	120.00	21.00	T1	N	0.00	N	-	
52	SI	20/08/2011	RS001	4000	1	10017	Translation of shipping docs	100.00	17.50	T1	Y	117.50	N	-	
53	SI	20/08/2011	RT001	4000	1	10018	Translation of sales	320.00	56.00	T1	N	0.00	N	-	
54	SI	22/08/2011	SC001	4000	1	10019	Translation of sales	160.00	28.00	T1	N	0.00	N	-	
55	SC	31/08/2011	HD001	4000	1	501	Refund of 10% discount .	52.00	9.10	T1	N	0.00	N	-	
56	SI	22/08/2011	RT001	4000	1	10020	Translation of contract	1,200.00	204.75	T1	Y	1,404.75	N	-	
57	PI	15/08/2011	TD001	5001	2	2561	Beginners French CDs	500.00	87.50	T1	N	0.00	N	-	
58	PI	15/08/2011	TD001	5001	2	2561	Advanced Italian CDs	300.00	52.50	T1	N	0.00	N	-	
59	PI	20/08/2011	BB001	5000	2	11231	German First Coure	297.00	0.00	T0	N	0.00	N	-	
60	PI	20/08/2011	BB001	5000	2	11231	French Second Course	267.75	0.00	T0	N	0.00	N	-	
61	PI	15/08/2011	RE001	5100	2	72/554	Same day delivery to	100.00	17.50	T1	Y	117.50	N	-	
62	PC	28/08/2011	TD001	5001	2	1919	Beginners French CDs	50.00	8.75	T1	N	0.00	N	-	

Task 1 (continued)

Interlingo Translation Services

Page: 2

Audit Trail (Summary)

No	Type	Date	A/C	N/C	Dept	Ref	Details	Net	Tax	T/C	Pd	Paid	V	B	Bank Rec. Date
63	SR	10/08/2011	HD001	1200	0	100110	Sales Receipt	345.00	0.00	T9	Y	345.00	-	N	
64	SR	17/08/2011	PL001	1200	0	100112	Sales Receipt	795.00	0.00	T9	Y	795.00	-	N	
65	SR	24/08/2011	RS001	1200	0	100114	Sales Receipt	850.00	0.00	T9	Y	850.00	-	N	
66	SR	24/08/2011	RT001	1200	0	100114	Sales Receipt	1,210.00	0.00	T9	Y	1,210.00	-	N	
67	SR	31/08/2011	SC001	1200	0	100116	Sales Receipt	800.00	0.00	T9	Y	800.00	-	N	
68	SR	31/08/2011	RT001	1200	0	100116	Sales Receipt	1,374.75	0.00	T9	Y	1,374.75	-	N	
69	SD	31/08/2011	RT001	4009	0	100116	Sales Discount	30.00	0.00	T9	Y	30.00	-	-	
70	BR	10/08/2011	1200	4000	1	100111	Translations	96.00	16.80	T1	Y	112.80	N	N	
71	BR	10/08/2011	1200	4101	1	100111	CDs	240.00	42.00	T1	Y	282.00	N	N	
72	BR	10/08/2011	1200	4100	1	100111	Books	160.00	0.00	T0	Y	160.00	N	N	
73	BR	17/08/2011	1200	4000	1	100113	Translations	116.00	20.30	T1	Y	136.30	N	N	
74	BR	17/08/2011	1200	4101	1	100113	CDs	180.00	31.50	T1	Y	211.50	N	N	
75	BR	17/08/2011	1200	4100	1	100113	Books	107.00	0.00	T0	Y	107.00	N	N	
76	BR	24/08/2011	1200	4000	1	100115	Translations	104.00	18.20	T1	Y	122.20	N	N	
77	BR	24/08/2011	1200	4101	1	100115	CDs	220.00	38.50	T1	Y	258.50	N	N	
78	BR	24/08/2011	1200	4100	1	100115	Books	84.00	0.00	T0	Y	84.00	N	N	
79	BR	31/08/2011	1200	4000	1	100117	Translations	82.00	14.35	T1	Y	96.35	N	N	
80	BR	31/08/2011	1200	4101	1	100117	CDs	190.00	33.25	T1	Y	223.25	N	N	
81	BR	31/08/2011	1200	4100	1	100117	Books	113.00	0.00	T0	Y	113.00	N	N	
82	SR	31/08/2011	RS001	1200	0	CONTRA	Contra Receipt	117.50	0.00	T9	Y	117.50	-	N	
83	PP	31/08/2011	RE001	1200	0	CONTRA	Contra Payment	117.50	0.00	T9	Y	117.50	-	N	
84	PP	06/08/2011	TD001	1200	0	120006	Purchase Payment	780.00	0.00	T9	Y	780.00	-	N	
85	PP	06/08/2011	BB001	1200	0	120007	Purchase Payment	420.00	0.00	T9	Y	420.00	-	N	
86	BP	07/08/2011	1200	0040	2	120009	Office furniture	140.00	24.50	T1	Y	164.50	N	N	
87	BP	08/08/2011	1200	6201	2	120010	Advertising	600.00	105.00	T1	Y	705.00	N	N	
88	BP	15/08/2011	1200	7100	2	120011	Rent	250.00	43.75	T1	Y	293.75	N	N	
89	BP	17/08/2011	1200	7504	2	120012	Stationery	126.00	22.05	T1	Y	148.05	N	N	
90	BP	20/08/2011	1200	7103	2	120013	Rates	129.00	0.00	T2	Y	129.00	N	N	
91	BP	22/08/2011	1200	7502	2	120014	Telephone	186.00	32.55	T1	Y	218.55	N	N	
92	BP	24/08/2011	1200	7200	2	120015	Electricity	84.00	14.70	T1	Y	98.70	N	N	
93	BP	30/08/2011	1200	7501	2	120016	Postages	45.60	0.00	T2	Y	45.60	N	N	
94	BP	31/08/2011	1200	7003	2	BACS	Salaries	2,240.00	0.00	T9	Y	2,240.00	-	N	
95	JC	06/08/2011	1200	1200	0	120008	Bank Transfer	80.00	0.00	T9	Y	80.00	-	N	
96	JD	06/08/2011	1230	1230	0	120008	Bank Transfer	80.00	0.00	T9	Y	80.00	-	N	
97	CP	07/08/2011	1230	7504	2	0001	Copy paper	16.00	2.80	T1	Y	18.80	N	N	
98	CP	07/08/2011	1230	7501	2	0002	Postage stamps	24.00	0.00	T2	Y	24.00	N	N	
99	CP	15/08/2011	1230	7504	2	0003	Box files	20.00	3.50	T1	Y	23.50	N	N	
100	CP	22/08/2011	1230	7501	2	0004	Postage stamps	12.00	0.00	T2	Y	12.00	N	N	
101	BP	10/08/2011	1200	7104	0	DD	Suresafe Insurance	98.50	0.00	T2	Y	98.50	N	N	
102	BP	25/08/2011	1200	7901	0	STO	Albion Bank (standing	15.00	0.00	T2	Y	15.00	N	N	

End of Report

Task 2

Interlingo Translation Services
Customer Activity (Detailed)

Date From:	01/01/1980
Date To:	31/08/2011
Transaction From:	1
Transaction To:	99,999,999
Inc b/fwd transaction:	No
Exc later payment:	No

Customer From:	RT001
Customer To:	RT001
N/C From:	
N/C To:	99999999
Dept From:	0
Dept To:	999

** NOTE: All report values are shown in Base Currency, unless otherwise indicated **

A/C: RT001   Name: Rotherway Limited   Contact: Tel:

No	Type	Date	Ref	N/C	Details	Dept	T/C	Value	O/S	Debit	Credit	V	B
3	SI	17/07/2011	10012	9998	Opening Balance	0	T9	1,210.00		1,210.00		-	-
53	SI	20/08/2011	10018	4000	Translation of sales contracts	1	T1	376.00 *	376.00	376.00		N	-
56	SI	22/08/2011	10020	4000	Translation of contract tender	1	T1	1,404.75		1,404.75		N	-
66	SR	24/08/2011	100114	1200	Sales Receipt	0	T9	1,210.00			1,210.00	-	N
68	SR	31/08/2011	100116	1200	Sales Receipt	0	T9	1,374.75			1,374.75	-	N
69	SD	31/08/2011	100116	4009	Sales Discount	0	T9	30.00			30.00	-	-
					Totals:			376.00	376.00	2,990.75	2,614.75		

Amount Outstanding	376.00
Amount Paid this period	2,584.75
Credit Limit £	3,000.00
Turnover YTD	2,730.00

Task 3

Interlingo Translation Services
Supplier Activity (Detailed)

Date From:	01/01/1980
Date To:	31/08/2011
Transaction From:	1
Transaction To:	99,999,999
Inc b/fwd transaction:	No
Exc later payment:	No

Supplier From:	TD001
Supplier To:	TD001
N/C From:	
N/C To:	99999999
Dept From:	0
Dept To:	999

** NOTE: All report values are shown in Base Currency, unless otherwise indicated **

A/C: TD001   Name: TDI Wholesalers   Contact: Tel:

No	Type	Date	Ref	N/C	Details	Dept	T/C	Value	O/S	Debit	Credit	V	B
6	PI	05/07/2011	2347	9998	Opening Balance	0	T9	780.00	0.00		780.00	-	-
57	PI	15/08/2011	2561	5001	Beginners French CDs	2	T1	587.50 *	587.50		587.50	N	-
58	PI	15/08/2011	2561	5001	Advanced Italian CDs	2	T1	352.50 *	352.50		352.50	N	-
62	PC	28/08/2011	1919	5001	Beginners French CDs	2	T1	58.75 *	-58.75	58.75		N	-
84	PP	06/08/2011	120006	1200	Purchase Payment	0	T9	780.00	0.00	780.00		-	N
					Totals:			881.25	881.25	838.75	1,720.00		

Amount Outstanding	881.25
Amount paid this period	780.00
Credit Limit £	5,000.00
Turnover YTD	1,530.00

Task 4

Hill & Dale & Co, Solicitors

17 Berkeley Chambers

Penrose Street

Mereford

MR2 6GF

Playgames PLC

Consul House

Viney Street

Mereford

MR2 6PL

RS Export Agency

46 Chancery Street

Mereford

MR1 9FD

Rotherway Limited

78 Sparkhouse Street

Millway

MY5 8HG

Schafeld Ltd

86 Tanners Lane

Millway

MY7 5VB

INDEX

Access rights, 25,44
Account list, 153,159
Accounting system, 205-208
Accruals, 166
Activity report, 153,158
Aged creditor analysis, 153,157
Aged debtor analysis, 153,156
Audit trail, 153,155

Back-up, 4,27-29
BACS, 109
Bad debt, 178
Bank accounts, 106-107,137
Bank payments on a 'cash' basis, 127,130-131
Bank receipts on a 'cash' basis, 126,129-130
Bank reconciliation routine, 160-165
Bank transfers, 137
Batch entry, 90

Cancelled cheques, 180
Capital items, 100
Card accounts, 143
Cash receipts account, 144
Cash sales, 51,125
Charts, 8-9
Chart of accounts, 73-74
Cheque, 112
Closedown, 31
Comma Separated Values (CSV), 10
Company credit cards, 143
Company preferences, 43-44
Computer
    access rights, 25
    closedown, 31
    dates, 26
    hardware, 2-4
    logging-on, 24,26
    networks, 3
    passwords, 24
    security risk, 32
    software, 4-15
    start-up, 23-24
Computer accounting
    export of data, 17
    facilities, 11

financial year, 27
integrated system, 13
ledger system, 12,46
output, 16-17
packages, 10
setting up the company, 40-44
transaction types, 14-15
Computer care, 22
Corrections, 173-174
Corrupt data, 30
Credit limits, 53
Credit note
    allocation, 115
    batch, 94
    elements of, 88-89
    product, 193
    service, 193
Credit purchases, 98-104
Credit references, 52
Credit sales, 51,84-95
Credit terms, 53
Creditors, 99
Creditors control account, 99
Customer accounts
    sales ledger, 51
    set-up, 54-58

Data export, 166
Data Protection Act, 35
Data security, 31-33
Data storage, 4
Database, 6
Dates, 26
Debtors, 89
Debtors control account, 89
Depreciation, 166
Discount
    cash/settlement, 194
    customer defaults, 199
    trade, 198
    VAT calculation, 194
Display Screen Equipment Regulations, 35
Double-entry
    accounts, 209-210
    balancing off accounts, 215

credit sales and credit purchases, 213-215
dual aspect, 210
manual system, 204-215

Electronic Data Interchange (EDI), 10
Email management, 9
Expenses, 100

Financial documents, 85-89
Financial year, 27
Firewall, 34

Hardware, 2-4
Hardware failure, 30
Health & Safety at Work Act, 35

Internet, 3
Intranet, 3
Invoice
    batch, 90,92,189
    computer printed, 91,189
    elements of, 86-87
    product, 190-191
    service, 192-193

Journal, 174-175

Logging-on, 24,26

Network, 3
Nominal ledger
    accounts, 71
    amending account names, 79
    chart of accounts, 73-74
    relationship to bank, 71
    setting up, 70-80
    trial balance, 76,78

Passwords
    protection, 32
    software, 24,25
    system, 24
Payments
    accounting system, 112
    BACS, 109
    cash, 108
    credit, 108

credit notes, 115
customer and supplier, 106-121
input, 110-111
overpayments, 116
processing, 112-113
remittance advice, 109,114
underpayments, 116
Petty cash account, 138-140
Petty cash voucher, 138
Prepayments, 166
Printer, 3
Purchases, 100

Rebuild, 177
Records amendment, 62
Record deletion, 63
Recurring entries, 165
Recurring payments, 145,146
Recurring receipts, 147
Refunds, 179
Remittance advice, 109,114
Restore, 29
Returned cheques, 179-180

Saving data, 27
Security risk, 32
Setting up the company, 38-47
Software, 4-15
Software failure, 30
Spreadsheet, 7
Statement of account, 159-160
Supplier, 52
Supplier accounts
    purchases ledger, 52
    set-up, 54,55,59,60

Trial balance, 61,76,79

VAT
    calculations and discount, 198
    rates and codes, 126,128
    set-up, 43
Virus protection, 34-35

Wizard, 41,45
Word processing, 5
Write-offs, 178

for your notes

for your notes

for your notes

for your notes

for your notes

for your notes

for your notes

for your notes

for your notes

for your notes